GHOSTOLOGY

GHOSTOLOGY

The Art of the Ghost Hunter

by

STEVEN T. PARSONS

www.whitecrowbooks.com

Ghostology
The Art of the Ghost Hunter

Published and printed in the United States of America and the United Kingdom
by White Crow Books; an imprint of White Crow Productions Ltd.

For information, contact White Crow Books
at 3 Hova Villas, Hove, BN3 3DH United Kingdom,
or e-mail to info@whitecrowbooks.com.

Cover Designed by Butterflyeffect
Interior design by Velin@Perseus-Design.com

Paperback ISBN 978-1-910121-72-6
eBook   ISBN 978-1-910121-73-3

Non Fiction / Body, Mind & Spirit / Unexplained Phenomena

www.whitecrowbooks.com

DEDICATION

This book is dedicated to all those individuals who have over the decades and centuries past set out to study the phenomenon called ghosts and who have inspired me and guided my own quest. It is also dedicated to my long-suffering family and friends who have supported my interest in ways too numerous to mention over the years. Finally it is dedicated to the deceased and discarnate ghosts and apparitions for their continued efforts at haunting me with so many questions.

CONTENTS

DEDICATION V

FOREWORD IX

INTRODUCTION. XI
    What is a Ghost? xi
    Ghosts Exist xii
    Ghostology xiii

CHAPTER 1: A BRIEF HISTORY OF GHOST INVESTIGATING... 1
    The First Ghost Hunters...1
    Enlightened Investigators 2
    Men of Science and Learning.......................................4
    Psychical Scientists..7
    Storytellers and Ghost Hunters.................................. 11
    Technology Takes Over... 15
    Ghost Investigating in the 21st Century 17
    What of the Future?.. 20

CHAPTER 2: CRITICAL THINKING 23
    How Do We Go About Doing That?...................................... 24
    Question Everything... 25
    Avoid Personal Bias When Obtaining or
        Evaluating Information. 25
    Watch Out for Qualifying Statements........................... 25
    Do Not be Intimidated 26

CHAPTER 3: EVIDENCE 29
   The Investigation Process.................................. 31
   The Scientific Method....................................... 31
   Psychic Methods.. 32
   Subjective Information and Objective Information......... 33

CHAPTER 4: PEOPLE AND PLACES 37
   Questioning the Witness.................................... 40
   Beginning the Process of Investigation................... 44
   Public Access Investigations and Locations.............. 45
   Historical Perspective 47

CHAPTER 5: AMAZING THINGS AND AMAZING PEOPLE 53
   The Maglite Theory.. 56
   Psychics and Mediums 59
   The Human Pendulum 62

CHAPTER 6: MONITORING AND MEASURING 67
   Should We Measure Anything at All? 74
   Making Measurements 75
   Recording Measurements.................................... 77
   Baseline Measurements...................................... 77
   Analogue or Digital... 78
   Excessive Measurement 80

CHAPTER 7: TEMPERATURE 83
   Liquid in Glass Thermometers.............................. 84
   Thermocouple Thermometers................................. 85
   Resistance Thermometers 86
   Infrared Thermometers...................................... 88
   Thermal Imaging... 90
   Other Methods.. 91
   Measuring Temperature 92
   Temperature, in Conclusion................................ 93

CHAPTER 8: ELECTROMAGNETIC GHOSTS 97
   Electromagnetism... 97
   Why are investigators Interested in electromagnetism?... 99
   EMF Meters 103
   Limitations of Use and Practical Considerations........ 104
   Very Special EMF Meters? 107
   Is it More Than Just Ghosts Inside the Machine? 110
   Ionising or Nuclear Radiation?......................... 113

Radio Frequency Radiation 114
Negative and Positive Ion Detectors 115
Static Electricity 118

CHAPTER 9: MONITORING AND MEASURING THE ENVIRONMENT ... 121
Local and Regional Weather 121
Air Pressure 124
Humidity 126
Air Movement 127
Infrasound 129
Other Environment Monitoring 130
Environment Monitoring: Final Thoughts 132

CHAPTER 10: ELECTRONIC VOICE PHENOMENON AND
    INSTRUMENTAL TRANSCOMMUNICATION 133
Historical Attempts at Spirit Voice Communications
    using Electronic Methods 134
EVP Some Key Dates 141
EVP Methods 141
Basic Methods 142
Spiricom 144
The Frank's Box 145
Simple EVP Experiments 147
The Voices 148
Current EVP Research 151

CHAPTER 11: SOUND RECORDING AND SOUND EQUIPMENT ... 153
Sound 154
Analogue Recording 154
Digital Recording 156
Microphones 159
Further Considerations When Recording Sound 161
Some Sound Terminology 162
Paranormal Sounds? 162

CHAPTER 12: INVESTIGATION SOUND RECORDING 165

CHAPTER 13: SOUND RECORDING, WHAT NEXT? 171
Listening Test 171
Analysis 172

CHAPTER 14: OBTAINING STILL IMAGES 175
Tools of the Trade 175

Choosing the Camera 176
RTFM... Read The Flipping Manual 176
Film Cameras 177
Film - Pros and Cons 179
Digital Photography 180
Digital Film 180
The Digital Darkroom 184
Digital Camera Types 185
Digital Conclusions 190

CHAPTER 15: VIDEO PHOTOGRAPHY 193
Analogue or Digital? 195
Some Useful Features 197
Night Vision and Low Light Systems 197
Interval Recording and Motion Detection 199
Progressive Scan Video 200
Still Pictures 201
High Definition (HD) Video 202
Photography and Video Overall Conclusions 202

CHAPTER 16: TECHNIQUES FOR VIDEO AND PHOTOGRAPHY ... 205
Tripods and Other Supports 205
Lenses and Lights 208
Technique 212
Set the Date and Time Correctly 212
Be Familiar with the Camera and How to Operate it. ... 213
Positioning the Camera 213
Viewpoint 214
Camera Care 214

CHAPTER 17: IMAGES: WHAT NEXT? 217
Can Ghosts be Photographed? 221

CHAPTER 18: LET THERE BE LIGHT 225
The Invisible Light Spectra 225
Photographing the Invisible - Ultraviolet 226
Photographing the Invisible, Infrared 228
Sources of Invisible Light 229
Digital Photography and Video 229
Some Problems with Invisible Light Photography 232
Image Aberrations 232
Full Spectrum Photography and Video 235

Invisible Light Options and Considerations 245
Other Methods of Invisible Light Imaging......................... 246
Thermal Imaging... 247
Thermal Conductivity 249
Emissivity.. 249
Thermal Reflectivity.. 250
Fraud.. 253
Searching for the Invisible 256

CHAPTER 19: ORBS, SOME DEFINITIVE EVIDENCE 261
Early Experiments 262
Stereo Camera Experiments... 264
Orbs Are Dust.. 267

CHAPTER 20: SMART GHOST HUNTING.................. 269
Ghostly Apps... 270
Smart Sensors 272
Smart Apps 274
Smart Users... 277

CHAPTER 21: AND FINALLY... 279

SUGGESTED FURTHER READING........................ 281

FOREWORD

Ghosts have been a common companion to man throughout the centuries, fascinating and terrifying in turn. But are we any closer to understanding and defining them? Many have tried, and as yet no one has succeeded, although many claim to have done so. Explanations range from the sceptical (ghosts cannot possibly exist) to the mystical and apparent proof of an afterlife (ghosts are spirits of the deceased who communicate messages to us). In recent years, the number of people interested in the field of paranormal investigation has increased significantly, and many of these people claim to carry out scientific investigations into the nature of ghosts and the paranormal. But are the techniques used by these ghost hunters truly scientific and investigative, or are their apparent results built on a foundation of unscientific misunderstanding?

Steve Parsons is acknowledged to be one of the leading paranormal investigators in the UK by both ghost hunters and academics alike, and has spent most of his life researching and carrying out field investigations. Steve has a scientific and medical background, and is well-known for his ground-breaking work on infrasound and its relationship to the paranormal. In this book, he provides the reader with an in-depth look at the field of paranormal investigation in a straightforward and easily readable way, whilst providing a wealth of knowledge about techniques and equipment.

I first started working with Steve over 20 years ago, when we discovered we had a mutual passion for applying scientific techniques to investigating the paranormal. I have always been impressed with the depth of his knowledge of the paranormal, and his scientific understanding is second to none. Over the years he has tested and critiqued nearly every item of ghost hunting kit that has emerged, from highly technical electronic gadgets to Ouija boards, and has built a number of devices himself to aid in the search for the elusive ghost. Over the years we have seen methodology that has impressed us, confused us, and amused us but no matter how apparently outlandish the methodology, Steve has always tried it, tested it, and determined its validity (or otherwise).

This book is a must-read for any paranormal investigator, whether they are new to the field or have many years experience. It explores the techniques used on many ghost hunts, from the very first contact with a witness through to methodology for measuring, monitoring and recording. It provides what should become a standard reference book for any ghost hunter.

Will this book help you to "catch" a ghost? Probably not. Will this book assist you in using equipment appropriately, ethically and scientifically, and therefore help increase our knowledge about paranormal phenomena? Most definitely, and I recommend that anyone who investigates the paranormal reads this book.

Ann Winsper BSc. (Hons)
Parapsychologist, Psychical Phenomenologist and
co-founder of Para.Science.
Chester,
August 2015

INTRODUCTION

GHOSTOLOGY

What is a Ghost?

That infernal question that all who are engaged in psychical research and specifically spontaneous cases of apparitions and hauntings have been striving to answer for hundreds, if not thousands of years. Some may say that serious science really only took an interest in trying to answer the question in 1882 following the formation of the Society for Psychical Research (SPR). Before then the question wasn't asked, as society generally accepted ghosts and spirits as part of their (unseen) world or was only occasionally considered by philosophers and men of religion. This notion is untrue, for as long as mankind has existed ghosts have been part of our shared human experience and there have always been those who would seek to try and understand such experiences. Of course there are many who already claim to know what ghosts are. Spiritualists inform us that they are the trapped souls of the deceased unable or unwilling to move on to the higher planes of existence. Parapsychologists offer the opinion that ghosts represent nothing more than hallucinations or some other unkind trick of the mind. There are countless paranormal investigation teams, throughout the USA, Britain, and further afield. Many of these amateur investigators have developed their own theories and notions about the nature of ghosts and how they manifest, theories they derive from their investigations or television ghost hunting shows and from sharing their ideas and evidence via social media and the internet.

Ghosts Exist

Every day people experience ghosts. They see ghosts, they hear ghosts, and, they interact with ghosts. There are many definitions of what ghosts represent and most of the definitions make assumptions that are based upon general notions or sometimes the beliefs of the person writing the definition. According to the Oxford dictionary a ghost is: "An apparition of a dead person which is believed to appear or become manifest to the living, typically as a nebulous image".

But there are plenty of examples in which apparitions of living people have appeared and plenty more in which the apparition is far from nebulous. Parapsychology considers the study of ghosts to be related to aspects of survival beyond death but there is little to indicate ghosts are visions of the returning dead. They may equally well be hallucinations, anomalies of time and space, or something else entirely. In 2002, parapsychologist Ian Baker[1] offered the definition of a ghost as being: "A sensory experience in which there appears to be present a person or animal (deceased or living) who is in fact out of the sensory range of the experient..."

But people have witnessed ghosts of vehicles and described smells of burning timber, and oil, and by what mechanism can a person have a sensory experience that is in fact outside of their sensory range?

In truth, all these definitions show that when it comes to the experience of ghosts we are usually either just guessing or imposing our own beliefs and ideas onto the question. Whenever we talk or write about ghosts, are we actually considering the same phenomena? The flitting shape seen out of the corner of our eyes, the solid appearance of an armour clad Roman soldier, translucent figures that walk noisily or glide silently across floors only to disappear through solid walls; all are described as ghosts. The word 'ghost' may therefore best be considered to be a generic expression; an all-encompassing term to describe

---

[1] Baker, I. S. (2002). Do Ghosts Exist? A Summary of Parapsychological Research into Apparitional Experiences. In J. Newton (Ed.). *Early Modern Ghosts*. Durham, UK: University of Durham.

some sensation or sensory experience that we are unable to explain by normal means.

In the hunt for ghosts many different methods have been employed. Good old-fashioned séance techniques and other methods drawn from Spiritualism still prevail. Ouija boards and dowsing with pendulum, crystal, or rods continue to be popular tools of the ghost investigator. Modern technology has allowed us to peer into the darkest cellar and the spookiest hiding place of ghosts using infrared and thermal imaging. The electromagnetic spectrum is routinely scanned for the energy used or manipulated by ghosts and spirits using a variety of meters; whilst the voices of the dead are listened for intently using modified radios and audio recorders. All so far (sadly) to no avail. Despite claims to the contrary by numerous investigators, we still lack that most crucial item of equipment - the ghost detector! But, that is hardly surprising when one considers that it would be impossible to create a device that has the ability to detect or measure something we know virtually nothing about.

It is a truth, perhaps not universally acclaimed, that after so many centuries of study by countless investigators and amounting to millions of man-hours of research we still do not have an answer to the question, *what is a ghost*?

But should that mean we should cease searching? No, of course not.

Ghostology

People continue to see ghosts and ghosts continue to be a fascinating aspect of our humanity and one that deserves to be studied. Such phenomena are generally described as being spontaneous i.e., they are unplanned, unexpected, or unsolicited. Ghosts and their associated phenomena and experiences represent a unique subject for investigation and study. Ghost investigation is often confused with Spiritualism (which is in reality a religion), mediumship, or the survival of bodily death. Ghost investigating is also frequently confused with parapsychology, which is the academic study of psychological or mental phenomena that are generally ignored by orthodox psychology. Ghost investigating certainly takes account of both spiritism and parapsychology but it out of necessity it also draws upon the sciences, engineering, and humanitarian disciplines too. In reality, ghost investigation is an area of research that is distinct and separate. Those who investigate ghosts are required to conduct much of their research in conditions that lack many of the formal experimental controls that science usually demands. Ghosts do not appear on demand in the laboratory, they cannot be predicted. Ghosts are reported in busy modern shopping precincts, derelict and ancient castles, in fact, ghosts are reported by night and by day under almost every imaginable circumstance. Such situations do not lend themselves to the rigours of scientific control, yet the ghost investigator must be able to work through the chaos in order to obtain useful and usable information. Ghost investigators have to take account of the need to record and document unusual and unexpected human experiences and they may have to document and examine the history and geography of a location. They are required to obtain and record objective measurements of environmental changes and they have to be able to conduct their research under conditions that most others would consider to be chaotic and un-conducive to accepted methods or techniques.

The study of ghosts, or *Ghostology*, is not trying to capture apparitions on camera, although that is sometimes a part of it. It is not trying to record the sounds and the voices of the deceased or of spirits, although that too is a part of it. Ghostology is the holistic study of a fascinating aspect of our humanity, a shared human experience that dates back to the earliest civilisations and is common to all of them.

CHAPTER 1

A BRIEF HISTORY OF GHOST INVESTIGATING

The First Ghost Hunters

Ghosts and apparitions have haunted man since the very beginning of recorded time. There are many references to ghosts in Mesopotamia. The religions of Sumer, Babylon, Assyria, and other early states considered that ghosts were created at the time of death, taking on the memory and personality of the dead person. There was also widespread belief in ghosts in ancient Egyptian culture in the sense of a continued existence of the soul and spirit after death, with the ability to assist or harm the living, and also the possibility of a second death.

The Greeks and the Romans had specific words to describe ghosts. In the Roman religion 'Manes' (*pronounced 'Man-Ess'*) were spirits of the deceased who continued to wander the earth and could in many circumstances harm or at least disrupt normal life. Accordingly, they needed to be placated and honoured by feast and sacrifice to prevent them from returning to haunt the living. The dead were buried outside the town and city limits, usually at the junction of several roads, which served to both confuse any ghost set upon returning to his former home and to protect the township from unwelcome visitors, both the living and the dead!

Ghosts in medieval Europe tended to fall into two categories, the souls of the dead, and demons. The souls of the deceased returned for a specific purpose. Demonic ghosts were those that existed only to torment or tempt the living. The living could tell them apart by demanding their purpose in the name of Jesus Christ. The soul of a dead person would divulge their mission, while a demonic ghost would be banished at the sound of the holy name.

From the earliest days there were men of learning who set themselves the challenge of seeking to understand these ghostly visitors. Pliny the Younger wrote an account of a haunted house in Athens in 50. AD haunted by a chain-rattling ghost. The ghost was so troublesome that no one would occupy the property. Pliny described how Athenodorus the philosopher took over the abandoned property and in time communicated with the ghost, subsequently discovering a shackled and chained skeleton buried within the garden. Upon the mortal remains being given a proper burial the haunting ceased.

In the same era, the Greek essayist Plutarch describes what might be considered as a test of the veracity of spirit communications. The Governor of Cilicia who was sceptical and critical of the supernatural resolved to test a soothsayer. He wrote his question on a wax tablet, sealing it and handing it to a trusted servant to take to the soothsayer without revealing the question or the identity of the Governor. Plutarch writes that a correct answer to the question was received.

Enlightened Investigators

In the twelfth century Giraldus Cambrensis (Gerald of Wales) wrote of several ghosts, "unclean spirits" in his *Journey Through Wales* (Itinerarium Cambriae, 1191) including one that affected the home of William Not. The account bears a close resemblance to what we might describe today as being a poltergeist:

> They have been in the habit of manifesting themselves, throwing refuse all over the place, more keen perhaps to be a nuisance than to do any real harm...they were a cause of annoyance to both host and guests alike, ripping up their clothes of linen, and their woollen ones too, and

even cutting holes in them. No matter what precautions were taken, there seemed to be no way of protecting these garments, not even if the doors were kept locked and bolted.

Other ghostly phenomena also get a mention by Gerald including the corpse candle (canwyll corff), small glowing balls of light often associated in Welsh culture with the spirits of the deceased. Not merely content with writing second-hand accounts of these supernatural occurrences, Gerald often took pains to visit the location and speak to those affected in order to obtain accurate information. He considered the causes of such manifestations, but professed to not know. However, he observed that in the case of William Not and in another similar manifestation at the home of Stephen Wiriet, in the same county there were some common features:

> It has often been the presage, as they call it, of a sudden change from poverty to wealth, or more often still from wealth to poverty and utter desolation, as indeed, it was in both these cases. It seems most remarkable to me that places cannot be cleansed of visitations of this sort by the sprinkling of holy water, which is in general use and could be applied liberally, or by the performing of some other religious ceremony.

The investigation of seemingly ghostly activity tended to be the domain of the church or men of religion, most often with a desire to remove or exorcise the offending ghost or demon. In the Middle Ages being seen to be too interested in ghosts or supernatural phenomena was however likely to encourage charges of witchcraft or necromancy. Such was the case of Dr John Dee, a noted mathematician, astronomer, astrologer, occultist, navigator and consultant to Queen Elizabeth I. In 1582, Dee and his companion Edward Kelley were accused of raising a spirit or ghost in order to learn its secrets. A more enlightened approach toward exploration of the supernatural began to take hold following the restoration of Charles II in 1660. Men of science and learning increasingly turned their attention to the question of ghosts and apparitions and attempted to discover by more methodical means what they could be and what they may represent. Religious beliefs still weighed heavily on their thoughts and many came out critically against ghosts and apparitions as being the agents of either God or the Devil. A small number of educated men opted for a more measured approach and thought the subject should be studied in order to gain a better understanding of what they might represent.

One of these was Joseph Glanvill the English writer, philosopher, and clergyman, well known for his work *Sadducismus Triumphatus* (1681), which decried scepticism about the existence and supernatural power mainly relating to witchcraft but in which he also dealt with a collection of seventeenth century ghost lore. Glanvill argued that the evidence for the existence or otherwise of ghosts should be judged without bias, being guided only by the evidence:

> Matters of fact well proved ought not to be denied, because we cannot conceive how they can be performed. Nor is it a reasonable method of inference, first to presume the thing impossible, and thence to conclude that the fact cannot be proved. On the contrary, we should judge of the action by the evidence and not the evidence by the measures if our fancies about the action... Frequency of deceit and fallacy will warrant a greater care and caution in examining; and scrupulously and shyness of assent to things wherein fraud hath been practised, or may in the least degree be suspected: but to conclude, because that an old woman's fancy abused her, or some knavish fellow put tricks upon the ignorant and timorous; that therefore whole assizes have been a thousand times deceived in judgements upon matters of fact, and numbers of sober persons have been forsworn in things wherein perjury could not advantage them. I say such inferences are as void of reason as they are of charity and good manners.

In 1696, English philosopher and Fellow of the Royal Society John Aubrey published his *Miscellanies* that contained many historic and contemporary accounts of apparitions and seemingly ghostly phenomena such as disembodied sounds. Largely consisting of brief accounts, frequently without additional comment by Aubrey, it provides researchers with a valuable resource although it did little for Aubrey who was seen as superstitious and credulous by many of his contemporaries when it was published.

Men of Science and Learning

The calls for a qualitative approach to the study of ghosts and apparitions increased throughout the eighteenth and nineteenth centuries.

In 1727, Daniel Defoe writing under the pseudonym of Andrew Moreton penned *The Secrets of the Invisible World Disclosed or A Universal History of Apparitions*. Defoe cautioned his readers to not blindly accept that all apparitions represented the work of supernatural forces but that they may have more mundane causes and it is only by a process of investigation that they may be distinguished. In the preface to his book he writes:

> That we may be perfectly easy about this undetermined thing called apparition, I have endeavoured here to bring the thing into a narrow compass and to set it in a true light. I have given you several specimens of real apparitions well attested, and the truth of them so affirmed, that they may be depended upon: If in any of these I am not so well assured of the fact, though they may as certain, yet as I have frankly told you so and adhered to the moral only. But all together may convince the reader of the reason and reality of the thing itself.
>
> On the other hand, I have given you specimens of those amusements and delusions which have been put upon the world of apparitions; and you may see the difference is so notorious, (whether the cheat be political or whimsical, magical or imaginary) that no man can be really deceived that will but make use of the eyes of his understanding, as well as those of his head.

The nineteenth century brought about renewed calls for science to take an interest in ghosts and apparitions. In 1819, Pierre-Simon, Marquis de Laplace remembered as one of the greatest scientists of all time wrote his *Analytic Theory of Probabilities (Théorie Analytique des Probabilités)* in which he discussed apparitions and the need for careful investigation to be conducted:

> That 'any case, however apparently incredible, if it be a recurrent case, is as much entitled under the laws of induction, to be a fair valuation'. Determined sceptics may indeed deny that there exists any well-authenticated instance of an apparition. But that, at present, can only be a mere matter of opinion, since many persons as competent to judge as themselves maintain the contrary; and in the meantime I will arraign their right to make this objection till they themselves have qualified themselves to do so by a long course of patient and honest inquiry; always remembering that every instance of error or

imposition discovered and adduced, has no positive value whatever in the argument, but as regards that single instance; though it may enforce upon us the necessity of strong evidence and careful investigation....

A few scientists were intrigued enough to study some of the phenomena that were being exhibited at this time. In 1846, the Paris Academy of Sciences examined Angeliqué Cottin, who had demonstrated the extraordinary ability to cause heavy tables and chairs to move or even overturn in her presence.

Known throughout France as the 'Electric girl' the scientists were at a loss to explain her abilities but decided that she was charged with an excess of electric fluid. It was some time before the truth was finally revealed that she was in fact moving the table by using her leg muscles. In America in the mid nineteenth century, a number of committees were established at different times to study the claims of the Fox sisters, who for some time had been using a series of raps and other phenomena to contact the ghost of a murdered pedlar at their home in Hydesville, New York State. The various committees all failed to reach any conclusive decisions regarding the sister's abilities but in 1888 two of the sisters, Margaret and Kate, publicly stated that the raps were fraudulently produced, made by cracking their toe joints. However, one year later Margaret recanted her confession.

In 1848, Catherine Crowe, an English author, challenged science to conduct proper studies of psychical phenomena in her book *The Night Side of Nature*. As she saw it, the reason why ignorance about ghosts and other psychic experiences existed was due to the intransigence and arrogance of contemporary science:

> To minds which can admit nothing but what can be explained and demonstrated, an investigation of this sort must appear perfectly idle, for while on the one hand, the most acute intellect or the most powerful logic can throw little light on the subject, it is at the same time – though I have a confident hope that this will not always be the case – equally irreducible within the present bounds of science. Meanwhile, experience and observation must be our principal if not our only guides...

> The Pharisaical scepticism which denies without investigation is quite perilous and much more contemptuous than the blind credulity which

accepts all that is taught without enquiry. It is indeed but another form of ignorance assuming to be knowledge. And by investigation I do not mean the hasty, captious, angry notice of an unwelcome fact that too frequently claims the right of pronouncing on a question; but the slow, modest, painstaking examination that is content to wait upon Nature and humbly follow out her disclosures however opposed to preconceived theories or mortifying to human pride. If scientific men could but comprehend how they discredit the science they really profess by their despotic arrogance and exclusive scepticism they would surely, for the sake of that very science they love affect some liberality and candour...

No one who lives can assert the reappearance of the dead is impossible; all he has a right to say is, that he does not believe it and the interrogation that should immediately follow this declaration is "Have you devoted your life to sifting all the evidence that has been adduced on the other side, from the earliest periods of history and tradition?...

The observation of any phenomena, therefore, which enabled us to master the idea, must necessarily be extremely beneficial and it must be remembered that one single thoroughly well established instance of the reappearance of a deceased person would not only have this effect, but it would afford a demonstrative proof.

Psychical Scientists

Eventually the calls for science to take an interest in psychical studies started to take hold. Much of this renewed scientific interest in psychical research was driven by the claims being made by the Spiritualist movement, which began in 1848 in America and had spread rapidly throughout the United States and into Europe. Prior to the nineteenth century the investigation of ghosts and apparitions had relied solely upon eyewitness testimony and personal experience as the primary method of study. As science started to understand the natural world and instruments for measuring it became available, it was only a matter of time before scientists started to use these instruments and attempt to measure the reported phenomena and collect objective rather than merely subjective information. In the 1850's, American chemistry professor Robert Hare began his own investigations into the claims of the Spiritualist movement and devised a number of instruments which, contrary to his expectations, conclusively proved that a power and intelligence, not that of those present, was at work. His book, *Experimental Investigation of the Spirit Manifestation* published in 1855, summed up the results as follows:

> The evidence may be contemplated under various phases; first, those in which rapping's or other noises have been made which could not be traced to any mortal agency; secondly, those in which sounds were so made as to indicate letters forming grammatical, well-spelt sentences, affording proof that they were under the guidance of some rational being; thirdly, those in which the nature of the communication has been such as to prove that the being causing them must, agreeably to accompanying allegations, be some known acquaintance, friend, or relative of the inquirer.

By the mid 1860's, the main issues had become clear. One either had to accept the occurrence of psychical phenomena, however astonishing or incredible, as a type of physical phenomena that had previously gone undetected or admit that the senses of seemingly sane people could deceive them in an unprecedented manner. Whatever view was taken, the facts remained; phenomena were being reported and observed which merited further investigations. It was therefore unfortunate that almost to a man the orthodox scientists of the day turned their backs on the problem. Fortunately, a small number did take up the challenge presented by the claims of Spiritualism. In the 1870's, chemist and physicist Sir William Crookes reached the conclusion that science had a duty to study the psychical phenomena associated with spiritualism. He was determined to conduct his impartial inquiry and described the conditions he imposed on mediums as follows: "It must be at my own house, and my own selection of friends and spectators, under my own conditions, and I may do whatever I like as regards apparatus".

Crookes developed experiments, some of which were based upon the earlier experimental designs used by Robert Hare, in order to test a number of mediums. Among those he studied were Kate Fox, Florence Cook, and Daniel Dunglas Home. Crookes used delicate spring balances in his sessions with Home and he pioneered the use of further equipment including photography and the observation of pulse rate and temperature for testing the claims of the mediums. He reported on this research in 1874 and concluded that these phenomena could not be explained as conjuring, and that further research would be useful.

Established in 1867, the London Dialectical Society passed a resolution in January 1869: "To investigate the phenomena alleged to be spiritual manifestations and to report thereon".

The Society appointed a committee of thirty-three people including several leading academics and scientists to examine the evidence. The committee reported in July 1870 and included the following statements:

1. That sounds of a very varied character apparently proceeding from articles of furniture, the floor and the wall of the room – the vibrations accompanying which sound are often distinctly perceptible to the touch – occur without being produced by muscular action or mechanical contrivance.
2. The movements of heavy bodies take place without mechanical contrivance of any kind or adequate exertion of muscular force by the persons present, and frequently without contact or connection with any person.
3. That these sounds and movements often occur at the times and in the manner asked for by persons present and by means of a simple code of signals; answer questions and spell out coherent communications.
4. That the circumstances under which the phenomena occur are variable; the most prominent fact being that the presence of certain persons seems necessary to their occurrence and that of others generally adverse; but this difference does not appear to depend upon any belief or disbelief concerning the phenomena.
5. That nevertheless the occurrence of the phenomena is not insured by the presence or absence of such persons respectively.

Upon its release, it was claimed by some that the report was biased and that little evidence had been considered from those who opposed such phenomena. The press were also generally highly critical of the Society's findings. The Dialectical Society report concentrated solely upon the actual phenomena and did not consider the question of survival. However, the report drew the attentions of many qualified investigators to the subject, which must be its most important and lasting legacy.

Around the same time, a small group lead by the Cambridge philosopher Henry Sidgewick began to examine the question of ghosts and other psychical questions. As an undergraduate, Sidgewick had been a member of the Cambridge University Ghost Club which existed mainly for the collection and telling of ghost stories. In 1863, he had investigated a number of mediums and, although these early studies were inconclusive, he continued his interest and by 1873 had formed a small group of fellow researchers including Frederick Myers. In 1882, Myers was to lead this small group along with Edmund Gurney, Sir William Barrett and Frank Podmore in the formation of the first real organised attempt by science to study psychical phenomena with the founding of The Society for Psychical Research (SPR). Its stated purpose given in the first Proceedings of the Society was: "...To approach these varied problems without prejudice or prepossession of any kind, and in the same spirit of exact and unimpassioned enquiry which has enabled Science to solve so many problems, once not less obscure nor less hotly debated."

Initially six committees were established on Thought-Transference, Mesmerism, and similar phenomena, Mediumship, Reichenbach Phenomena (Odic Force), Apparitions and Haunted Houses, Physical Phenomena associated with Séances, and the Literary Committee which studied the history of these phenomena.

One significant undertaking was the Census of Hallucinations, in which 15,000 persons were asked to report on hallucinatory experiences while awake and in good health. Around ten per cent of those responding reported such experiences, and a small number of veridical hallucinations were also reported - that is hallucinations that appeared to convey information not known to the person hallucinating at the time, which was believed by the authors to be suggestive of telepathy. Critical SPR investigations into mediumship and the exposure of fake mediums led to a number of resignations in the 1880s by Spiritualist members. However, the Society continued to investigate mediums, studying Leonora Piper and Eusapia Palladino among others.

The SPR's first substantial involvement in the investigation of a seemingly haunted house took place in the winter of 1897.

Ballechin House in Scotland had developed a reputation for being haunted. Members of the SPR were part of an invited group who took several months rental of the property in order to document and investigate the reports of ghosts and other phenomena. SPR member and medium Ada Goodrich-Freer, writing under the Nome de plume of 'Miss X' together with the Marquess of Bute published a book in 1899, *The Alleged Haunting of 'B' House*, that provides a detailed description of the investigation and the numerous experiences of the investigators and visitors. A very public dispute conducted in the letters column of The Times newspaper resulted in the credibility of the case being damaged. The dispute meant that the investigation of 'B' house was discontinued and plans to bring in phonographic and temperature recording equipment had to be abandoned. However, this does represent the first attempt at trying to conduct a long term and well-documented study of ghostly and haunting phenomena. Unfortunately the investigation was never recommenced and the building no longer exists.

Storytellers and Ghost Hunters

Meanwhile the Church did little or nothing to discourage the popular belief in ghosts as being the shades of the murder victims, suicides, and other unfortunates returning to haunt the living. The ghost story was one of the most popular forms of literature. The few amateur ghost investigators of this period pursued a subjective approach preferring to concentrate upon personal experience rather than objective measurement of any phenomena. Elliot O'Donnell and Marchioness Lady Townsend in the first half of the twentieth century had long and fruitful careers as ghost investigators. Both were content to visit haunted houses in the hope of seeing and experiencing the ghost for themselves and took no further action by way of investigation other than to simply document their own various experiences and those of their acquaintances in their numerous books. Lord Halifax was another who was passionate about collecting and re-telling ghost stories. His son produced several volumes of his father's collected stories and tales of ghosts and the supernatural entitled *Lord Halifax's Ghost Book*. The book provides accounts of hauntings at well-known locations such as Glamis Castle and Burton Agnes Hall but its style is one of mystery and romance and clearly has more than a touch of artistic licence, designed to exploit the growing fascination within the wider public of the supernatural.

Born in 1881, Harry Price was to become possibly the best known of all the ghost investigators. In time Price would establish ghost investigation as a meaningful pursuit in the minds of both the public and the media, writing a number of books and many more articles for newspapers and magazines on the subject. Price was first and foremost a man interested in investigating and understanding psychical phenomena. His first ghost investigation took place when he was just fifteen. Together with a school friend, Price attempted to capture photographic evidence of ghostly activity at an empty Shropshire house, an investigation which led to his claim to have "Shot the poltergeist to pieces!" following his misjudgement of the amount of powder required for the camera flash. From the very beginning, Price was interested in developing equipment that could be used to obtain objective information to verify and test the paranormal claims that were being made both within the séance room and more importantly in haunted houses. Price will forever be remembered for his investigation of Borley Rectory in Essex, which he first visited in 1929, at the invitation of the Daily Mirror newspaper. He continued to visit the site from time to time throughout the next decade which culminated in him hiring the rectory for a full year in order to conduct the fullest investigation possible. Through a newspaper advertisement, Price recruited a team of forty-eight volunteers to carry out the year-long investigation and he produced a book of notes and guidance for the investigators. Known as *The Blue Book* on account of the blue cardboard cover, this was the first attempt to set down some ground rules for the standardisation of ghost investigating methodology. Price was passionate that psychical research should become an academic pursuit and a recognised science in its own right, a cause he championed constantly throughout his life:

> I said that it was our primary object to turn psychical research into a science, and it is of course, a corollary of that that psychical research is not or at any rate has not been up to the present, a science, at least in this country. As you probably know, official science tends to regard psychical research with a certain amount – I will not say of fear, but of disapprobation. There is a certain pulling up of the skirts on the part of official science when psychical research passes by. Now our object is to make an honest woman of psychical research. If you look back over her past, it has been, I fear very dubious; so dubious that directly the word is mentioned, whether to scientists or to journalists, there is a tendency to raise the eyebrows, or to giggle, or to think of ghosts and spooks or to become factitious at the expense of those who are investigating this highly equivocal territory...

> ...Official science, as I have said regards psychical research as something disreputable. But those who believe that here is a territory in which the methods of science, if carefully and scrupulously applied, would bear valuable and important fruit; those who believe that here are phenomena – perhaps not many, because when you sift the grain from

the chaff there is not very much grain left, but there is some – those who believe that there is some grain that wants sifting and investigating cannot but regard this attitude of official science with regret...

Now wishes may father thoughts, but they do not breed evidence, and in my view there is no evidence from the séance room, whatever evidence there may be from other quarters, for the particular view, that abnormal psychical phenomena somehow point to or establish even the fact of survival... I have made many efforts to introduce psychical research into the universities and transform it into an official science. I have reason to be satisfied with the results to date:

The University of London, when discussing my offer to endow and equip a department of psychical research, declared that the investigation of paranormal phenomena was 'a fit subject of university study and research (1934).

The formation of the University of London Council for Psychical Investigation (1934).

The acceptance by London University of my psychic library and records, and the housing of the laboratory of the University Council (1936).

The German Government recognises psychical research as an official science (1937).

The German government and the University of Bonn seek my assistance in forming a Department of Parapsychology (1937).

Trinity College, Cambridge, accepts the Perrott bequest and establishes a Studentship in Psychical Research (1940).

New College, Oxford, accepts the Blennerhasset Trust for the promotion of Psychical Research (1941).

Since 1933, advances can be recorded in certain other universities e.g., Duke, North Carolina; Utrecht, Leiden and John Hopkins so my fight for academic recognition has borne fruit. Further advances would have been made had it not been for the Second World War.

Price was frequently accused of courting publicity and seeking personal fame, charges that led some within the SPR to try to discredit both his work at Borley and also Price himself. In 1956, the highly critical posthumous book *The Haunting of Borley Rectory* (E. Dingwall, K. Goldney, T. Hall) was published. Two of the authors Eric Dingwall and Kate Goldney had been former colleagues of Price. Their claims went largely unchallenged and were accepted as fact for over a decade by many until another SPR member Robert Hastings re-examined the original claims made by the three authors. In March 1969, the SPR produced his findings in an edition of their *Proceedings (Vol. 55, Part 201)*. In *An Examination of the Borley Report* Hastings dismisses many of the claims made against Price but the damage done to Price's reputation as a ghost investigator was considerable and continues to this day despite a reassessment and posthumous apology proffered to Price in recent years by the SPR.

Although lacking formal academic qualifications, Price was nonetheless a skilled engineer and inventor, abilities that served him and psychical research well. He designed and built many items of equipment such as the Telekinetoscope, which he used to test the abilities of medium Stella 'C' during the 1920's. He used highly sensitive recording thermometers at Borley Rectory during which he documented some seemingly inexplicable temperature fluctuations. Price also put together what is the forerunner of all current ghost-hunting kits. Some of the items that Price included such as a bowl of mercury or the hanks of bell wire might not be in a modern ghost investigator's flight cases but we still need the notebook and pens, torch, and many other items that were to be have been found in Price's battered fibreboard suitcase. Price extensively used photography for psychical investigation and developed methods of photographing phenomena in low light using infrared film and adapted cameras. One of his stated wishes was to have the capability of recording movement using movie camera and infrared movie film, an ability almost every ghost investigator now has readily available in the form of infrared assisted night vision video cameras.

Price was not the first psychical researcher to use instrumentation for the study of psychic phenomena. As already mentioned, Robert Hare, William Crookes, and several others had taken instruments into the séance room and in 1915 a lecturer in mechanical engineering at Belfast University Dr W.J. Crawford began a two year study of physical phenomena taking place at a home séance circle in Belfast. His use of properly calibrated scales and other measuring equipment, together with a well thought out methodology and detailed recording of his many experiments must stand as a landmark in psychical investigation and the results still offer a challenge to the modern researcher. A series of phonograph recordings of the raps and other sounds were made but it is not known if they survive today.

Technology Takes Over

Following the Second World War, ghost investigation progressed slowly. As a body, the SPR took little interest in the active investigation of hauntings and apparitions. However a number of SPR members did undertake ghost investigation and the study of haunted houses. Their methods were still in the main experience orientated, with comparatively few attempts to obtain objective information to support the claims under investigation. Leading ghost investigator of the time, Peter Underwood visited and investigated many locations including the site of Borley Rectory and its adjacent church. Like Price, Underwood also wrote and broadcast extensively on the subject of his investigations. Underwood also revived The Ghost Club that had lapsed in 1948 following the death of Harry Price who had been an active supporter and of this prestigious group which claims to be the oldest surviving ghost group in the World, tracing its formation to 1862.

Another notable and highly acclaimed investigator during the post war years was Andrew Green, who was known as 'The Spectre Inspector' by the media. Green was an active ghost investigator for over sixty years until his death in 2004. Green wrote many accounts of his investigations that emphasised a scientific approach to the subject. His books include *Ghost Hunting, A Practical Guide* which was published in 1973. The book considers many aspects of ghost investigation such as the use of equipment, site examination, and the interviewing of witnesses; it remains a highly relevant book for the modern investigator although sadly Green is now almost a forgotten figure by many ghost investigators. Green's book, now long out of print, contains a great deal of helpful information and it is pleasing to discover that there are plans for it to be re-issued.

Like Andrew Green, other investigators from within the SPR sought to develop a more objective approach to ghost investigations. The late Tony Cornell together with Alan Gauld developed *'SPIDER'*

(Spontaneous Psychophysical Incident Data Electronic Recorder) recognising that spontaneous cases had largely become ignored by the parapsychologists' preference for laboratory work studying psi:

> We need to know much more about the physical effects that are alleged to occur in many cases. Do objects really levitate as described at the time witnesses? From which direction do they come and at what speed? Do things really mysteriously disappear, only to be found later? Are the often-reported thumps, bangs, and temperature changes the result of paranormal forces or not?

SPIDER consisted of a linked series of sensors and recorders that could be triggered remotely, either manually or automatically. It was portable (just about) and many cases were monitored, photographically and electronically, using this equipment for over more than twenty years. Unfortunately, SPIDER failed to obtain the hoped-for definitive objective proof of paranormal phenomena but a number of inexplicable events were documented over the years. Prior to his death in 2010, Tony Cornell provided modern investigators with a lasting if sometimes overlooked legacy with the publication of his book *Investigating The Paranormal (2002)*, one of the most considered accounts of modern ghost investigation and psychical research that has been compiled and one that should be considered as essential reading for everyone with an interest in the practical study of ghosts. Cornell and Gauld, together with a small number of SPR members, did continue with their efforts towards objectively investigating and documenting haunted locations. Maurice Grosse, along with Guy Lyon-Playfair, were responsible for the detailed investigation of the Enfield poltergeist case in 1977, one of the most interesting cases ever investigated by the SPR. Extensive use of sound recording and photography, together with the pioneering but ultimately unsuccessful use of video recording equipment at Enfield meant that many of the phenomena associated with poltergeist manifestations were for the first time properly recorded and made available for detailed examination. The objective information meticulously collected by Playfair and Grosse still remains as a thorn in the side of the sceptics and demonstrates the importance of properly gathered objective information.

The SPR meanwhile has continued to shift its emphasis towards a more psychologically orientated study of psychical phenomena although they did produce a set of guidance notes for investigators of spontaneous cases, including cases of apparitions and poltergeists. These guidance notes are long out of print but the Society maintains a 'Notes for Investigators' page on its Internet site, www.spr.ac.uk/page/notes-investigators-paranormal.

Founded in 1981, ASSAP (Association for the Scientific Study of Anomalous Phenomena) set itself the challenge of investigating a broad range of paranormal subjects including ghosts but also UFO's, earth mysteries, and cryptozoology. ASSAP focussed on the use of equipment in support of its ghost investigations. It also established a methodology that is still widely used by many ghost investigators. Location investigations were divided into set periods, typically of forty-five minutes of investigating followed by a break of equal duration before relocating for the next investigating period and so on. Notes of personal experiences were maintained and compared, but a strong emphasis was placed upon the information obtained by means of mechanical and electrical equipment. ASSAP also provided accreditation for investigators, and its members were encouraged to participate in organised training and investigation events. Alongside the SPR and ASSAP, there were a handful of amateur ghost investigation groups throughout the 1960's, 70's, and 80's. Many undertook investigations of local haunted properties and revisited notorious sites including Borley, where the subject of their visits had become the church, the rectory having been demolished in 1944, following a fire in 1939. These amateur investigators used a mix of psychic techniques including many that were recognisable as being derived from the Spiritualism and the séance room supported by an ever-increasing use of technology such as tape recorders, cameras, and thermometers.

Ghost Investigating in the 21st Century

In recent years there has been a huge increase in the number of people and groups who are investigating ghostly goings on. Driven by the media and by the Internet, the number of ghost investigation groups has soared from a mere handful of teams in the 1970's to more than one thousand within the UK and almost double that number in the USA by 2010. Spurred on by television programmes such as *Most Haunted* in the UK and *Ghost Hunters* in the USA, thousands of people now devote their weekends to visiting and investigating haunted locations. All too frequently a poor understanding and knowledge of the subject, gained predominantly from the media or from theories popularised by social media, guides the actions of many of these willing amateurs. Often, despite claims to the contrary on their various websites and social media pages, many of these groups prefer to use a combination of pseudo-science and methods derived from Spiritualist or new age studies to support their investigations rather than adopting a more rigorous and critical methodology.

Ghosts and apparitions generally cannot be studied. The reality is that most people with an active interest in such spontaneous experiences usually only ever encounter verbal or written reports or images of alleged phenomena. Investigation is therefore in reality the study of second-hand and secondary sources of information. Such a situation leaves room for a great deal of doubt in the minds of some as to whether the phenomena we call ghosts has ever been genuinely encountered and properly documented. Much of the claimed evidence being presented as factual is poorly understood or has little to do with the actual subject at all. Dowsing for ghostly energy and the channelling of spirits by sensitives and mediums have become inexorably intertwined with modern gadgetry in the search for proof of the existence of ghosts and the survival of death. The overused depiction of such methods as providing scientific proof of the claims that are made by ghost investigators only adds to the state of confusion that currently exists. Central to all aspects of ghost investigation is the notion that there is a series of phenomena that can be easily studied simply by spending time in haunted locations. Virtually this entire premise of investigation assumes that there is intelligence behind these phenomena.

A popular viewpoint amongst those who undertake the investigation of ghosts is that the human spirit can survive death in some way and can return at will to locations frequented during their lifetime. A second equally popular view, suggests that the environment can in some way record a traumatic event or memory into the fabric of its surroundings to be played back at some later time. Often these two notions may be mixed together and presented as definitive explanations by those who champion such ideas. There may be some logic and rational thought behind both of these concepts but there is also much disagreement and a current lack of any coherent study being undertaken to test such ideas. The truth about ghost investigations is that the bulk of anomalous reports are continually being appropriated and hijacked by people with their own agendas, be they a believer, or a sceptic. Whilst individual motivations may be well meaning, the results serve only to scatter the subject and cause disagreement. Evidence of ghosts and related paranormal activity is widely presented on the Internet, published in magazines and books, or shown on television. The major casualty of all this information is undisputed truth. Many interesting cases are now badly tainted by the poor standard and sensationalist nature of the evidence that is being presented by the investigators. The sceptical voices often display a poor understanding of cases they dispute and readily dismiss those who continue to investigate claims of ghosts and apparitions as scientific heretics.

There are a small number of more thorough investigations being undertaken, some of which are producing vital and challenging work. However, the continued sensationalist approach by the majority has left the subject of ghosts and hauntings, or as it used to be called spontaneous case investigation, largely in an academic limbo. Well documented reports of ghost and apparition encounters are fascinating and more substantial that many of the sceptics would like to admit but many of those researchers employed in university parapsychology and anomalous psychology departments regard amateurs in amateur investigation groups almost as a kind of 'care in the community' branch of the study, and, who can blame them given the current approach that most amateurs seem to be taking. Spontaneous case study is often seen as a sure route to career suicide for scientific researchers. Research undertaken in psychology, physics, and sociology have made substantial contributions to the debate but have often failed to impress those involved in gathering field reports. In most cases, those active within investigation groups either don't have access to or fail to understand the academic research, normally only to be found in obscure journals and written in a form that seems to be almost purposefully designed to exclude the non academics. Occasionally, the investigators get the gist of new ideas and theories but there is little encouragement and support from the mainstream sciences. Instead of guidance and the provision of solid foundations upon which to develop their investigations, the amateurs are abandoned, free to interpret the ideas, sometimes in novel or bizarre ways.

The modern ghost investigator has adopted a vast range of equipment for the task. Often, it is apparent that there is little substantive knowledge of why or what the equipment is actually measuring. Theories abound and increasingly bizarre claims for what the gadgets can achieve are being made. We now have meters that apparently can measure the energy emitted by ghosts or that can be utilised by the dead to communicate with the living by manipulating the ambient electromagnetic fields, sometimes both, using the same device. Simple portable AM and FM radios have also been modified for the purpose of direct communication with spirits and ghosts. Digital photography using either modified or unmodified cameras allows ghosts and spirits to be photographed or recorded onto video seemingly with results that are being claimed as offering convincing proof for the existence of ghosts. Another popular claim for producing convincing evidence is the extensive use of digital sound recording in haunted locations, it is frequently claimed that the voices of the deceased together with other discarnate entities can be recorded. The celebrity ghost hunter too has survived from the days of Harry Price and Peter Underwood, although their celebrity status is more often the result of their media persona instead of any actual contribution towards a greater understanding of the subject. Mainstream science has largely turned its back on ghosts and instead prefers to concentrate its efforts into areas of psychologically based study. Fortunately, there remain a bare handful of academic researchers who do have an active interest in hauntings and apparitions. Another comparatively recent development in ghost investigation is that psychics and mediums would traditionally confine themselves to conducting their activities within the séance room or Spiritualist meetings but they have now moved extensively into conducting ghost investigations. Many mediums now lead or take an active role within ghost investigation groups, often proclaiming their personal sceptical viewpoint but all too often using the ghost hunt and the presented evidence obtained as a means of promoting their own survivalist or assorted new age beliefs as factual and evidential.

Modern ghost investigation has now become primarily the domain of poorly informed amateurs and commercially driven ghost event companies who cater for a market more intent upon having a spooky night out rather than truly investigating and trying to understand what ghosts might actually represent.

What of the Future?

Is there a future for ghost investigating? To be honest, it seems a bleak one at present. Ghost hunting has become mass entertainment rather than the intriguing new branch of science that many of the earlier investigators hoped that it would in time become. The very popularity of the subject looks likely to condemn it even further into the fringe world of entertainment and thrill seeking. With so many groups now active and so many people spending their leisure time in pursuit of ghosts and apparitions it has become increasingly difficult to find cases and locations that have not been trampled in the rush to enjoy a personal encounter with a ghost or spirit. Genuine cases have become lost and buried under a deluge of ghost hunters. Savvy venues have realised that they are sitting on a goldmine and now routinely charge extortionate amounts for a few hours access. No serious researcher begrudges paying a reasonable amount toward the costs of maintaining a location or paying for overnight staffing but does it really cost up to £1,000 to allow a few people to spend a night in an alleged haunted ruin?

If spontaneous case investigation is to continue it needs to alter its approach radically. Sound practical and ethical guidelines need to be adopted by all investigators. It would be useless to try and impose such conditions upon the groups as too many hold tight to their entrenched beliefs and would fiercely resent the intrusion into their hobby and, in some cases, income. Fortunately, for ghost hunting there are still a number of researchers and investigators who continue to follow the route of using critical thinking and good methodology and who continue to contribute toward extending our knowledge of this often maligned and misrepresented area of study into what remains a fascinating human experience.

CHAPTER 2

CRITICAL THINKING

M ichael Scriven and Dr Richard Paul defined critical thinking
to the 8th Annual International Conference (1987) on Critical
Thinking and Education Reform as:

> The intellectually disciplined process of actively and skillfully
> conceptualising, applying, analysing, synthesising, and / or evaluating
> information gathered from, or generated by, observation, experience,
> reflection, reasoning, or communication, as a guide to belief and action.

Learning to think critically is perhaps the most useful skill a ghost
investigator can hope to develop. Unfortunately, most of our thinking
when left unchecked becomes distorted, biased, poorly informed, or
simply prejudiced.

Many people will consider themselves to be excellent at critical
thinking, however, the reality is that critical thinking doesn't come
naturally to most people. Fortunately, it is something that we can train
ourselves to do better.

Critical thinking raises important questions or highlights problems
formulating them precisely. Critical thinking gathers and assesses all
of the relevant information. It tests ideas against relevant criteria and
standards to reach a well-reasoned conclusion. Critical thinking is
open-minded, takes consideration of alternative points of view, and

assesses their implications and consequences. In short, critical thinking is self-disciplined, self-monitored and self-corrective thinking that applies rigorous standards when considering any information that may help to form an opinion or reach a conclusion.

How Do We Go About Doing That?

Every single day we are exposed to so much information and so many different opinions that it is really easy to get lost in the detail. We therefore need to train ourselves to learn which details matter and which do not. Start by listening to your gut instinct, if something doesn't sound quite right, that should be a warning sign. Examine the information for its completeness and consistency and be wary when finding problems. However, it is unsound to disregard information solely on the basis of a lack of completeness or any inconsistency, particularly when dealing with personal testimony. Sometimes the experience may have had unsettling or profound effects upon the witness that may render their testimony as seemingly at odds with your own expectations of such an experience. Sometimes, the witness may be simply confused or unsure about their experience and this can also affect the way that they present their testimony.

When you read an account or listen to an opinion consider whom, if anyone, might gain or benefit from the statement that is being made. If someone is making a claim or stating an idea, there is usually a good chance that they hope to benefit from it in some way.

Question the source of the information. Particularly if it is the Internet, which is mainly unregulated, and where original source material may not be immediately apparent. Whenever possible, attempt to track down the original material together with any alternative sources or accounts. Be aware that claims or ideas are often just repeated, appearing on multiple sites, sometimes reproduced verbatim or with additions and modifications.

With personal testimony and witness accounts always try to speak to the original witness and obtain a first-hand account. Be wary of those accounts, which come to you via a friend or even a friend of a friend.

Question Everything.

The first and possibly the best question to ask is *how does the person know what they know?*

When someone provides an account, a statement, or refers to a study or an experiment, all too often they are rarely challenged. By asking them to explain how and where they obtained their information important light can be shed upon the original information, allowing it to be checked further and more thoroughly.

Sometimes the response to any further questioning response might be: "this is purely my opinion" or "it's possible, because nobody can really know for sure". These are extremely weak claims that most people will typically use if they are uncertain or they are simply repeating something that they have picked up elsewhere. Learn to identify someone's opinion as being speculation rather than as a fact.

Look out for obviously true statements. It is a common tactic in debates, reviews, and even personal accounts to couch a critical argument inside a series of obviously true statements. These sorts of arguments are easy to miss, by the time they come along you may have already started agreeing with a statement. For example: "So, now we know that the sky is blue, that grass is green, that clouds are white and the sea is always turquoise".

Avoid Personal Bias When Obtaining or Evaluating Information.

Personal belief can easily lead to the investigator assigning a greater or lesser value to an account or item of information. Intrinsically believing in something makes it far more likely that the investigator will believe what they are being told and all the more likely to overlook signs that an account is unreliable. Likewise, being highly sceptical of something that is said makes it much more likely to that the information will be disbelieved and dismissed.

Watch Out for Qualifying Statements.

Critical thinking is not just about training oneself to think, it is also about training the ear to listen and notice subtle words and phrases that should set off warning bells. Generally speaking, a warning bell should sound whenever the speaker uses a qualifying statement at the beginning of their account. Some examples of qualifying statements might be:

"To tell you the truth."

"To be perfectly honest."

"I hear what you are saying."

"Don't take this the wrong way."

"I agree with you, but."

"As far as I know."

"I'm thinking that."

"You have to understand."

"It stands to reason."

Do Not be Intimidated

Often, a person will try to use their qualifications or experience, real or otherwise, to attempt to persuade others that their testimony, information, or opinion is more plausible or reliable. They may also play down the ability or experience of others with reference to their own. They will usually emphasise their special status by reminding people about it prior to giving their testimony, information, or opinion. For example:

"Speaking as a scientist (medium)."

"Speaking as someone who has experienced this before."

"I have been studying this for (x) number of years."

"I have attended a course run by (insert name of well-known person or television ghost hunting celebrity)."

"I was told this personally by a medium (scientist)."

"You weren't there, so you cannot possibly know."

"You cannot be an expert in something that is not properly understood."

Thinking critically is not simply the accumulation of information; it is using the information that has been acquired to solve problems. Critical thinking assists in the formulating of hypotheses and the construction of arguments. That is not to say that critical thinking should be considered as being argumentative or critical of others but it can be used to expose weaknesses and poor reasoning. It is a valuable asset and tool and forms the very core of scientific method.

CHAPTER 3

EVIDENCE

Evidence is a term that requires some consideration. Evidence is testimony or facts in support of or for a conclusion. In science it usually refers to data in support of a hypothesis. In relation to ghosts, the general hypothesis is that an unknown phenomenon commonly referred to, as 'ghosts' exist. Of course there are many other hypotheses, ideas, and theories that then seek to explain how it is that ghosts can exist. The hypothesis that ghosts do exist may indeed be true; it could neatly explain many alleged anomalous phenomena that are reported within a particular location. On the other hand, it may also be the case that all the reported phenomena considered as ghostly has normal explanations, in which case ghosts do not exist at all and a null hypothesis is instead appropriate. Many ghost investigators believe that there is sufficient evidence for the existence of ghosts to satisfy a scrupulous historian or physical scientist. But what constitutes evidence? As Henry Bauer, emeritus professor of chemistry and science studies at Virginia State University said; "It is by no means obvious what is evidence and what is not; what is thought to be evidence by one person will be thought to be irrelevant by another".

Much of the evidence for ghosts is circumstantial and it is generally not easy for other investigators to gain access to the original evidence. It may at first seem logical to take as the primary evidence that which is presented by the ghost investigator who has examined the case, spoken to witnesses, perhaps visited the location, and/or has conducted an investigation for themselves. Such evidence, presented as fact, is often the basis for many reports of hauntings and ghostly experiences within the media. However for completeness, we must acknowledge all the known reported evidence in a case. Evidence that does not support the hypothesis that ghosts exist is frequently given less space than that which the ghost investigators themselves consider to be important proof. Thousands of people each year search for ghosts or visit haunted locations but they do not see ghosts; thousands of people take photographs at haunted locations that do not show ghosts. The onus of proof must therefore always be on those who claim to have discovered some evidence, and in this case the burden rests on those who claim to have evidence for the existence of ghosts. Despite the fact that frequently they have not thoroughly proved their case, the evidence they present still deserves to be thoroughly examined.

Something also needs to be said about negative evidence. Science regards a hypothesis as being valid only if it produces testable predictions. If a test produces a positive result then it does not necessarily prove the hypothesis is correct, although it might be. It only shows that it has not been found to be incorrect. Equally if a test produces a negative result that does not mean the hypothesis was wrong, although it might be. Following any such test, there is bound to be what is considered both positive and negative evidence. However, all too often, the negative evidence tends to be overlooked or played down as it either is not considered to be supportive of the hypothesis or it fails to conform to the expected outcome.

Strictly speaking, evidence has little or no value until it has passed a number of stringent tests. For instance in a court of law, a witness may provide their evidence, however, their statement is normally only regarded as being reliable evidence if it withstands a process of rigorous cross-examination. In science, prima facie evidence must always be regarded critically and only if it withstands critical examination can it be regarded as reliable. Critical examination normally takes the form of a peer review of the results prior to publication within a journal. Replication of the experiment by others may also be used to test the evidence. It is worth stating that peer reviewed journals and books may contain misleading or out-dated information that has been successfully challenged or revised by additional research and study.

Currently, the evidence for ghosts stands as prima facie evidence. There are many difficulties in testing the evidence that has so far been presented and, until such time that it has been examined, it remains to be seen whether or not there truly is any reliable evidence for the existence of ghosts.

The Investigation Process

Investigation is really all about discovery, the act of detecting something new.

With reference to science, discovery is the observation of new phenomena, new actions or new events. Discovery also seeks to provide new reasoning and understanding to explain that observation. With respect to ghosts, there can be no question whatsoever, even by the most ardent of critics, that people experience ghosts. To claim otherwise is to totally disregard the vast collection of human testimony and experience that has been assembled over thousands of years. It is the role and function of the investigator to seek to understand why it is that people have such experiences. There are two well-established methods that are used by those seeking to study such experiences. Regardless of any pre-disposing beliefs that the investigator may have, both methods need to be fully considered and addressed by the investigation process.

The Scientific Method

Science has an established methodology that has been proven to work and can be used by anyone. It uses a defined logical series of stages that need to be followed in order to produce a conclusion or result.

1. Asking a question about some phenomenon
2. Making observations of the phenomenon
3. Hypothesising an explanation for the phenomenon
4. Test the hypothesis by experiment, observational study, or field study
5. Evaluating the results and perhaps modifying the hypothesis
6. Creating a conclusion with the data gathered in the experiment.

(Steps 4 – 6 may need to be repeated as often as necessary as the process of discovery continues).

The scientific method does not make use of, or support, what may be considered to be questionable techniques and practises including:

a) Pre-determining the nature of the phenomena based upon personal belief
b) The deliberate misuse of equipment. For example, using an electromagnetic field meter as a device to attempt to effect communications with supposed discarnate entities.
c) Aimless wandering around a location, calling out for the supposed discarnate entities to show themselves or perform some acts of proof.
d) Devising pseudo-scientific experiments i.e., using trigger objects.
e) Placing an over emphasis on claims of psychic experiences or accounts.

Psychic Methods

Paranormal investigation has, from the earliest times, made use of psychic techniques and methods in an attempt to understand the nature of the phenomena being reported within haunted locations.

These have included methods adopted from Spiritualism and divination, such as the use of the Ouija board, table tipping, automatic writing and mediumship. All of these methods are subjective and rely chiefly upon human testimony or involvement in order to obtain information. It is important that the investigation does not place any undue emphasis on the value of these methods and techniques. However, that does not mean that any information offered or obtained by such means should be disregarded either. Instead, whenever such techniques are employed, they should be carefully documented as part of the general information gathering process. Wherever possible, appropriate controls should be applied to the use of such methods and techniques.

When conducting any experiments that involve psychic methods, the investigator must be aware that they are dealing with a person's beliefs including their own. The investigator must also be aware that it is generally much easier to gain acceptance for the value of any information obtained in this manner. This includes instances where objective information appears to confirm a subjective account or experience, such as might be the case with EVP or photography. This is because people generally prefer to give additional weight to information that confirms their own pre-existing views or opinions or appears to support an experience that they may have had, or that they may have read about, or heard about from someone else. It is unfortunately the case that information that appears to contradict any prior held beliefs or ideas is considerably less likely to be accepted.

In the search for evidence and when considering any case under investigation ghost hunting takes account of two types of information:

Subjective Information and Objective Information

Taken together, these two information strands provide the investigator with the very best opportunity of determining and understanding what may be taking place or what has been experienced and reported.

Subjective information relates to the actual experiences that are reported, for example, "I saw a ghost", or "I felt a chill". Subjective information is used to provide information to the investigator, normally in the form of witness interviews, personal accounts, and testimony or from researching archives and historical sources. In all cases the information that is provided should be thoroughly checked and properly documented and referenced to any additional sources whenever possible. Often the investigator has only the subjective account of the witness. The entire basis for any investigation is invariably a claim that someone (perhaps multiple persons) has had an experience that they (or someone else) considered to be anomalous, possibly paranormal. It is therefore important that subjective information is obtained accurately and assessed properly.

Sometimes the original witness will seek out the services of the investigator in order to try and provide an explanation for their experience or perhaps they are seeking confirmation of their own belief of what the experience represents. Such scenarios are generally to be found within cases that involve domestic and residential properties. In other cases, the investigator may learn about claims for anomalous experiences through advertising and promotion of a location, from the media or the reports of previous investigators. This is more generally the case at locations that are non-residential or commercial premises and attractions. Increasingly, investigators are pro-actively seeking potential haunted locations based upon the physical appearance of the site, its age or simply the belief that it might be haunted. This latter method is seriously flawed in that it alters the entire foundation for ghost investigation. In such instances the ghost hunters are no longer seeking to test reported claims and experiences but are instead seeking to have an experience for themselves prior to any attempt at understanding or testing of their experience.

Objective information is information that is independent of human experience, opinion, or judgement and typically refers to the measurement of physical variables within a location. Such information can only be obtained using a range of equipment that has been specifically designed to monitor and record changes within the physical or environmental variables that may be present at the location and of interest to the investigation. Typically, this might include: sound recordings, pictures or video information, temperature measurements or some other form of data obtained using equipment or instrumentation. Once again, any such information that is obtained needs to be correctly documented. Things that need to be considered when addressing any information or data is the means by which it was obtained and under what circumstances it was obtained, for instance by the use of appropriate items of equipment.

Equipment can be used to:

1. Check that an observed phenomena or event actually occurred.

2. Quantify the amount of change or the rate of change of a particular variable over time.

3. Observe and record events that may go unnoticed by human observers.

Using any item of equipment requires that certain precautions need to be taken in order to ensure the quality and reliability of the observations and measurements. The equipment must only be used when these criteria have been fully met.

a) The correct item of equipment must be selected for the variable that is being observed and measured.

b) The equipment must be used in accordance with the manufacturers designed limitations and instructions for use.

c) If necessary, calibration should be carried out before and after use.

d) It is critical that anyone using an item of equipment learns the correct use and placement of each item they will be using.

e) The operator must be familiar with the setting up and positioning of the equipment in a manner that ensures its correct operation and its ability to accurately measure the intended variable.

f) The operator should have an awareness of the operating principles of the equipment and also the principles of the particular variable that is being observed.

g) The operator must be alert to error, misuse, fraud, or other situations that could result in the measurements obtained being contaminated.

h) Information must be recorded in an appropriate manner so that the information can be recalled at a later date and interpreted correctly.

i) The operator must know the correct manner in which to record and document the information that is presented by a particular item of equipment.

The information that is collected by the investigator ultimately may or may not form part of the evidence. The information is not in itself evidence, but is merely the subjective testaments and objective data used to formulate or test a hypothesis or support a conclusion. Information is often used selectively, either to support or deny the case being made. Often information may be discarded if it fails to conform to the investigator's desired outcome and the evidence they present, using selected information reflects that desire. The objective investigator needs to be led by the information rather than selecting the information that best fits their notions, beliefs, and opinions.

CHAPTER 4

PEOPLE AND PLACES

The first contact with any witness or potential witness should generally be relaxed and informal but not overly friendly. Such a first contact may take the form of a telephone call or more likely these days, email or message by social media. At this stage neither the investigator or the witness know each other well and, for any subsequent action or outcome to be successful, it is important that both parties are prepared to cooperate and work together. This is especially the case in instances in which the location is residential.

The investigator should also ensure that they do not attempt to make pre-judgement about what might have transpired or what the witness claims to have experienced. Any personal beliefs that the investigator might have should be completely disregarded at this stage and it is important to listen and accept the testimony of the witness. In the case of residential locations and, in some instances, commercial locations it is also important to try and ascertain why the person has made contact and why they are requesting the involvement of the investigator. It might also be useful, if possible, to try and discover the person's expectations in terms of any hoped for investigation or other outcome. Generally speaking, it is wise to carefully avoid offering any suggestions about what may have transpired or try to diagnose any experiences at this stage.

At all times the investigator needs to be mindful of the ethical considerations of their involvement, even down to what is said to the witness. It is all too easy to inadvertently cause more harm than good with a poor choice of words or an inappropriate response. Should the witness and the investigator decide to proceed beyond this initial contact then it will become necessary to arrange a meeting, which is generally held (although not exclusively) at the location under consideration. The first meeting should also be informal, continuing the intention of developing a good relationship with the witness and determining their expectations, but it should also consider the expectations of the investigator. It is worth re-stating the necessity of thinking carefully about the ethical considerations, anything that may be said or any actions that are proposed by either party. It is important that the investigator does not attend any meeting alone, nor should a large number of people turn up. When picking a partner for the meeting the investigator should be mindful of the witness's age, gender, and any other relevant considerations. If the witness is female, for example, it is good practise to ensure that one of the investigators is also female. Likewise, in the case of a child or adolescent, particular attention should be given to selecting those who are to attend the meeting. The witness should be invited and encouraged to have someone accompany them during the meeting. This provides them with some support and reassurance and adequately ensures the well-being of both parties. The investigator needs to consider the manner of their personal appearance and dress. Witnesses to ghostly experiences come from all walks of life and all ages. The investigator needs to develop a good relationship with the witness and it is a true saying that "first impressions count". It is not always a good idea for the investigator to demonstrate their allegiance to a particular heavy metal band. Neither is it always appreciated that the investigator shows up at the witness's home or workplace wearing their investigation group logo proudly emblazoned on a fleecy jacket or with a collection of flight cases. Sometimes a witness may not have mentioned their experiences to family members or work colleagues, or they may not wish colleagues and neighbours to know that they have requested assistance. In cases where the witness has sought out the investigator and requested their involvement they will undoubtedly have certain expectations, expectations that the investigator may or may not be able to attain. Such expectations may be as a result of television ghost hunting programmes but it is just as likely that they will have based their expectations on the investigator's media or Internet presence. Such sites and pages often emphasise the serious intent of the investigator and often are liberally peppered throughout with terms such as *scientific, professional, and expert.* The investigator needs to be aware that these words will create both an impression and an expectation within the witness. Some witnesses may consider the investigator to be less skilled because they do not act like the television role models or they might be put-off by an over-zealous investigator who arrives burdened with an enormous quantity of ghost hunting equipment. Most importantly, at all times the investigator must act courteously and professionally. It is unfortunately the case that investigators will often overlook the basic pleasantries and there is no need to immediately begin questioning the witness about their experiences. Instead, the investigator should make their introductions, talk about the weather, share some small talk, and initially keep the conversation informal. The investigator should use appropriate words and language when speaking to the client and avoid ghost-hunting jargon. Do not offer or suggest a diagnosis or opinion about the experiences of the witness at this stage. The investigator should maintain an impartial and non-judgemental attitude regardless of personal beliefs or anything what the witness might say.

Often the witness will launch into a full description of their experiences, usually with a jumbled chronology. A witness may have a friend or family member present who may prompt the witness to describe events or add information and opinions of his or her own. It is all too easy for the investigator to become overwhelmed by this torrent of information and to miss important details or lose track of the events and the timeline. Occasionally the witness may be reticent to describe their experiences and the investigator may need to draw the information from the witness. Every witness is a human being and every witness and meeting will be different. The investigator needs to assess the situation carefully and adjust their approach accordingly. The investigator needs to be guided by the witness but not end up being led by the witness. Witnesses may already have strong opinions about the nature of their experiences and what they represent, the reasons and the causes. The investigator must listen to what the witness is saying and use that to guide their response but they should avoid it becoming a situation in which the witness demands an explanation for their experiences or any confirmation that it is paranormal.

Questioning the Witness

The way in which questions are asked can have a large bearing on the outcome of any interview and the resulting value of the information that is obtained. The investigator must always avoid asking leading questions such as "Whereabouts did you see the ghost?" This can be replaced by a more general question that will usually elicit the same information such as "Can you tell me about your experience?"

Certain methods may be usefully employed to help the witness recall information. These include:

1. *Limiting cognitive resources.* This considers simply the number of items a person can be expected to concentrate upon at any given time. It is recommended that interviews be conducted in a suitable non-distracting environment where the witness's ability to focus upon answering the questions and recalling information is not being diminished by competing distractions.

2. *Context recreation.* This takes account of the possibility that memory might be improved by recreating the context in which the experience occurred. This might take the form of visiting the specific location, the showing of photographs and plans or simply asking the witness to recreate the scene in their minds eye.

Documenting any conversation is important and nowadays it is common to also record the conversation. This is generally a good practise as it allows the investigator to focus upon their dialogue with the witness without the constant distraction of needing to write copious notes. However, it is important that the witness consents to the conversation being recorded beforehand and that they are also encouraged to record the conversation or are offered a copy of the recording by the investigator. Some investigators prefer to work through a list of prepared questions or even a questionnaire. In some situations this may be appropriate and helpful, but it can often become a tick-box exercise in which questions are asked simply because they are written on the form. Having some prepared questions is helpful as it forms a memory aide for the investigator. It is all too easy to overlook asking important questions, which are sometimes the most basic of all, particularly when faced with a witness who is keen to share their experiences with a torrent of information and mixed up detail.

The investigator must treat the witness ethically at all times and show both the witness and their property due respect. The investigator has no right to be there without permission. A principle of informed consent must apply to every action undertaken by the investigator. The witness must be guaranteed complete confidentiality together with the right to withdraw from the process at any time and have all records either handed over to them or destroyed.

The witness must be considered to have moral ownership of every item of information, including all recordings, documents and material relating to the investigation. The investigator must waive all rights to use any of the material without the prior written consent of all the witnesses. Such an agreement must explicitly state how and where the investigator intends to use any material. It is unfortunately the case that investigation groups continue to regularly post pictures and video recordings that are taken at private homes and workplaces onto their social media or Internet sites. Often these images will contain sufficient detail to permit the identity of the location or witnesses to be ascertained, even though the investigators state that the case is anonymous.

In many cases there may be additional witnesses or people involved. For example, this might be neighbours, friends, or relatives of the primary witness. They may have had experiences of their own that might corroborate or contradict the primary witness's account. However, the investigator must be cautious when considering such sources. These people may not wish to participate and assist the investigation or the primary witness may not wish them to get involved or even be consulted. These wishes must be given priority over any desire on the part of the investigator to consult or question these additional people. Moreover, the investigator must ensure that from the very outset that they do not draw any attention to their presence, their interest in the location, or the phenomena that have been reported, until they have ensured that they have the full prior consent of all the parties involved. When interviewing witnesses it is important that all possible sources of potential information are considered and not just those who claim to have had some experience. It is frequently found that some people who may live or work at the location may never have had any experiences at all. This information relating to non-experience is just as important and significant for any investigation as the testimony of those who have had an experience.

Finally, it worth bearing in mind that sometimes a person will deny having any experience, they may even be dismissive of the experiences of others that took place whilst they were present but some time later reveal and describe experiences to the investigator.

At this stage it is important that the investigator merely documents the testimony of the witness, however strange it may sound and does not seek to question the veracity or integrity of the witness directly. In the majority of instances the witness will be providing a truthful account of their experiences. Immediately challenging the witness, suggesting that they were mistaken, or even fabricating their account is a sure and certain way to destroy the investigator / witness relationship that is necessary for the investigation. Instead, immediately following the initial conversation or meeting, the investigator needs to begin the process of trying to understand the witness's experience and seek to test the claims that are being made. This involves reviewing the information, not just the information that has been provided by the witness about the experience, but also taking into consideration how the information was obtained during interview process. Consider if the account or the testimony is plausible. Does the information make sense? Could it have happened the way it is being described? For example, from their position or vantage point could the witness actually have seen what they tell you they have seen? Was the witness reluctant to provide information or uncertain about any aspects of their experience?

Sometimes, the investigator may consider that it is appropriate to request information that is of a personal or sensitive nature. Unfortunately, this sort of information is often routinely requested by investigators for no other reason than the investigators are merely following the example of others or a belief that by asking such things they are being thorough with their investigation. There are some investigators who produce questionnaires that go into extraordinary detail about every aspect of the daily life of the witness. Often, these questionnaires will also include questions about the mental health of the witness, that of their family members, medications, and even the sexual orientation of the witness. This is not only highly intrusive but, in the majority of cases, such questions are completely unnecessary in terms of carrying out an effective investigation. There may be some very limited instances when it might be relevant to consider the drug and alcohol intake of a witness but these are questions that should not form a routine part of any witness interview. Moreover, it is meaningless to ask any such questions without the necessary expertise to understand the responses.

For example, understanding about how a particular medication may affect a witness is not something that can be gained by just using the Internet to look up the side effects of the drug and relating those side effects to the experience of the witness. Such methods will inevitably lead only to assumptions being made by the investigator that are, at best, misleading. Questioning the mental health or well-being of a witness can have no justification whatsoever by any investigator except in special circumstances in which the investigator has the necessary training and expertise to fully understand the response that may be provided and the training and expertise to respond accordingly. It has frequently been the case that unwitting investigators have caused actual psychological harm to a witness by ill thought questions and poor responses to the answers.

Following the initial meetings, time should be taken for a proper consideration of the information that has been obtained. This period of consideration should also be extended to the witness and they may wish to amend the terms of their involvement, or even withdraw from the investigation altogether. It may equally be the case that the investigator cannot meet the expected outcome desired by the witness in which case it much wiser to withdraw and state honestly that they are unable to proceed. If it is decided by both parties to continue with the process, then it will become necessary to begin to more formally document the information that is being provided. Here it might be appropriate to utilise a questionnaire in order to ensure that all the necessary information is obtained and recorded. All of the foregoing described requirements relating to ethical considerations and the principles of informed consent and ownership and use of the information must continue to be adhered to by the investigator. It must also be remembered that the witness may, at any time and without notice, alter or change those conditions or withdraw from the process.

Some investigators operate in the belief that they are providing a service to the witness or their community by conducting an investigation. This is a mistake. Certainly, the investigator should be mindful of the needs of the witness and try to assist them meet those needs but they are not the primary function of any investigation. The function of investigation is to attempt to seek and understand an unusual and interesting experience that the witness claims to have had. Investigators are not well placed to act as counsellors or spiritual advisors, neither should they be there to conduct any form of clearance or treatment for either the witness or the location. Such functions have no place in ghost investigation and they should never be offered or provided by responsible investigators.

Subsequently, if it is agreed by all parties that an active investigation is deemed appropriate, then the client should be fully informed prior to every stage of the process and be given the opportunity to remove their consent or amend the terms of the investigation at any time. Any investigation generally requires the investigator or a group of investigators to spend time at the location. This requirement is two-fold:

1. To seek to replicate if possible the experience of the witness.

2. To seek an explanation if possible for the experience of the witness.

The witness must at all times remain an integral part of the investigation process. In many instances they will be spending a great deal more time at the location than the investigators and their on-going testimony and reports should be fully considered and integrated into the overall investigation. Upon completion, the witness must be given full and complete access to any and all the investigation notes, documents, and findings except in special circumstances where it might infringe upon the privacy of others but generally excluding that of investigators.

Beginning the Process of Investigation

Once it has been agreed that some form of active investigation is required, then it is often the case that the witness is asked to begin to keep a diary of their experiences. This can be a helpful step and assists the investigator with information about the on-going events. A diary should include simple details and provide information relating to who had the experience, where the experience occurred, when the experience took place, and a basic description of the experience. However, the investigator must be aware that their request for the witness to maintain a diary will almost inevitably affect the witness's perception of any subsequent events and experiences. Requesting that a diary be kept is a sign of the investigator's interest and it may result in the witness attributing a greater significance to experiences than might have previously been the case. Events that previously had been ignored or overlooked as mundane or irrelevant may now become noteworthy.

Other family members or work colleagues may also become aware of the diary that is being kept or may themselves be asked to note their own experiences. People who previously had no interest in the events and who had never even considered the events, may start to make attributions of a paranormal cause for unrelated experiences or events. Commencing and maintaining a diary of events is a useful step but it can often cause an increase in the apparent number of experiences and events that take place and the investigator needs to be aware of this likelihood.

If it is decided that the witness should maintain a diary, then this should be for a reasonable period of time before the active investigation begins. The diary should also be maintained throughout the period of the investigation. A second diary kept by the investigator should also be commenced in order to document their personal experiences and thoughts during each visit to the location. The diaries will hopefully provide some insights into the nature of the reported events and experiences, the time and locations where they occur, and who (if anyone) was witness to the events. The investigator can use this information in order to better target their resources in terms of timing of visits and placement of investigation personnel and / or items of equipment.

Whilst there may be common features, there are no two cases that are alike. The events will differ, the experiences will differ, and the perception and response of witnesses to their experiences will differ. Some people may be scared, others accepting and nonplussed. The expectations and desired outcome of the investigation will also be different case to case. Some people will seek to have the events and experience stopped whilst others are happy for them to continue. It is the role of the investigator to adapt their investigation methods and approaches to suit the particular case and most importantly the people involved. Accordingly, there can be no prescribed method or technique for undertaking the investigation other than further re-stating that the primary consideration must always remain the moral and ethical treatment of the witness, their property, and their privacy.

Public Access Investigations and Locations

Due to high demand we have managed to secure new dates for our Ghost Hunt at T... in G... Available Spaces are limited. Saturday 4th July and Saturday 25th July.

It is highly advisable that any guest that practices witchcraft thinks very long and hard before booking this ghost hunt especially due to the encountered paranormal encountered here on previous investigations. Some of the entities in this location are formidable, and this location requires guests to have full protection before the event starts. This is non-negotiable. Any guests that "opts" out of this will not be permitted to continue / start the investigation.

T... is harrowing, and this location has very dark entities that still remain in this building. Witches...Murderers...Pirates...are just some of the people that have been through these doors! This haunted Gaol is eerie, dark, and bloody frightening. Some of the paranormal reported here such as ghostly apparitions, guests being pushed, as well as voices being heard, is just a small fraction of the paranormal encountered here. For further information or other dates please go to:

(SOCIAL MEDIA ADVERT PROMOTING PUBLIC GHOST HUNT EVENT)

There is another type of investigation commonly undertaken by investigators that needs to be briefly considered. These generally take place at locations which permit investigations to take place for profit or gain. Locations such as historic buildings, tourist attractions, and public houses often come into this category. Sometimes the location will approach the investigators and request an investigation but equally the investigators may approach the location and suggest that an investigation be permitted. In some instances the investigator and the location have very different expectations and desired outcomes. The location may be seeking to gain financially or in some other way, such as increased publicity (usually with the aim of also gaining financially), whilst the investigator may be seeking to understand more about the nature of the reported events and experiences. In recent years there have been an increased number of commercial companies who offer ghost-hunting opportunities to members of the public. The aim of these business enterprises is solely to make a profit from running the event and, despite the advertising and promotion of such events as investigations, this is usually far from the reality and any discussion regarding such events can have no place within this book.

A final complication is the trend by ghost investigation groups to also sell ghost-hunts to the public. It is now very much the case that the majority of locations charge the investigators, often a great deal of money, to access the particular location and there are increasingly fewer investigators who can afford to pay these high fees. While it is clear that some groups are seeking to gain financially from organising these types of events, there is a case to consider whereby a mutual agreement can exist between the investigators and the location that satisfies both parties. For instance, an arrangement might be made, that permits the investigators to gain access to a location in order to conduct their own research and study whilst organising separate public access events that generates revenue for the location. Such an arrangement can be of mutual benefit, although investigators who use such arrangements must fully consider the implications carefully. Approached with diligence, such arrangements have proved to be helpful to both parties. The primary advantage is of course gaining access to a location of interest that would otherwise be unavailable due to the cost; the possibility of obtaining the additional experiential information from participants may also be advantageous. If investigators opt for this approach, then it is still important that the individual privacy and ethical treatment of participants is ensured.

Historical Perspective

Psychical research is full of well-attested cases in which apparitions, ghosts of the living, have been reported. Unsurprisingly, there are numerous theories that attempt to account for those experiences; time-slips, hallucinations, thought transference, spontaneous telepathy, and bi-location, etc., have all been proposed and argued over. But it is the general belief that ghosts and apparitions represent deceased persons and events from the past that prevails. This belief is rooted deep within the folklore and traditions of ghosts and is reflected in many of the stories attached to haunted homes and locations. Drawing upon the same traditions, many also believe that, in order for a ghost to attach itself to a location, the site must have been the place in which some traumatic event took place such as a murder for example. It is this widespread belief that ghosts and hauntings represent some historical remnant that leads ghost investigators toward studying the history of a location that they are investigating. Investigators are seeking a reason and an explanation for why a ghost haunts a location. To do so is a normal human trait; we like to seek out explanations for the things that we experience. For many ghost investigators it is not a question of what a ghostly experience might represent in terms of a human experience, but instead it becomes the search for a historical reason why a particular ghost would wish to appear. They may have been murdered or be the murderer, the may have been deeply unhappy, or have had fond memories of their mortal life at a location. The ghost may still be attached to the location because their mortal remains lie unclaimed, such as was the case with Athenodorus and his chain-rattling spectre.

To facilitate their historical study, investigators access local, regional, and even national archives, a task now made much easier by many of these records being available online. They seek out significant people and events, searching for clues that link together the reported experiences and the past.

A recent development has been a reversal of this process; investigators now visit and conduct investigations at locations purely on the basis of its history frequently with little or even no prior witness information to support a belief that it must be haunted because something terrible or significant took place.

Of course, other than conjecture and speculation, it is impossible to determine why ghosts haunt locations, so it might be that they return to places that in life they loved, hated, were murdered, or took life, were incarcerated, or spent their final happy hours of freedom. It may be entirely logical to consider that the dead do return and are witnessed, and there are numerous instances in which the apparition has been positively identified as being someone who is known to be deceased. Equally, there are many cases in which the identity of the phantom is based entirely upon speculation or a perceived link to some significant historical event. Researching and studying the history of a haunted site is a part of the overall investigation process but there becomes a real danger that any perceived significant events or individuals that are discovered will affect the investigation.

An example of this distortion is the case of Borley Rectory, notoriously known as the most haunted house in England. Investigated by Harry Price from 1929 until his death in 1948 and studied by ghost investigators and sceptics ever since; the rectory was built in 1863 by the Reverend Henry Bull. The site already had local stories of a ghostly nun and her lover attempting to elope and being caught. With some variations between accounts, the lover was hanged; the nun bricked up and left to die. The case has been extensively written about and discussed with many theories and speculations being proposed. Several ghosts including the former incumbents, animals, and ghostly coaches

drawn by headless horses or driven by headless coachmen are reported to haunt the location. But the ghostly figure of a nun is the one that
has endured from the earliest days up to the present. Many speak of
her identity as a certainty, her name, Mary Lairre is well known. There
have been many who claim to have witnessed the apparition of the nun;
sometimes more than one witness such as famously took place on the
evening of 28 July 1900 when three young female members of the Bull
family who were returning from garden party saw the nun. One of the
girls rushed to call an older sister who also witnessed the ghostly figure. Based upon the number of experiences there is certainly a case to
be made for the appearance of the figure at various locations within
the small area surrounding the rectory site but the identity of the nun
is the significant problem that most tend to overlook. On 28 October
1937, Helen Glanville, the daughter of Harry Price's assistant Sydney
Glanville, used a planchette to experiment with automatic writing,
she was alone in the family home in Streatham, South London. Harry
Price reproduced an extract of her scripts in *The Most Haunted House
in England*:

[No question was asked, but the name Marianne was written]	
Is it someone using this name?	[Indistinct]
Could you tell me your own name?	[Indistinct]
Are you buried in the garden?	Yes.
Can you tell us where?	Der re Ind.
Do you mean under the fir tree?	No.
Near a tree?	Yes.
Is there anything to tell us where?	Stone.
Can you tell me the rest of your name?	La.... [then indistinct]
Are the first two letters 'L a' ?	irre.
Do you mean 'Lairre'?	Yes.

A second séance was held on 31 October 31 1937 at the same location,
this time attended by Mr Glanville, his son and daughter Helen, together with another investigator Mark Kerr-Pearse who provided further
information about the identity of the nun. The participants obtained
the nun's full name 'Mary Lairre' together with details of her death by
strangulation in 1667 apparently by a member of the prominent Waldegrave family. In his second book relating to the case of Borley Rectory
The End of Borley Rectory published in 1946, Harry Price devotes an
entire chapter to what he describes as a "brilliant analysis of the Borley

drama" supplied by the Reverend Canon W. J. Phythian-Adams, Canon of Carlisle. The Canon goes on to construct an entire narrative about the haunting and the reasons why the nun continues to be seen. That she was a young French woman brought to England in the seventeenth or eighteenth centuries, a member of the Waldegrave family becoming infatuated with her, possibly even marrying her. Later, she becomes an impediment to a more suitable or profitable marriage and is murdered. Price clearly found Phythian-Adams' assessment of the case to be highly satisfactory and the events suggested by Phythian-Adams have become the basis for almost all the accepted versions of the nun's tale. It has been recounted in many books and articles and has become almost an accepted fact by many. But it is just the opinion of one man, based upon his interpretation of the events and the name Mary Lairre came from the participants at an automatic writing séance.

Of course, it might well be the case that a young French girl was brought to England and ultimately murdered, it may also be the case that her name was Mary Lairre and that she was strangled in 1667. It may equally be the case that the entire story is completely different, perhaps even that there was no story at all. What is clear is that a lot of people have had unusual experiences at the rectory and the adjacent area. A number of the experiences pre-date the building of the rectory and post-date its demolition. Most of the experiences were subjective, a much smaller number have been objectively documented, but virtually all have been distorted by an almost unwitting desire on the part of the investigators to link them to the Phythian-Adams story. Any consideration of the actual experiences of the numerous witnesses to the many different events now tend to always be judged against the story of Mary Lairre and her tragic death. It is a common error; investigators continue to seek significance in the history of a location where in reality there may be little or nothing to suggest any connection. Often, the identity of the ghost or spirit is revealed by a medium or as in the case of Borley, during an automatic writing séance. Increasingly, it is because a name is heard uttered in an EVP session. The validity of these sources of information must be questioned, as it is possible that the investigators will already have heard about significant people or events associated with a location beforehand.

One final point to consider is that the history of the location may just as equally affect the witness perception of what they experienced. A fleeting figure in a religious setting may easily be interpreted as being the ghost of a monk or a priest. The same experience in a castle might be interpreted with certainty as being a knight or a warrior. People's perception of events and experiences is often coloured by their expectations and their personal beliefs. This becomes especially true in cases in which the history of the location is well known, such as historic landmarks, or where the location is the subject of local stories and folklore. There are numerous places in which there is a tale of murder or intrigue or an association with a prominent historical figure but a lack of any supporting historical documents or facts to be found. This assumed knowledge relating to a location may lead to witnesses describing an apparition as wearing a particular period costume or resembling a portrait but that doesn't prove the identity of the apparition, most people in the past tended to wear similar clothing and appeared alike.

Researching the history of the location, the building, and the people that have been associated with it, might reveal information that is relevant to the investigation process but investigators must ensure that it does not become a search for an easy explanation as to why people claim to have ghostly experiences.

CHAPTER 5

AMAZING THINGS AND AMAZING PEOPLE

Ghost investigators have embraced technology. Technology has allowed them to peer into the darkest recesses of haunted buildings, to accurately measure the smallest temperature fluctuations, and record every creak of the floorboard. But this conventional technology has failed to deliver up the ghosts. In their continuing quest for proof, ghost investigators have increasingly turned toward new devices that, according to the manufacturer and seller's description, provide new capabilities and ghost detecting opportunities. Investigators can now use the Geo-Phone, the REM-Pod, and the EMF Pump and have discovered that the spirits seemingly have developed a preference to speak in distorted monosyllables over modified radios and have even adapted their communication skills in a bid to master the smart phone and tablet. Do any of these new pieces of equipment really work and prove the existence of ghosts? Many investigators will tell you they do.

In some instances, conventional equipment is used in novel new ways, investigators have observed that the dead and discarnate can communicate by causing the bulb in their torch to flicker and the LED's on their meters to flash. Do any of the new uses found for older technology prove the existence of ghosts? Again, many investigators will say they do.

Most people understand how a torch works but in the majority of cases it is actually quite difficult to discover much about the mechanics of the new devices. For example, many paranormal investigators use the REM-Pod, a device retailing between £100 and £200 and which the manufacturer describes as being:

> Designed exclusively for professional paranormal investigators. REM-POD monitors its electromagnetic environment, alerting you with sound and multi-coloured lights when a change has occurred. To enhance the effect, it uses a mini telescopic antenna to emit its own independent electromagnetic field around the instrument. The emitted EM field can be easily influenced by objects that conduct electricity... and this influence will be detected as well. Based on source proximity, strength and EM field distortion... 4 colourful LED light columns can be activated in any order or combination. This new feature is intended to further help promote and advance paranormal research.

All of which sounds impressive, more so when investigators see the REM-Pod being used on several of the television ghost hunting shows. Hundreds of five star reviews by investigators attest to its usefulness as a ghost investigation tool, so useful in fact, that the manufacturer has extended the 'POD' range. There is the E-Pod that "detects the e-field that surrounds static electricity", the Temp-Pod that provides "hot and cold spot audible detection with red and blue trend LED", the Vibe-Pod, the PSA-Pod, REM-Pod SDD, and REM-Pod EMT etc. But returning to the original REM-Pod, exactly what is the nature of the electromagnetic field it produces? No information about the field frequency or strength is provided. The technical information is sparse; in fact it's non-existent. The manufacturer and ghost stores inform buyers that it was designed for a particular television ghost hunting programme and that it uses a 9-volt battery but that is just about all that they tell the buyer. There are several manufacturers who offer similar devices, all making vague but amazing claims and all offering little or no technical information about the manner in which the device works. However, it is possible by examining the advertising to determine that:

> A moving electric current is transmitted from the antenna creating an electromagnetic field. Each time the current changes direction the polarity of the field changes. This constantly changing field interacts with any electrically conductive object it encounters and induces

within it an opposing electric field that is detected, amplified and used to drive an indicator.

The foregoing was not a description of a ghost-detecting device however, but of a metal detector used by treasure hunters or security staff. Other varieties of ghost detectors use capacitance sensing, the same as used in DIY pipe and stud detectors, while others use a principle borrowed from the Theremin, a musical instrument that dates to 1928, invented by Russian Leon Theremin. A Theremin uses an antenna as one side (plate) of a variable capacitance circuit; the other side (plate) of the capacitor is created by the performer's hand (or any electrically conductive object). The capacitance varies according to the distance between the two plates. This antenna / performer capacitor forms part of a circuit that detects and measures these changes in capacitance. In the case of the Theremin, the changes drive an oscillator circuit that produces changes in tone or volume, in the case of a ghost detector; the changes are used to drive a light display, sometimes with an audible buzzer too. Actually, ghost investigators have explored the use of Theremins in the past and some continue to do so, theorising that instead of the performer's hand altering the capacitance of the circuit, the ghost or spirit does this. The current crop of devices that utilise all these simple and well-understood principles of proximity sensing are offering nothing to ghost investigators that will assist them in understanding the nature of their surroundings and absolutely nothing in terms of assisting them to detect the presence of ghosts or spirits despite their claims and the claims of those writing the five-star reviews. They all fall at the very first hurdle, that of defining what exactly a ghost or spirit is, or even if ghosts exist at all. As already stated, it is an impossible task to detect or measure something that we know absolutely nothing about. Ghost investigators leap at using every new device, desperate for proof or greater proof. Those who investigate ghosts are constantly seeking new ideas, adapting theories picked up from television, Spiritualism, and one another via social media but rarely ever truly considering the questions that the devices and the theories pose. Devices don't have to appear to be highly technical in order to have some amazing ability to detect or interact with ghosts and spirits either; sometimes the most basic item of equipment can be put to good use.

The Maglite Theory

Those who regularly watch television ghost hunting shows might already be familiar with this comparatively new technique for spirit communication. Using an AA mini Maglite torch, the investigator turns on the torch and places it unattended onto a table or some other surface. The ghosts and spirits are then called upon to interact and respond to the investigator's questions by switching the bulb on and off. Generally, this demonstration produces dramatic and intriguing results as the light is turned off and on, or flickers and flashes as questions are put to the ghost or spirit by the investigators. The reaction of those witnessing these responses is generally a mixture of amazement and disbelief. Sometimes, the torch is dismantled and sceptics are encouraged to examine and verify that the torch is absolutely standard, with no hidden devices or wires connected to it. Returned to the table, the spirits will begin once again to affect the device. The torch is only capable of two basic responses i.e., on or off, so questions must be simply put, requiring only a yes or no answer. The flickering and flashing is sometimes interpreted as an uncertain response by some investigators. Sometimes the torch is used alongside more conventional séance methods, the investigators sitting in a darkened circle surrounding the torch. It is a well-established convention that spirits prefer red light and fitting a red filter to the torch satisfies this and, fortunately, Maglite make a set of filters that can be quickly pushed onto the front of the torch. Investigators using this new communication method claim that it is often more reliable than other techniques that require ghosts and spirits to affect an electrical device. It is a widely held opinion amongst investigators that spirits and ghosts are able to manipulate energy and this belief forms the basis of the Maglite theory; the communicating spirit merely has to manipulate the electricity flowing from the batteries and illuminating the bulb.

The use of a simple electrical circuit that uses a light bulb as an indicator of spiritual phenomena is far from a new idea. Harry Price and several other psychical researchers included a small bulb, wire, and batteries in their ghost hunting kit. Similar techniques were also often included in séances as a simple test for a materialising spirit. Sometimes elaborate anti-fraud measures were taken, such as placing the equipment under a glass dome. Price took fraud prevention to the next level by additionally placing the switch beneath a soap bubble, which would readily burst if anyone attempted to tamper with the switch. Used in séances with the

Medium, Stella C., the device called a Telekinetoscope was a development of a similar device used by researcher Dr W. J. Crawford at séances with the Golligher circle in Belfast between 1915 and 1920.

The AA Maglite is a simple device; two batteries supply power to the small three-volt bulb. There is no switch in the AA Maglite model, it is turned on and off by simply twisting the bulb housing. As the user turns the bulb housing, the bulb is moved into contact with the batteries against an opposing spring, making the circuit and turning the lamp on. Rotating the bulb housing in the opposite direction causes the bulb to break contact with the batteries and the light is extinguished. The Internet has many pages and forums dedicated to the Maglite theory and of course there are lots of YouTube videos showing investigators apparently communicating with spirits using this method. The Maglite theory has many supporters who believe that the spirits are able to communicate by causing the bulb to switch on and off. However, the true explanation is more mundane and simply the result of the Maglite's design and its switchless method of illuminating the bulb. The Maglite demonstration is an easy trick to perform. The investigator needs only to rotate the head of the Maglite until the bulb just illuminates. The bulb, now lit, produces heat as well as light. When the light is on, the bulb heats the metal carrier that surrounds it, which expands slightly. This small amount of expansion is just sufficient to cause the contact between the bulb and the batteries to be broken and the bulb turns off. Once off, the metal cools and contracts. When it has sufficiently cooled, contact between the bulb and batteries is once again restored and the bulb once more illuminates. The cycle of heating and cooling, expansion and contraction, continues at fairly regular intervals. The actual frequency of the on / off cycle will vary slightly from location to location as it is partially dependent upon the temperature of the torch body and also the ambient temperature of the location. Once the cycle has been determined it then becomes a simple step for the investigator to time the questions they ask and work with the sequential switching of the light. The reliability and reproducibility of this effect is such that it is commonly demonstrated on public access ghost hunting events and periodically appears on television ghost shows too. There are some investigators who unquestioningly use the method perhaps believing that it does represent an actual demonstration of spirit interaction. This simple demonstration of physics may not teach us anything about the spirit realm but it may teach valuable lessons about the manner in which people react to seemingly paranormal events.

I was asked to participate in a public ghost hunt, to demonstrate some of the techniques used by investigators. In the introduction, I showed how to surreptitiously manipulate an EMF meter using a simple magnet, making it seemingly respond to a series of questions and I cautioned the participants that often-simple tricks can be used to create the illusion that something paranormal is taking place. Afterwards, during a group séance session led by a medium, I set up my AA Maglite torch, turning the head until the bulb just lit and placed it, without comment, near to the group. After several minutes, the light on the torch flickered and went out and after a few more moments it turned itself back on. Immediately, the group took notice and diverted their attention toward the torch, which after a short pause extinguished and illuminated once again. Without prompting, the medium leading the séance asked aloud if the spirit had caused the light to flash and began to question the interacting spirit and she interpreted the spirit's responses. The spirit was male, trapped after being murdered and unhappy at being contacted. It promised to make further demonstrations by moving objects and touching people. The effect of the bulb's response to questioning was further accentuated for the participants when several of the group stated that they had become suddenly cold and had felt shivers running through them. Over the next fifteen minutes the medium and group were able to piece together a tale of murder and intrigue and the name John. Throughout the séance, nobody questioned that the response of the torch may have any other explanation and as the session concluded the medium explained that it was one of the best séances she had led and participants talked openly about how impressed they had been by this demonstration of spirit interaction. At the end of the evening I explained that a communicating spirit had not affected the torch and that the flickering of the bulb was in reality completely explainable, demonstrating this by reproducing a short spirit conversation of my own using another AA Maglite belonging to a member of public. The group reacted well to my explanation and I believe understood the point that I was making. However, the medium was less pleased, complaining that I had used the torch to demonstrate that she was in some way fraudulent. During the séance she, like everyone else in the group had believed that a spirit called John was communicating, responding to her questions; but this was not a test of mediumship, neither was it a demonstration of fraudulent mediumship. It was, however, an excellent demonstration of human fallibility and the medium like everyone else in the séance group was human. Previously, as part of my infrasound studies another medium had been asked to walk around a building and note down his psychic impressions onto a location plan. Later, when the measured levels of infrasound were compared with the notes of the medium it was noticed that there was a strong correlation between the psychic impressions of the medium and the levels of infrasound. Regions in which infrasound was strongest corresponded to the medium sensing a "dense psychic energy"; whilst in areas of lower infrasound the psychic energy was also less. Discussing these results afterwards with the medium, we both appreciated that he was simply interpreting the psycho-physiological effects of the infrasound in terms of his own psychic beliefs, the medium pointing out that he "was just human and was of course judging his experiences in the light of his beliefs". The Maglite experiment also demonstrated that mediums are just like the rest of us, they are normal human beings, complete with all our normal human failings and fallibilities. The Maglite did not demonstrate that the medium was behaving fraudulently or lacking psychic skills. In actual fact, like tests that seek and constantly fail to prove the existence of ghosts, there are no tests that are able to conclusively prove that mediumistic abilities exist. The converse is also true and we completely lack proof that ghosts and mediums are not true examples of paranormal phenomena. When it comes to all these devices that claim to detect ghosts, contact ghosts, and capture proof of ghosts, the reality is that sometimes it becomes all too easy for investigators to be drawn in by something that appears to be amazing.

Psychics and Mediums

In 1848, in a seemingly haunted house in Hydesville, New York State, a series of strange raps and knocks heralded the start of the Spiritualist movement. Claimed to be the attempts by the spirit of a dead peddler to communicate with two young sisters, Kate and Margaret Fox, the sounds continue to resonate to this day. The Fox sisters were not the first mediums but their experiences came at a time when a receptive world took notice. Spiritualism grew rapidly and, following the example of the Fox sisters, many people discovered that they too were psychic with a special ability to act as mediums between the dead and living. Despite the first footsteps of Spiritualism taking place in haunted houses, psychics and mediums for the most part confined themselves to the séance room, communicating directly with the spirits of the deceased, seeking their own forms of proof and rarely venturing into haunted houses to seek out the ghosts. There were of course some exceptions, one of which took place in Preston, Lancashire, in December 1934, when a small group of Spiritualists and mediums visited a haunted house to investigate a ghost. After their visit, during which one of the group claimed to have witnessed the apparition of a woman, the owner of the property concluded that the ghost was "a myth... caused by the lights of a passing motor". Periodically, mediums and psychics have also offered their services or have been called upon to assist ghost investigators, such was the case at Borley Rectory and the Enfield poltergeist, for example, but for the most part they have tended to steer clear of haunted locations. In 2002, the television programme *Most Haunted* portrayed the use of a medium as a key role in their ghost hunt and this appears to have directly changed the manner in which ghost investigation groups have used mediums. Prior to this, a medium was rarely part of the investigation team, and ghost investigation groups were rarely led by a medium or had a resident medium as part of their group. Following the show going to air, the concept of mediums, sensitives, and psychics being integral and/or essential to ghost investigating, has increasingly become the norm. This is not the place to begin a discussion about the abilities or otherwise of mediums and psychics and there are strong cases put by both sides. It is worth, however, considering the manner in which the information that is provided by those who claim to have such abilities is used and treated by ghost investigators. The investigator is totally reliant upon the testimony of the medium, there is no way in which the claim can be tested or verified. The medium may claim that they can see or sense the ghost; they may then describe their experience in great detail. The investigator relies upon that testimony and often uses it as a keystone of the investigation and the basis for setting up equipment, locating personnel, or for judging other experiences.

The lights flash on some device or other and the team's resident medium confirms it indicates the presence of a spirit. A team member describes that they are feeling chilled and the medium confirms that this is due to the proximity of a ghost. Both the foregoing are commonly encountered scenarios of modern ghost investigation and both are seriously flawed in the manner they are usually dealt with by investigators. As was pointed out during my infrasound experiments, mediums are human. They, like the rest of us, have thoughts and impressions all of the time. They get disorientated in the dark and fooled by shadows; the difference is that they may allow the belief that they have additional abilities to colour and affect the way in which they interpret their personal experiences. Investigators need to take account of everyone's experiences; the entire basis for investigating any haunting or ghost is based upon the testimony of someone's experience. If the witness makes no special claims about their ability then their testimony is usually documented without giving it any undue status but when the person claims to have special abilities, such as psychic abilities, then generally ghost investigators tend to give that testimony a greater degree of credibility and place a greater reliance upon its worth. This becomes increasingly true if the person with psychic abilities is a part of the investigation team, perhaps even the leader of the team. A greater emphasis is therefore placed on the medium's testimony with little questioning of the information that they provide.

It is not the role of the ghost investigator to seek to test anyone who is claiming special abilities and to attempt to do so would in all probability be pointless. Parapsychologists and others have been undertaking such tests for over a century with inconclusive results. Certainly, some mediums have been shown to be fake and acting fraudulently but that does not mean that they all are charlatans. It is almost certainly the case that many believe that their psychic abilities are totally genuine, their experiences a direct result of their abilities, or gift, but that does not prevent them from being tricked by their senses and led by their beliefs into making assumptions that may be false. But, there may be people who do in fact have an ability to sense or communicate with ghosts and spirits.

The role of the ghost investigator is to examine the claims of witnesses and of experiences and events. Documenting the experiences of every witness is a crucial part of every investigation. It makes no difference if the witness is a household member, location worker, or an investigation team member; their subjective testimony is usually the only information that the investigator has in most instances. Information that is provided by a medium is subjective i.e., their opinion and their description of their experience. It is important and must not be disregarded but it is no more and no less important than the subjective testament from anyone else. Like the existence or otherwise of ghosts we cannot show the existence of psychic abilities, and that must mean that the investigator should not place a greater degree of reliability or a greater emphasis on the testimony of anyone simply on the basis that they claim to have some special ability. To do anything otherwise will only compromise the outcome of the entire investigation process.

The Human Pendulum

It is not just amazing items of equipment or even amazing people that ghost investigators have to deal with; they are often faced with amazing methods too. Some time ago I witnessed the human pendulum experiment being conducted by ghost investigators. For those who are unfamiliar with this technique, the human pendulum is supposed to be a means by which spirits are able to communicate with the investigators by causing a person or people to move in response to questions that are asked. When I first heard of this technique my initial thoughts were of the ethical problems that might be created by dangling one of the investigation team or a member of the paying public from a rope secured to the rafters and swinging them to and fro, so I was relieved to discover that this isn't in fact the case. In near or total darkness, the participants are required to stand in a circle, sometimes with their hands linked. As in any séance, protection and grounding forms an important part of the ritual. Once protected, the spirit communicators are requested to select a person from within the group that they wish to use as their pendulum. The method of selection is simple: The chosen individual is moved (pushed?) by the spirits either forwards or backwards to indicate that they have been selected. The chosen human pendulum moves into the centre of the circle and stands alone, surrounded by their fellow investigators. It is then usually necessary to establish the correct relationship between the subsequent movements of that person and the spirit's answers. This would typically be forwards (or backwards) for a 'Yes' or positive response and backwards (or forwards) for a 'No' or negative response. Swaying around from side to side is generally considered to be an uncertain or 'Don't know' answer. Questions are then asked aloud by members of the group. Questions such as: "Are you a male spirit?"... "Is your name John?"... "Were you murdered?" Obviously, only questions with a simple yes or no answer can be asked. Using a series of posed questions, the identity, relationship, and reason for the spirit's presence can be established, a process that is inevitably time consuming, and at times confusing, both for the investigators trying to understand the responses and seemingly for the spirit communicator too as the responses are often ambiguous and incoherent. A variation on the question and response format can take the form of the human pendulum being moved in the direction of a person standing in the enclosing group to whom the spirit feels drawn or is connected. This latter variation is more puzzling as one might wonder why the spirit communicant didn't just select that person earlier when they were asked. Some groups like to combine the human pendulum with other experiments, as was the case with the particular experiment I witnessed. The location for the investigation was an old dockside warehouse converted into a nightclub, complete with a powerful in-house sound system. The investigation group made good use of this and throughout the human pendulum experiment they provided a background of authentic dockside warehouse sounds; heavy barrels being moved and rolled, horse-drawn carts and the creak of ropes, and timbers from the ships and sailing vessels moored alongside. Their idea being that by using appropriate background sounds they might provoke or induce a greater response from the ghost or spirit. The dockside sounds, played through the professional audio system sounded very convincing, and it was easy to imagine the ships swaying gently on the tide as one listened to the endless creaking of their mooring lines, while gangs of men laboured to load and unload the barrels and bails of cargo.

The investigators formed themselves into a circle and waited with an obvious mixture of eager anticipation and nervous trepidation to discover which of them would be selected by the spirits to be the human pendulum. The lead investigator asked for the spirits to indicate their choice, at which point around three quarters of those standing in the circle swayed inward then back upright again. Their coordinated movements assisted by the spirits and encouraged by the loud pleading of the lead investigator for the spirits to make their choice clear and move the appointed person resembled a weird slow motion Oki-Koki dance. Either the spirits were undecided or they were indicating that the session was to be an exercise in mass communication. The question was again asked "Spirits will you indicate your choice by moving someone? Please choose just one person." This time around only about half the participants lurched forward but one of the group also declared that she felt that she had been touched, clearly the chosen one. To the subtle but obviously disappointed murmurings of several of the circle the human pendulum moved to the middle of the circle. The human pendulum now stood alone in dark, exchanging a few nervous comments with her fellow investigators as she waited to be used by the spirits as their means of communication with the living, the darkness of her surroundings lit only by the dazzling light on a camcorder. Before the business of questioning the spirit could begin it was necessary to establish which way the spirits would move their human pendulum, once this was achieved, the questions began. At several points throughout the session it was unclear which answer the spirit was giving as the human pendulum swayed forwards and backwards in the light and the moving shadows cast by the rest of the investigation group. The human pendulum herself said several times that she was unsure if she was moving forwards or backwards or by how much. In response to this confusion the lead investigator gave repeated instructions to the spirit to make the pendulum give a more definite movement "Move the person, move further.... further ...further...." until at last, as the human pendulum almost toppled into the surrounding group, a clear answer was ascertained. The confusion of spirit replies was not helped by the swaying to and fro of several other members of the circle, possibly the spirits had not yet fully committed themselves to using just one of the group but, nonetheless, as the session progressed and the human pendulum rocked precariously back and forth, a series of answers to the questions was extracted "Are you John?" "Are you connected with someone here?" Showing consideration for the remainder of the group, the spirits provided additional proof of their presence by apparently gently touching and stroking the hair of several members of the circle. Others felt the temperature around them become suddenly icy. It was clearly a very intense experience for all. Unfortunately, the spirit's answers to the questions soon began to lack clarity and became confused until at last the lead investigator in some despair asked if the spirit was telling the truth? The response was discerned to be a NO.... Nonplussed, the leader asked, "Will you now give us truthful answers?" Fortunately for the investigation, the answer was swayed out in the form of a "yes" and the session proceeded. The lead investigator soon ran out of questions and at this point other questions were then encouraged from the surrounding group, leading to a volley of questions. These were mostly answered using the multi-directional swaying of the human pendulum, and an occasional collision between the pendulum and those in the surrounding circle. After fifteen minutes the session drew to a close. The communicating spirits were dutifully and respectfully thanked and the circle was broken as people headed en-mass for the exit for a welcome cigarette and to discuss excitedly what just took place. The lead investigator and several of the investigation group proclaimed the great success of the experiment. The investigators who undertook the human pendulum described it as a demonstration of genuine spirit interaction, especially in the context of the experiences of other participants i.e., the sudden sensations of cold and the feelings of being touched or moved. No one within the group of investigators questioned the validity or purpose of the human pendulum, or offered the suggestion that, by asking someone to stand still in the dark in the middle of the night, when they are tired, scared, excited, and probably full of caffeine, they will almost inevitably start to rock to and fro or sway around, no doubt helped by the added maritime sound effects. None of the investigators pointed out that the human pendulum relies on the heady mixture of suggestion, compliance, and fulfilled expectation. The human pendulum is a technique that is growing in popularity. It is regularly demonstrated (performed?) on stage as part of a theatre tour that is hosted by several ex-members of a well-known television ghost hunting series and features in numerous YouTube video clips. I was pleased to have witnessed the human pendulum experiment being conducted but dismayed at the manner in which it was used as part of a serious investigation of a haunted location. I was even more disappointed to listen to the conversations that took place between the investigators and those who participated afterwards. It was obvious that there was no consistency between the experiences. Some believed the spirit to have been male; others decided that it was a female. Several different names were discerned and there was even some confusion about whether the spirit was that of a former warehouse worker or a monk from a nearby priory. Several of the investigators emphasised the perceived temperature changes as further confirmation of spirit presence, although nobody in the group had thought to use one of several thermometers that were available or indeed anything other than the single camcorder during the entire proceedings. Nevertheless, all those who participated in the human pendulum experiment departed afterwards with a sense of personal fulfilment and satisfaction that they had interacted with the haunting spirits of the old warehouse. In due course, the names that they received were published in the group's investigation report and the video appeared on their YouTube channel, receiving lots of likes and positive comments from other ghost hunters.

In many ways the human pendulum is representative of modern ghost investigating. Investigators who seek only to have an interaction and confirmation that ghosts are evidence of survival, overlook numerous contradictions in the apparent spirit responses. The human pendulum is theatre and, together with locking people alone into rooms, dressing up in costumes, or calling upon the resident ghosts and spirits to throw and move items, has no real value or worth in terms of increasing the knowledge about the location or the case. Perhaps, the only positive that can be said is that such methods exploit and demonstrate several interesting aspects of human psychology and physiology and provide investigators with an opportunity to discover more about human responses to such situations. An opportunity that is overlooked by the investigators who forget that all ghost investigating is in reality the study of a human experience.

CHAPTER 6

MONITORING AND MEASURING

T he use of technology in the search for evidence of apparitions, poltergeists, and spirits has been in vogue since the advent of scientific ghost investigation in the late nineteenth century. Each succeeding generation of ghost investigators has made use of the latest inventions and technologies available, in many cases adapting and even inventing their own when it was not.

In Chapter 1 it was briefly mentioned how scientists such as Robert Hare, William Crookes, and others developed objective tests for the claims being made by the Spiritualists. Physicist, Professor Michael Faraday was so intrigued by the claims relating to table turning he set about devising experiments to determine the nature of the forces being applied. In a letter to *The Times* newspaper in June 1853, Faraday described his findings:

SIR: — I have recently been engaged in the investigation of table-turning.

I should be sorry that you should suppose I thought this necessary on my own account, for my conclusion respecting its nature was soon arrived at, and is not changed but I have been so often misquoted, and applications to me for an opinion are so numerous, that I hoped, if I enabled myself by experiment to give a strong one, you would consent to convey it to all persons interested in the matter. The effect produced by the table-turners has been referred to electricity, to magnetism, to attraction, to some unknown or hitherto unrecognized physical power able to affect inanimate bodies, to the revolution of the earth, and even to diabolical or supernatural agency. The natural philosopher can investigate all these supposed causes but the last; that must, to him, be too much connected with credulity or superstition to require any attention on his part.

Believing that the first cause assigned namely, a quasi-involuntary muscular action (for the effect is with many subject to the wish or will) was the true cause, the first point was to prevent the mind of the turner having an undue influence over the effects produced in relation to the nature of the substances employed. A bundle of plates consisting of sand-paper, mill-board, glue, glass, plastic, clay, tinfoil, card-board, gutta percha, vulcanized caoutchouc, wood, and resinous cement, was therefore made up and tied together, and being placed upon a table under the hand of a turner, did not prevent the transmission of the power; the table turned or moved exactly as if the bundle had been away, to the full satisfaction of all present. The experiment was repeated, with various substances and persons, and at various times with constant success and henceforth no objection could be taken to the use of these substances in the construction of apparatus. The next point was to determine the place and source of motion i.e., whether the table moved the hand, or the hand moved the table; and for this purpose indicators were constructed. One of these consisted of a light lever, having its fulcrum on the table, its short arm attached to a pin fixed on a card-board, which could slip on the surface of the table, and its long arm projecting as an index of motion. It is evident that if the experimenter willed the table to move toward the left, and it did so move before the hands, placed at the time on the card-board, then the index would move to the left also, the fulcrum going with the table. If the hands involuntarily moved towards the left without the table, the index would go towards the right and if neither table nor hands moved, the index would itself remain immovable. The result was that when the parties saw the index it remained very steady when it was hidden from them, or they looked away from it, it wavered about, though they believed that they always pressed directly downwards and, when the table did not move, there was still a resultant of hand force in the direction in which it was wished the table should move, which, however, was exercised quite unwittingly by the party operating. This resultant it is, which, in the course of the waiting time, while the fingers and hands become stiff, numb, and insensible by continued pressure, grows up to an amount sufficient to move the table or the substances pressed upon. But the most valuable effect of this test-apparatus (which was afterwards made more perfect and independent of the table,) is the corrective power it possesses over the mind of the table-tamer. As soon as the index is placed before the most earnest and they perceive, as in my presence they have always done, that it tells truly whether they are pressing downwards only or obliquely, then all effects of table-turning cease, even though the parties persevere, earnestly desiring motion, till they become weary and worn out. No prompting or checking of the hands is needed — the power is gone; and this only because the parties are made conscious of what they are really doing mechanically, and so are unable unwittingly to deceive themselves. I know that some may say that it is the cardboard next the fingers which moves first, and that it both drags the table and also the table-turner with it. All I have to reply is, that the card-board may in practice be reduced to a thin sheet of paper weighing only a few grains, or to a piece of goldbeaters' skin, or even the end of the lever, and (in principle,) to the very cuticle of the fingers itself. Then the results that follow are too absurd to be admitted the table becomes an incumbrance, and a person holding out the fingers in the air, either naked or tipped with goldbeaters' skin or card-board ought to be drawn about the room, etc.; but I refrain from considering imaginary yet consequent results which have nothing philosophical or real in them. I have been happy thus far in meeting with the most honorable and candid though most sanguine persons, and I believe the mental check which I propose will be available in the hands of all who desire truly to investigate the philosophy of the subject, and, being content to resign expectation, wish only to be led by the facts and the truth of nature. As I am unable, even at present, to answer all the letters that come to me regarding this matter, perhaps you will allow me to prevent any increase by saying that my apparatus may be seen at the shop of the philosophical instrument maker - Newman, 122 Regent Street.

Permit me to say, before concluding, that I have been greatly startled by the revelation, which this purely physical subject has made on the condition of the public mind. No doubt there are many persons who have formed a right judgment or used a cautious reserve, for I know several such, and public communications have shown it to be so; but their number is almost as nothing to the great body who have believed and borne testimony, as I think, in the cause of error. I do not here refer to the distinction of those who agree with me and those who differ. By the great body, I mean such as reject all consideration of the equality of cause and effect who refer the results to electricity and magnetism yet know nothing of the laws of these forces ; or to attraction — yet show no phenomena of pure attractive power or to the rotation of the earth, as if the earth revolved round the leg of a table; or to some unrecognized physical force, without inquiring whether the known forces are not sufficient ; or who even refer them to diabolical or supernatural agency, rather than suspend their judgment, or acknowledge to themselves that they are not learned enough in these matters to decide on the nature of the action. I think the system of education that could leave the mental condition of the public body in the state in which this subject has found it must have been greatly deficient in some very important principle.

I am, sir, your very obedient servant,

Royal Institution, June 28, 1853. M. FARADAY.

Inspired by the work of Faraday, American Robert Hare, a chemistry professor developed a series of devices known as Spiritoscopes. Several variations were built but all used a principle of levers, wires, and counterweights in order to attempt to determine the source of the physical forces that caused tables to tilt and tip and letters to be selected, apparently by the spirits.

Spiritoscope 1855

Hare also constructed other devices such as the water test device that sought to try and measure the forces being applied.

Another chemistry Professor Sir William Crookes FRS drew upon the work of Hare and also made use of delicate spring balances and thermometers in his experiments with the Medium D. D. Home. Crookes described his extensive experiments, together with the equipment and results in his *Researches in the Phenomena of Spiritualism* that was published in 1874.

> In another part of the room an apparatus was fitted up for experimenting on the alteration in the weight of a body. It consisted of a mahogany board, 36 inches long by 9½ inches wide and 1 inch thick. At each end a strip of mahogany 1½ inches wide was screwed on, forming feet. One end of the board rested on a firm table, whilst a spring balance hanging from a substantial tripod stand supported the other end. The balance was fitted with a self-registering index, in such a manner that it would record the maximum weight indicated by the pointer. The apparatus was adjusted so that the mahogany board was horizontal; its foot resting flat on the support. In this position its weight was 3 lbs., as marked by the pointer of the balance.

> Before Mr. Home entered the room, the apparatus had been arranged in position, and he had not even the object of some parts of it explained before sitting down. It may, perhaps, be worthwhile to add, for the purpose of anticipating some critical remarks, which are likely to be made, that in the afternoon I called for Mr. Home at his apartments, and when there he suggested that, as he had to change his dress, perhaps I should not object to continue our conversation in his bedroom. I am, therefore, enabled to state positively, that no machinery, apparatus, or contrivance of any sort was secreted about his person. The investigators present on the test occasion were an eminent physicist, high in the ranks of the Royal Society, whom I will call Dr A. B.; a well-known Serjeant-at-Law, whom I will call Serjeant C. D.; my brother; and my chemical assistant. Mr. Home sat in a low easy chair at the side of the table. In front of him under the table was the aforesaid cage, one of his legs being on each side of it. I sat close to him on his left, and another observer sat close to him on his right, the rest of the party being seated at convenient distances round the table.

For the greater part of the evening, particularly when anything of importance was proceeding, the observers on each side of Mr. Home kept their feet respectively on his feet, so as to be able to detect his slightest movement.

The temperature of the room varied from 68° to 70° F.

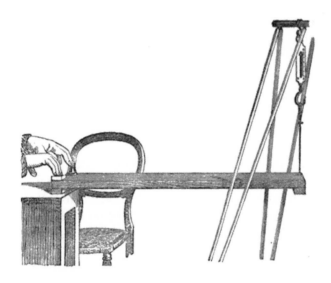

Spring balance apparatus used by Crookes to test D.D. Home
(Researches in the Phenomena of Spiritualism p.22)

It might be thought that ghost investigators were somewhat slow to make use of these new recording and measuring opportunities that science had provided than those seeking to test the spiritualist claims. In truth, ghost investigation wasn't a popular pursuit by men of science and was limited to a few amateur investigators who either could not afford the expense of equipment or preferred not be hampered by the often heavy and cumbersome equipment. In the main, the investigators preferred merely to document their own and others experiences in haunted houses. The Society for Psychical Research did attempt to monitor some of the reported phenomena at 'B' House' in Scotland during the late 1890's. The group had planned to use a phonograph and also a seismometer in their investigation but were ultimately thwarted by a legal wrangle that broke out between the parties that resulted in the investigation being halted and all further attempts to continue denied. 'B' House (Ballechin House) was a shooting lodge in Perthshire in which a wide variety of alleged paranormal experiences had been reported. These included the sighting of apparitions and sounds that ranged from voices to the loud explosions of petards (small bombs). For several months in early 1897 the group made careful observations and took detailed notes of their many various experiences inside the house and it is to be regretted that they were prevented from pursuing the investigation more fully.

It is Harry Price, the legendary, and many would say controversial ghost investigator, who is perhaps best remembered for his contributions toward modern instrumented ghost investigation. Price devised and frequently carried with him an assortment of equipment and gadgets into haunted houses. Many of the items in Price's ghost hunting kit we would still recognise and use today, for instance, thermometers, movement alarms, and photography. Others have fallen out of regular use such as the vibration-detecting bowl of Mercury (perhaps for good reason!) and there are very few modern ghost investigators who will have a block of sealing wax and a hank of bell wire in their ghost kits. Price was aware that even back then, some people were claiming to have developed equipment that could detect ghosts as he describes in his book *The Most Haunted House in England*, published in 1940. Commenting on the response to his advert in *The Times* newspaper for investigators to join a year-long investigation of Borley Rectory he notes that the response was phenomenal and included replies from: "Cranks and inventors with machines to sell – pieces of apparatus guaranteed to detect a ghost a mile off."

While it is often said, "Clothes make the man", for ghost hunters perhaps it could be amended to say, "Flight cases make the ghost hunter". It appears that the more equipment they possess and the higher the perceived technology and value of the equipment they possess, the more credibility they have with their peers. Equipment is important and, properly used, it can provide objective information that may confirm or contradict the subjective claims made by witnesses and experients. Improperly used, or when it is used by those with too little experience or the wrong supporting information, it can often create many more problems than it will solve. It is a fact that many anomalies presented as evidence of paranormal claims by investigators when correctly analysed are in reality the result of an operator error and misunderstanding or much more rarely an equipment malfunction. Many items of equipment have an unproven value to paranormal study. For instance, the usefulness of the negative ion detector (NID) and to a large extent the ubiquitous electromagnetic field (EMF) meter as investigative tools has not been demonstrated much beyond conjecture and supposition. Other less esoteric items, such as the thermometer have on the other hand been used to objectively measure unusual and seemingly inexplicable ambient temperature changes both in haunted locations and in the séance room.

The following chapters should not be considered to be a comprehensive guide to ghost hunting gadgets but notes for guidance. For those seeking more information they should consult other reference materials perhaps starting with a good basic high school physics textbook which will provide masses of useful information about the physical world ghost investigators seek to measure. This might be an appropriate moment to introduce an important note of caution into the proceedings: To date, and despite claims by many to the contrary, not a single item of equipment exists that is capable of detecting or measuring paranormal activity including spirits, ghosts, poltergeists.

Should We Measure Anything at All?

The vast majority of documented evidence relating to ghosts, apparitions and poltergeists continues to rely upon personal testimony, subjective descriptions of an experience. The investigator is therefore generally reliant upon the frailties of human perception and memory. Psychologists have discovered just how unreliable such faculties can be and whilst investigators cannot afford to disregard such records and accounts, they do need some additional means of verifying the information and seeking information to assist them with determining what might actually be taking place. The carefully targeted use of the right equipment can provide objective information which is free from the defects of the human senses and memory. Ghost hunters in their search for evidence now routinely measure temperature, electromagnetism and a range of other physical variables. While some measurements and observations may be potentially relevant and helpful to the investigator including temperature, audio, and video recording, other measurements such as radiation or air ions are highly dubious and of questionable benefit to paranormal investigation.

Making Measurements

Measurement is the process of making or determining the magnitude of a quantity. Units of measurement are arbitrary and generally defined on a scientific basis, which are established and regulated by national and internationally agreed standards. Whilst a number of standards exist for defining units of measurement such as the imperial system and the metric system, the majority of scientifically recognised measurements are now undertaken using the SI system of measurement, the abbreviation deriving from the French - Système International d'Unités. In addition, some variation of units also exists within equipment manufactured mainly for local markets and specialist applications. For instance, many items of measuring equipment that are manufactured and intended for the USA display measurements using the US Customary Unit system (derived from the British Imperial system), although most also offer SI measurements. With electromagnetic meters for example, it is common to see magnetic flux density expressed in terms of units of Gauss or milliGauss (mG) in preference to the SI unit of the Tesla or microTesla (uT). Likewise with thermometers, the Fahrenheit scale is still used for the majority of temperature measurement in the USA rather than the Celsius scale, which is standard throughout UK and Europe and in widespread use throughout the rest of the World. In terms of documenting any measurements that are made, it is therefore more important that the investigator chooses and uses one single system of measurement throughout and that measurement units are not mixed. For example, it is simply confusing to say that a room is 12 feet in length by 10 feet wide and is 3 metres in height. Likewise, it is unhelpful to have some instruments displaying mG whilst others use uT. Making measurements involves a series of steps that must be adhered to in order for any measurement to be considered meaningful.

- The correct instrument must be selected for the desired variable being measured.
- The proper **unit** has to be selected and agreed for the **variable** being measured.
- The measuring instrument must be used correctly to assure **accuracy** of the measurement.
- The calibration and **precision** of the measurement must be noted.

It is important that the person making the measurements understands exactly what they are measuring and what instrument is required to make the correct measurements. An electromagnetic field (EMF) meter for instance is designed for observing and measuring magnetic flux density. The manufacturer designs the device to work within certain frequency ranges and any measurements that are made outside that designed operating range cannot be assumed to be correct. Using the EMF meter as an example, once again, if it has been designed to measure at the electricity supply frequency of 50Hz or 60Hz then measurements made of EMF's having a frequency of 10Hz or 500Hz will be much less accurately expressed. Manufacturers of better quality instruments generally include an indication of the device's calibration, some may even provide or offer a calibration service and certificate of calibration (which requires the instrument to be regularly tested and checked). In terms of ghost investigating, all of the parameters that are routinely measured such as temperature and electromagnetic fields have defined standards for making measurements and documenting the results. However, some groups opt to adapt or build their own items of ghost hunting equipment. In such cases, the equipment in all likelihood lacks any form of accurate calibration and the data that is provided cannot be accurately related to any defined standard. For just about anything and everything that is required to be measured there is a series of standards that govern, not only how the measuring equipment should operate, but also how the relevant measurements are to be made.

The International Standards Organisation (ISO) governs these standards in over 160 countries and produces detailed standards for all measurements and measuring equipment. The individual standards are catalogued in the International Standards Catalogue (ICS), for example ICS 17.200.20 deals with standards for temperature measuring instruments. The ISO maintains a complete and up-to-date list of all the ISO standards online (www.iso.org).

Whilst it is impractical and unrealistic for many amateur ghost investigators to be able to measure and observe everything in accordance with the ISO standards it should be the aim of every investigator to monitor and measure effectively and to the highest standard that is possible. The careful and considered use of measuring equipment, rather than the more prevalent scattergun approach, is more likely to produce measurements that are at least meaningful and will withstand scrutiny. Such measurements are the only measurements that can ever hope to provide useful information that is helpful to furthering ghost investigation.

Recording Measurements

Once any measurement has been made, it is vital that the information is documented correctly and that those who are recording the information understand what recording method is being used. For investigators, this may take the form of a separate chart or may be included within personal notes but, whatever method is adopted, everyone included on the investigation must universally employ it. For example, if temperature is considered to be important, then those making the measurements must present their data in a form that can be related to everyone else making the same measurements and the data must be presented in a form that can be readily understood by the person who has to transcribe that information, usually at a later time or date. The units, either Fahrenheit or Celsius, must be agreed upon, as must the measuring method. Without this standardised approach it is almost impossible to relate one set of measurements to another. The location of the measuring instrument must also be documented; it is not very helpful to simply say "The temperature of the stairs was 21°C at 10pm". Whereabouts on the stairs was the temperature information obtained? Was it at tread level or somewhere above? At which point on the or above the staircase was the measurement made? What type of thermometer was used and how long was the measuring period? It can take several minutes for a thermometer to stabilise and be able to make a reliable temperature measurement. This information is normally provided by the manufacturer but is frequently ignored by the users. All of this information needs to be documented and presented if the subsequent measurements are to be considered reliable and accurate. Failing to adequately document, not only the measurements but also the method and context in which they were obtained, will only result in any resulting conclusions that are drawn from that data being questionable and unreliable.

Baseline Measurements

Baseline measurements are beloved of ghost investigators and they are essential in many types of scientific measurement too. A baseline measurement or series of measurements is undertaken to provide a known value or reference point against which all subsequent measurements of the same variable can be compared. However, when it comes to ghost investigation, all too frequently, the baseline measurements are made hours before the actual required measurements are obtained and often under very different conditions. Measurements obtained in the middle of a cold dark night are set against a baseline taken during the daytime. Measurements in empty buildings are set against a baseline obtained when the same building is full of people. Sometimes baseline measurements from earlier site visits are employed; these may have been obtained days or weeks in advance of the actual investigation measurements. In reality, such baselines can provide no usable information and are more likely to simply mislead the user. There are even examples in which the baseline measurement was obtained in a completely different location but one that the investigator deemed to be sufficiently similar – all castles are not the same! To be useful, the baseline measurements need to be made under circumstances that are as close to the actual investigation measurements as possible. Equipment that will be turned off during the investigation should be turned off, people who won't be there during the investigation shouldn't be there, and items such as windows, doors, heating, and lighting set to the conditions that they will be in during the actual investigation measurement period. It is also wrong to assume that baseline measurements are carried out only prior to an investigation. The baseline measurements should run continuously for a period prior to the investigation and throughout the entire duration of the investigation period. Modern technology allows many physical properties such as temperature, humidity, and electromagnetism to be recorded using data logging equipment so this need not be an onerous or time consuming task. Failing that, it is a simple method for members of the investigation team to manually record the information at a regular fixed timescale, for example, once every five or ten minutes using a chart or graph. By making the baseline measurements meaningful it becomes much easier to then describe and relate any subsequent measurements that seemingly deviate unexpectedly from those reference points.

Analogue or Digital

The use of equipment to support the investigation of hauntings and related cases such as poltergeists, etc., and within the séance room has a long history dating to the late nineteenth century. For the greater part of that period recording and measuring equipment used analogue techniques. An analogue system uses the information from a sensor such as a temperature probe or microphone and represents that information in the form of a continuously variable physical quantity such as voltage, etc. However, since the late twentieth century digital systems have now largely overtaken analogue methods to become the primary method of obtaining information. Digital systems sample the information from the sensor and present that information as a series of digits, (0 and 1) or states (on and off). Digital systems present the information in a discontinuous series of data. Both methods have their inherent advantages and disadvantages. Analogue systems generally provide a greater signal bandwidth and therefore are a truer representation of the actual sensor signal. Digital data is more readily compatible with modern techniques for using the information, such as the use of computers for interrogating the data. The clarity and quality of digital information is usually better as extraneous signal noise in the form of electrical and mechanical interference with the signal from the sensor can be removed. Digital systems are also more readily available as manufacturers have in the main discontinued many analogue devices particularly those relating to sound and imagery.

It is rare these days to find many analogue devices being used by ghost investigators. A few investigators still use analogue audio equipment such as cassette recorders for their EVP sessions alongside digital recorders and fewer still use film cameras and analogue thermometers. One type of analogue device that is still commonly found is the basic electromagnetic field (EMF) meter including models such as the CellSensor, K-II and the various Alpha Labs TriField models. This is not a discussion about the advantages or disadvantages of either system of obtaining information but it is worth asking the question as to whether the needs of the investigation are being best served by this paradigm shift in the way information is gathered? Many of the most interesting pictures that purport to show ghosts were taken (out of necessity) using film and there are countless EVP's made by the early researchers (out of necessity) using tape recorders. These pictures and recordings pose questions that still require answers; can ghosts be photographed? Can the dead communicate directly with the living? The evidence that supports the claims was obtained using analogue methods and may never be suitably answered using digital devices. In some measuring systems the sensor remains broadly the same or is identical; for instance, digital thermometers still use thermocouples and the design of microphones has barely changed in almost a century but the way a digital camera sensor sees light is very different to the way in which film does. The way in which information is captured and used by the investigators may be affecting the way in which the information is interpreted too. The software that is used to work with digital data may affect the manner in which information is interpreted, the modern computer interface generally encourages visual rather than auditory scrutiny and the editing of the information by the investigator is also encouraged by its simplicity. Altering a few sliders or clicking a mouse button can radically alter the way in which a picture or sound might be perceived. These are not in themselves a bad thing and in many ways they confer advantages to the modern investigator that were denied to their predecessors but they do need to be considered. Analogue methods of obtaining information tend to be more time consuming and expensive in terms of the consumables (tape, film, paper rolls, etc.,) therefore early investigators in all likelihood considered more carefully the usefulness of any measurements. Modern investigators have the luxury of little additional costs beyond that of the equipment and some small outlay for storage media. Equipment costs are comparatively much lower too. Twenty years ago it would be unlikely that an investigator could afford to have multiple cameras and a large number of audio recorders, these days the majority of ghost investigators will have several of each type. The amount of information that can be obtained has increased exponentially but just because it can be obtained, does that necessarily mean that it should be obtained?

Excessive Measurement

In their desire to obtain some proof of paranormal activity during their investigation, many ghost investigators use the technique of measuring everything all of the time. When they undertake an investigation they simply deploy every item of their ghost hunting equipment regardless of what it is they are seeking to discover. If temperature changes have never been reported by anyone at a location there seems little point in measuring the temperature, likewise with sound or visual phenomena, if nobody has ever reported having such experiences what purpose will be served by setting up equipment to detect such unreported experiences?

Over measuring may leave the investigator with an inordinately large amount of data that they have to wade through. In reality this only increases the potential for missing the important information buried under a weight of unhelpful and unneeded data. Perhaps the selective use of measuring equipment, appropriately targeted at the properties that are of real interest is more likely to lead to helpful data acquisition.

CHAPTER 7

TEMPERATURE

There is certainly a great deal of anecdotal evidence to link sudden or unexpected changes in ambient air temperature with reports of people experiencing unusual and possibly paranormal events. Of particular interest, there is also some objective data from calibrated thermometers that have recorded seemingly inexplicable large or sudden fluctuations of the temperature at some haunted locations or associated with paranormal experiences. Properly obtained measurements of temperature anomalies were demonstrated in séances with the medium Stella 'C' (Cranshaw) and also at Borley Rectory by Harry Price. Modern researchers using digital recording thermometers and state of the art thermal cameras have also reported similar strange temperature observations. Currently there are no suitable explanations as to how and why these apparent temperature anomalies can take place. Such anomalies are sometimes coincident with a report of paranormal activity or experiences but, apart from the coincidental nature of the measurement and the experience, the two cannot as yet be directly linked. Parapsychologists and sceptics often make a case for personal belief, suggestion, or expectation to be the link between a perceived temperature change and an experience that is described as being paranormal. Whilst this is likely to be true in a number of cases, perhaps the majority fail to take into account those rare instances where a proper objective measurement of temperature was made thus demonstrating that the temperature did indeed change in an unexpected manner or in a way that the recognised processes governing thermodynamics (the transfer of heat) does not apparently account for.

Liquid in Glass Thermometers

The earliest thermometers used the expansion of liquid in response to an increase in temperature as the principle of operation. The typical liquid in glass thermometer consists of a sealed stem of uniform small diameter tubing (capillary tube) made from glass or other transparent material and with a larger diameter reservoir (bulb) formed at one end. The bulb and part of the stem are filled with a liquid such as Mercury or alcohol, the remainder being evacuated of air and forming a vacuum. Graduations on the stem form a temperature scale. The first thermometer of this type, made by Swedish Astronomer Anders Celsius in 1742 used fixed points of reference, the melting point of ice (0°C), and the boiling point of water at atmospheric pressure (100°C). The scale was divided into 100 equal divisions, each being the equivalent of 1 degree (Celsius). There are several variations of this basic design such as the clinical thermometer, which is optimised to a temperature measuring range based around the human body but all use the same principle of operation i.e., the expansion of a substance in response to temperature change. Liquid in glass thermometers are simple in construction, relatively inexpensive, easy to use and portable and are still widely used in many temperature measuring situations. They tend to be fragile and can only be used when the liquid column is visible. They cannot be used reliably for surface temperature measurement and are slow to respond to ambient temperature changes due to the thermal properties of the glass, which first needs to be heated or cooled before the contained liquid can react.

Liquid in glass thermometers also relies upon a human operator to manually observe and record the temperature and as such are at risk to human factors such as simple errors when reading or interpreting the (often small) scale divisions. Versions exist that utilise small sliding indicators to show the maximum and/or minimum temperatures.

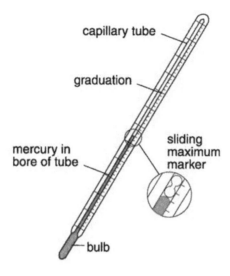

capillary tube

graduation

mercury in
bore of tube

sliding
maximum
marker

bulb

Liquid in Glass Thermometer

Thermocouple Thermometers

Thermocouple thermometers use the emf that is created when the junction between two dissimilar metals is heated. Some people may at this point be wondering what electromagnetic fields have got to do with temperature? There is, in fact, no connection, as emf is actually an abbreviation that has nothing to do with electromagnetic fields (more about this in Chapter 8). Here 'emf' is being used in its correct form, which refers to Electromotive Force. An electromotive force, or most commonly referred to as 'emf' (seldom capitalised), is the force or electrical potential (electrical voltage) that causes an electrical current (actual electrons and ions) to flow through a conductor.

Thermocouple thermometers use two different metals, usually Copper and Constantan joined together (normally) inside a protective sheath or probe. A difference in the electric potential, which varies with temperature, exists at their junction. If they complete a circuit containing a second similar bi-metal junction that is at a different temperature, an electric current will flow through the whole circuit and may be measured using a galvanometer. This is known as the thermo-electric effect or Seebeck effect after German physicist Thomas Seebeck who in 1821, discovered that when any conductor is subjected to a thermal gradient, it would generate a voltage. Most portable thermocouple thermometers are used with a battery powered circuit that amplifies the very small voltage from the bi-metal junction, and is used to drive a voltmeter that is directly calibrated with a temperature scale. Thermocouple thermometers are comparatively simple and robust and generally have a fast response time (depending upon the probe sheath material). Modern microprocessor controlled thermocouple thermometers can also be used to record temperature over time (data logging).

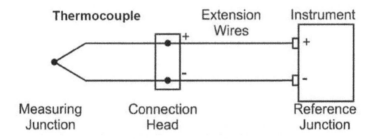

Thermocouple Thermometer

Resistance Thermometers

Resistance thermometer designs make use of the fact that most metals change their electrical resistance in response to a change in their temperature. Thus, the amount of electricity (current) able to flow through the metal alters as the temperature of the metal changes. This principle may be incorporated into a temperature sensor. The temperature sensing probe forms part of a circuit through which an electric current is passed. Measuring the amount of current flowing through the probe provides a value which can then be used to determine the temperature of the probe. Related to the resistance thermometer is the Thermistor. The thermistor is a semi-conducting material in the form of a bead of metal-oxide. As the temperature of the metal-oxide bead changes, the electrical resistance of the material changes altering the amount of electricity that can flow through it. Both types of resistance thermometer typically respond readily and rapidly to ambient temperature changes and are also sensitive to small changes in temperature. Using a meter or digital display, the amount of resistance can be measured and displayed using a scale that is calibrated in units of temperature. Microprocessor driven circuits can be used to record the temperature. Both types of resistance thermometer are comparatively simple to manufacture and can be highly portable using battery power and the majority of consumer digital thermometers use one of the resistance techniques to measure temperature. As with the thermocouple, it is the material that comprises the protective sheath that will ultimately affect the response time of such devices. Materials, like plastic, are relatively slow to pass on changes in ambient temperature to the sensor inside. Open sensors are available for both thermocouples and resistance thermometers, which dramatically speed up response times, but the lack of physical protection may result in the fragile sensor becoming easily damaged.

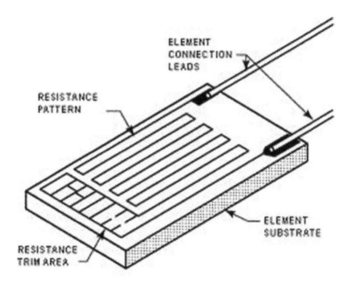

ELEMENT
CONNECTION
LEADS

RESISTANCE
PATTERN

ELEMENT
SUBSTRATE

RESISTANCE
TRIM AREA

Thermistor temperature sensing element

The types of thermometer described so far (liquid in glass, thermocouple, and resistance), all measure the temperature of the probe by measuring the physical changes within the probe material. By careful application of the probe the temperature of the medium it is attached to, or immersed in, can therefore be observed. Such devices are often known as direct reading or contact thermometers. It is important to note that the information these thermometers provide is actually a measurement of temperature for the sensor and a very small area that the sensor is directly in contact with or is surrounded by. It is therefore incorrect to assume that a larger surrounding area is of the same temperature. Regardless of the type used, using any single thermometer to measure the temperature of an entire room will almost certainly give an erroneous result. In order to obtain an accurate assessment of the temperature of a room it is necessary to carry out a series of individual measurements (simultaneously) throughout the whole room. The individual measurements may then be considered either as a temperature gradient across the space, or as a mean value for the entire space.

There is another method for judging or measuring the temperature of a material that has been exploited for thousands of years. Early metal workers and pottery makers used the colour of the heated object to judge its temperature. We are probably familiar with the principle that many metals when heated first glow red, then yellow, and finally white, as they get hotter. Most substances emit radiant (visible and infrared) energy when heated and the amount of energy emitted depends upon its temperature. The famous potter Josiah Wedgewood used this principle to invent his Pyrometer, which was an optical device that accurately measured the temperature of his pottery kilns. A common type of portable thermometer that is to be found in many ghost investigators kits also uses this principle of energy emission.

Infrared Thermometers

An Infrared thermometer does not measure temperature directly; instead it uses the infrared (IR) emissions from the material to obtain its temperature. As such, they are also known as non-contact thermometers. All objects emit IR in varying amounts depending on the materials emissivity and its temperature. The emissivity of a material (written 'e') is the relative ability of its surface to emit energy by radiation. In general, the duller and blacker a material is the closer its emissivity is to 1. The more reflective a material is then the lower its emissivity will be. For example, highly polished silver has an emissivity of about 0.02 and a brick wall an emissivity of about 0.96. The emissivity of most high quality non-contact thermometers may be adjustable and can be set to optimise the measurement of the temperature for a range of reflective and non-reflective surfaces. The most basic design of an infrared thermometer consists of a lens to focus the infrared radiation on to a detector. The detector then converts the radiant power into an electrical signal that can be displayed in units of temperature after compensation has been made for the ambient temperature. This configuration facilitates temperature measurement at a distance without physical contact with the object to be measured being necessary. The infrared thermometer is useful for measuring temperature under circumstances where thermocouple or other probe type sensors cannot be used or do not produce accurate data for a variety of reasons. Another factor that needs to be considered when using an IRT is the Distance to Spot (D:S) ratio; this is the ratio of the distance to the object and the diameter of the temperature measurement area. For instance if the D:S ratio is 12:1, measurement of an object 12 inches (30 cm) away will give an average of the temperature over a 1-inch-diameter (25 mm) area. As the D:S ratio increases, the area being measured will increase but the overall accuracy of the temperature information may be reduced.

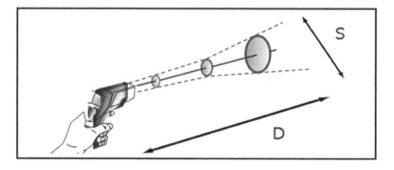

Many infrared thermometers use a laser pointer to indicate the region being measured, this usually takes the form of a simple red spot at the centre of the measuring region but on some advanced models the laser can be formed by a lens into a circle that more accurately indicates the area being measured. Microprocessor control can permit several measurement parameters to be recorded including the maximum and minimum, average, and data recording over time (data logging). Some models can be fitted with an additional thermocouple or resistance probe too as the infrared thermometer cannot be used to measure the temperature of the air. It is an all too common error by ghost investigators who describe capturing and even measuring a 'cold-spot' in the air within a location. Air is thermally transparent and has an emissivity value of Zero. Therefore, it neither absorbs nor radiates any infrared energy. As such, the temperature of the air cannot be measured using this technology.

Thermal Imaging

Related to the infrared thermometer is the thermal imaging camera, which also utilises the principle of infrared emission to infer the temperature of a material. Instead of simply displaying the result in terms of a temperature value, thermal imagers use the information from an array of individual infrared sensors (pixels) built onto a silicon chip to form a visual representation of the temperatures present within the field of view of the camera. Thermal imaging cameras use a specialised focal plane array sensor (FPA) that responds only to longer infrared wavelengths. Thermal imaging cameras are not a new invention and date back to 1947 and the infrared line scanner developed for the U.S. military. The newest technologies use uncooled FPA sensors. Resolution is typically considerably lower than that of optical cameras, mostly 160x120 or 320x240 pixels, up to 640x480 and higher for the most expensive models. Thermal imaging cameras are also much more expensive than their visible-spectrum counterparts, although recent improvements in microelectronics has resulted in thermal cameras becoming comparatively cheaper and they are now being increasingly used by ghost investigators. Most models can be used with additional software to extract additional thermal information such as maximum, minimum, and the spot temperature at any point within the picture. The resulting pictures (thermographs) can allow quick visual comparisons between different parts of the image to be made. Thermal imaging is more fully discussed in Chapter 18.

FLIR ® i3 Thermal Imaging camera

Other Methods

There are other techniques that can also be used for measuring temperature. These include temperature indicating paints, crayons, and liquid crystals which change colour in response to changes in temperature, bi-metallic thermometers which use the varying expansion of metals to move a pointer, and gas expansion thermometers in which the change in volume of a gas is used in place of the liquid in a liquid in glass thermometer. With the exception of the liquid crystal type, which is commonly, used for some industrial, medical, and nursery thermometers these techniques tend to be highly specialist in their use and are rarely used by ghost investigators.

Measuring Temperature

There are a number of ways that errors can be introduced into the measuring process seriously affecting the overall accuracy of measurements and it has already been noted that thermometers do not actually measure the temperature of the surface or material itself but instead measure either physical changes within the probe material or the thermal radiation emissions from an object.

Poor selection of equipment and poor positioning of the sensor can both lead to a misreading of the temperature. For example, an infrared thermometer or thermal imager cannot be used to measure the air temperature. Locating a thermocouple or resistance thermometer too close to a hot or cold object can result in the measured air temperature being affected by radiant heat from the adjacent surface. Probe type thermometers such as thermocouple and resistance devices are also only capable of taking the temperature from the material they are in direct or very close contact with and therefore cannot be used for temperature measurement over a large area. The actual region of temperature measurement is that which is directly in contact with the probe. Air has a poor ability to conduct thermal energy and so in reality only a region of perhaps a few cubic centimetres around the probe can be accurately sampled. Liquids tend to conduct thermal energy better and so permit a slightly larger region around the probe to be sampled. Thus, simply taking one or two temperature readings within a room will rarely result in an accurate temperature profile being obtained. A better method is to make a series of temperature measurements at regular (1 metre) intervals, both vertically (hot air rises, whilst cooler air falls) as well as horizontally. This will provide a range of ambient temperature observations for the entire room and an overall more accurate impression of the temperature within the space. This is obviously time consuming but in reality it is the only way that it is currently possible to obtain accurate information. Using a thermal imager can allow a rapid assessment of the surface temperatures to be made over a larger area, and a series of thermographs can be taken for later examination in detail. However, the thermal imager cannot be used for obtaining measurements of air temperature. The thermal imager and infrared thermometers also rely for their accuracy on the user correctly setting the device's emissivity calibration. Emissivity is dependent on the type and nature of the materials being measured and can vary by a large amount even over a small distance. For example, a wall may be partially painted or may have a mirror or painting hung upon it. Fabrics, plastics and many building materials all have different emissivity values, which will alter the accuracy of the overall temperature measurements made using these techniques. Generally, an emissivity setting with an average value (typically e=0.95) is used to deal with these situations and although absolute accuracy is sacrificed, the measurements will be useably accurate to within a few degrees. By understanding the shortfalls of temperature measurement and the particular requirements of the chosen thermometer it is possible for the investigator to develop a range of techniques and tools in order to be able to obtain generally accurate temperature measurements. Simply wandering around a location taking one or two temperature measurements in a fairly haphazard fashion will just result in inaccurate and misleading temperature data being obtained.

Temperature, in Conclusion

Temperature changes have been a regularly reported feature of paranormal encounters for centuries and indeed unusual temperature changes have been accurately measured by researchers in situations that have been associated with reports of paranormal experiences, or as having a significant correlation to other activity during séances. In cases of alleged hauntings, large numbers of seemingly trustworthy witnesses consistently report experiencing unusual phenomena, including sudden changes in temperature (Wiseman, Watt, Stevens, Greening, O'Keeffe, 2003).[1] Sitters at séances, have, since the earliest days of spiritualism also reported apparent falls in temperature (Randall, 2001).[2] Temperature drops seem to be the most commonly reported experience; temperature increases seem to be a much less common experience. This is shown in a survey of 813 people who had reported seeing a ghost: 36.6 per cent of the respondents said that

---

[1] Wiseman R. Watt C. Stevens P. Greening E. O'Keeffe C. (2003). *An Investigation into alleged hauntings.* British Journal of Psychology (2003), 94, 195-211.

[2] Randall J.L. (2001). *The Mediumship of Stella Cranshaw: A statistical Investigation.* Journal of the Society for Psychical Research Vol 65.1, No. 862. January 2001

they experienced a temperature drop coincident with the sighting, while 4.2 per cent reported that the temperature increased (Para. Science, 2005).[3] Anomalous temperature changes are characteristically sudden with a short duration. In one case, a sharp rise in temperature of 10 degrees Fahrenheit over a few seconds was measured before falling back and remaining constant for the rest of the investigation (Guiley, 2000, p.164).[4] Recognition of temperature change is a critical element of sensory perception, allowing the individual to evaluate their environment. Most people can discriminate changes in ambient temperature of several degrees. However, some researchers report anecdotal instances suggesting that some percipients may not accurately estimate or describe temperature changes associated with having an anomalous experience, e.g., "As they entered the house, they were met by a blast of cold air, they described it like walking into a refrigerator" (Wilson, 1981, p.143).[5] In some instances, researchers have observed that percipients report a sensation of coldness when no measured change in the ambient temperature has occurred (Spencer, Wells, 1994, p.130).[6] In some cases, percipients report large temperature decreases when the measured ambient temperature has increased by a small amount (Para.Science, 2005).[7]

Witnesses, even experienced investigators, can therefore be considered generally poor at judging temperature changes and, even when temperature changes are experienced, they will frequently misreport or exaggerate their perception of the amount, or the rate, of any temperature change. It is therefore unwise for any investigator to place great store on witness reports alone as a basis for documenting temperature changes during the investigation process. The proper selection of the thermometer type and its correct use is of great importance when measuring of temperature during an

---

[3] Para.Science (2005). Extracted from Internet survey of paranormal experiences 2004 to present. www.parascience.org.uk

[4] Guiley, Rosemary Ellen. (2000). *The Encyclopaedia of Ghosts and Spirits*, 2nd *edition*. New York, Checkmark Books.

[5] Wilson C. (1981). *Poltergeist! A study in destructive haunting*. London. New English Library.

[6] Spencer J. Wells T. (1994). *Ghostwatching*. London. BCA.

[7] Para.Science (2005).[2] Unpublished investigation report of haunt phenomena at a Merseyside Shipyard. Transcript of audio recording during séance & temperature records.

investigation and it can be shown that temperature measurement is an important consideration in many investigations of paranormal experiences that ghost investigators might wish to pay particular attention to.

CHAPTER 8

ELECTROMAGNETIC GHOSTS

Many ghost investigators will have heard of an EMF meter. They have probably seen them being used on their favourite television ghost hunting programme. They probably already have one or two in their ghost investigation kit. Generally, however, few seem to be fully aware of the reasons they are used or the way in which they work. As mentioned in Chapter 7 (Temperature) the expression 'emf' generally refers to a different physical force but it is now generally accepted by ghost investigators and even some of the equipment manufacturers that meters that measure electromagnetic fields are referred to as being EMF meters, in line with that convention the abbreviation EMF (capitalised) will be used here to denote electromagnetic fields and measuring devices. However, for the sake of completeness, it is worth mentioning here that, depending upon the type and nature of the field component that is being measured, a more accurate description of these devices would be Magnetometers, Magnetic Flux Density Meters, or Electromagnetic Radiation Meters.

Electromagnetism

The electromagnetic spectrum is the encompassing term for all the frequencies of electromagnetic radiation. It includes radio waves at the longest wavelengths, through microwaves and the light spectra in the middle regions up to x-rays and gamma radiation at the shortest wavelengths. Even matter may in some instances be included within the electromagnetic spectrum.

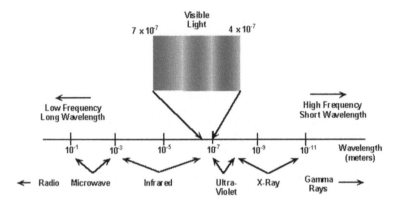

At the lowest frequencies the wavelengths can be of immense length, millions of kilometres and greater; whilst at the highest frequency the wavelength may be just a fraction the size of an atom. As the frequency increases the energy also increases, which can be simply demonstrated by considering microwaves, which are very high frequency radio waves, microwaves heat food but lower frequency radio waves do not. Electromagnetic energy is typically described by either its frequency or wavelength or by a description of its properties i.e., Radio, Light, Visible, etc.

As the name suggests, an electromagnetic field is actually made up of two separate component fields, an electric field and a magnetic field although each can also exist separately. An electric field surrounds electrically charged particles; this electric field exerts a force on other electrically charged objects. It was Michael Faraday who introduced the concept of an electric field. The electric field is usually described using SI units of volts per metre (V/m). An electric field also surrounds fluctuating or moving magnetic fields.

A magnetic field is produced by moving electric charges, by electric fields that fluctuate over time, and by the intrinsic magnetic field of some materials. Where both electric and magnetic fields exist together they are intrinsically linked, any changes within either of the fields causing changes within the other. The relationship between magnetic and electric fields, and the currents and charges that create them, is described by the Maxwell equations named after the Scottish physicist and mathematician James Clerk Maxwell who described them in his paper *On Physical Lines of Force*, published in 1861. In measuring terms, the two interlinked fields that comprise an electromagnetic field co-exist at right angles to one another.

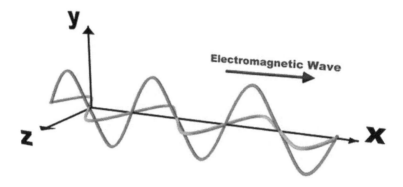

Schematic representation of an electromagnetic field.

Why are investigators Interested in electromagnetism?

Since the early 1980's, ghost investigators have become increasingly interested in various types of electromagnetism and they offer various ideas and suggestions as to why they are considered to be significant. Some may say that electromagnetism can be used or manipulated by the spirits and ghosts. Others may point out that ghosts and spirits exist as part of the electromagnetic spectrum. Many believe that by measuring EMF it is possible to detect ghosts or spirits or in some cases use this knowledge in order to effect direct interactions, such as having the spirit alter the reading of a meter and cause it to respond to questions. Many investigators may cite the work of Canadian Professor of Neurology Michael Persinger as justification for their methods. Working at the Laurentian University, Persinger has conducted a number of experiments which suggests that when certain parts of the brain, in particular the temporal lobes, (those regions of the brain located above and behind the ears) are stimulated by low frequency electromagnetic fields (typically less than 100Hz) of varying intensity and duration, test subjects reported experiences that were similar to those experiences often associated with reported paranormal activity.

Using his *"God Helmet"*, essentially a snowmobile or motorcycle helmet fitted with electromagnetic emitting coils, Persinger reported that many of his participants experienced a presence beside them in the room. These sensations ranged from a simple sensed presence through to visions of God. Many more had less evocative, but still significant experiences of another consciousness or sentient being. These experiments lead to the suggestion that some people may be more susceptible to these electromagnetic emissions. Persinger claimed that similar electromagnetic fields might be present within the environment and concluded that the source for the fields can be both natural and man-made. Natural sources of electromagnetism include variations within the Earth's inherent geomagnetism and interactions between the geomagnetic field and solar radiation. Man-made sources of electromagnetism include electrical wiring and electrical appliances. The ambient electromagnetism is also created by a combination and interaction from both natural and man-made electromagnetism. Persinger suggested that these interactions might be responsible for the production of a range of anomalous experiences, from the sighting of apparitions to poltergeist phenomena and even UFO encounters. Other researchers examining Persinger's work disagree with his conclusions, most notably a team from Uppsala University in Sweden, who used a second God helmet in a double blind experiment to try and replicate Persinger's experiments. Their conclusions published in *Nature* (2004) concluded that exposure to electromagnetic fields was not a significant factor in creating anomalous sensations; instead they concluded that suggestion and personality traits were more likely to account for Persinger's results. However, a more recent study carried out in Brazil and published in the *Journal of Consciousness Exploration & Research* (April 2014) has indicated a partial replication of Persinger's original claims but also pointed to the influence of expectation by the participants thus concluding that more research is still required.

Humans have evolved to use and trust our five normal senses and the human brain can only interpret any electromagnetic interference to its normal functioning in a sensory manner. Research suggests that the witness may therefore see, hear, taste, touch, or smell something, which they believe to be a real experience without any apparent cause and therefore is considered by them to be anomalous. Electromagnetic fields at 50 or 60Hz are mainly produced by the electricity supply. These frequencies are very close to those naturally found within the brain and it is therefore not surprising to discover that some people have suggested that exposure to these man-made fields can have a measurable effect on human physiology and behaviour. Some researchers have also suggested that electromagnetic field exposure may even be detrimental to health and well-being, which is the main reason why there are so many EMF detectors now being readily sold to an increasingly health conscious population. To date all this of this research has been mostly confined to laboratory studies with very few detailed studies ever being conducted in haunted locations. These few studies did however suggest that exposure to environmental electromagnetism may indeed be linked to some personal anomalous experiences. For example, in an experiment carried out in the Edinburgh vaults by a team lead by Professor Richard Wiseman, the test volunteers reported a higher instance of feeling that were being watched or described feeling uncomfortable in particular areas where the ambient electromagnetic field amplitude was higher. In areas where the ambient electromagnetism was lower, correspondingly fewer anomalous experiences were reported. Persinger investigated a location in Ontario, Canada, in which he claimed to have found a link between fluctuating man-made electromagnetism and it's interactions with the natural geomagnetic field and reports of paranormal experiences. A link was also strongly indicated at a farmhouse in Cheshire, England, between reported paranormal experiences and an abnormally high region of man-made electromagnetism from a damaged electricity supply cable during an investigation carried out by Para.Science and Bristol University, Human Radiation Effects Group.

Suggested links between electromagnetism and anomalous experiences predate Persinger. Harry Price described a possible electromagnetic theory in his 1945 book *Poltergeist over England*:

> It is thought by some people that the energy used in the poltergeist phenomena is of an electrical nature, obtained from the atmosphere. There is no evidence for this. It occurs to me that, though, the alleged new current recently discovered by Professor Felix Ehrenhaft might be an explanation. Professor Ehrenhaft, a Viennese physicist, demonstrated to the American Physical Society at Columbia University on 16th January 1944, that he had obtained experimental proof of the existence of pure magnetic current. This meant he declared, "That not only electric currents, but also magnetic currents flow through the universe". He said, "The discovery has terrific possibilities". It is possible that the poltergeist can utilise this current in some way.

A correspondent, Mr. Percy Piggot, of Kirk Ella, Hull, has sent me his views of how the manifestations might be explained. His speculations are ingenious and novel, and I have pleasure in reproducing them: "Is it not possible that the substance which pervades all space, interpenetrating and enveloping our Earth and our bodies, which scientists simply name ether, but do not pretend to explain, is capable of receiving and retaining pictures of our actions and the sounds which emanate from such actions and even of reproducing them when conditions are favourable, as for instance, the evening light, the temperature, and the weather generally? In other words, this little understood substance is perhaps capable of acting as a photographic negative. This is simply what a cinema film does. It reproduces form, motion and sound. Why should Nature not also do it?"

Unfortunately for poltergeists (the term Price used for the majority of ghost and haunting experiences) and also for ghost investigators, the claims relating to the existence of pure magnetic currents made by Professor Ehrenhaft have been demonstrated by physicists to be wrong.

It might therefore be argued that if investigators use EMF meters and locate unusual or unexpected electromagnetic fields at a site being investigated, they may be a little closer to determining a possible cause for some of the activity being reported. Unfortunately, many investigators have not fully read the published research or choose to simply ignore the parts they do not agree with. In time, the logic of measuring EMF has become diluted and lost.

EMF meters have become Ghost Detectors. Some investigators have proposed their own explanations as to why an EMF meter is a useful tool for paranormal investigation "Ghosts emit EMF's or distort the Earth's natural electromagnetism". "Ghosts use the electricity supply or the electromagnetic energy to obtain energy that allows them to manifest". There are many explanations and many books that earnestly declare that using an EMF meter will allow the investigator to detect the energy or presence of a ghost or spirit. These ideas have nothing to do with the actual existing research and represent nothing more than pseudo-science or a corrupt understanding of the actual reasons as to why EMF might be worth considering.

EMF Meters

EMF meters measure either the electromagnetic radiation flux density (DC fields) or the change in electromagnetic field strength over time (AC fields), essentially the same as a radio wave, but with different frequency characteristics. There are different types of EMF meters; some have the ability to measure the electric and magnetic fields separately. Measurement may also be made using single or multi-axis sensors. Single axis meters are cheaper but may be less accurate overall and take longer to complete a survey because the meter only measures one dimension of the field. A tri-axis meter measures all three axes simultaneously, but these models tend to be more expensive. Most EMF meters can only measure moving (AC) electromagnetic fields, which are usually emitted from man-made sources such as electrical wiring or radio transmitters. Gauss meters or magnetometers are normally used to measure DC fields, which occur naturally in Earth's geomagnetic field and occur around objects or material such as ferrous metal where inherent magnetism is present. Many ghost investigators use an AC EMF meter of a type that is designed and optimised to measure frequencies around of 50Hz or 60 Hz, which are the respective domestic electricity supply frequencies for the UK and the USA. Typically these meters will also measure electromagnetic fields at frequencies above and below this calibration point, although with a greatly reduced accuracy and sensitivity as the field's frequency moves further from the optimum point. The measurement data is normally provided using units of magnetic field strength, milliGauss or microTesla. Although these devices are often known as EMF meters, they are in fact only measuring the magnetic field component, with the electric field being interpolated from the magnetic field data. Some meters are available that can also measure the electric field component using a dedicated separate sensor, the measurement being expressed in Volts/metre.

Electromagnetic fields are directional and surround the source such as a cable or appliance. The primary field strength is dependent upon the direction of current flow. The field strength also diminishes as the distance from the source is increased, for ease of visualisation they may be likened to the ripples produced when a single pebble is dropped into a pond, the ripples diminishing in size as they move away from point where the pebble is dropped. Electromagnetic fields from several sources can also interact with one other, similar to the effect seen when two or more pebbles are dropped into the pond. This leads to areas where the strength may be much higher or significantly lower than would be expected from a single source. In order to obtain the maximum accuracy for any measurements it is important that the actual sensor within the EMF meter corresponds to the direction of maximum field strength at any given location. If it does not, then the user risks making measurements that may be much lower than the true field strength. One solution to this problem is to use a meter that has three sensors each set at right angles to the one another, an arrangement known as tri-axis or three-axis sensing (X-axis, Y-axis and Z-axis). By combining the information from all three sensors inside the meter, a much more representative measurement for the overall field strength can be obtained. Single axis meters are available and are often preferred by investigators, as they are generally much cheaper than three-axis models and also more readily available. A single axis meter needs to be used with care. By carefully moving the meter around when making the measurements it is possible to discover the orientation of the field at a given location and then align the meter's sensor with it to obtain the most accurate measurements.

Limitations of Use and Practical Considerations

One serious problem that does present itself when obtaining electromagnetic field measurements is that, with very few exceptions, the meters that are used provide only information that relates to the amplitude of the field. Every electromagnetic field has two defining characteristics, its amplitude, which is a measure of the overall strength and its frequency. Frequency information is vital when determining the source or cause of the field. Failure to measure frequency means that the investigator is unable to state anything about the electromagnetic field except that it exists and that it has amplitude. To make any statement about cause or source without the frequency information becomes speculation and guesswork. In those cases where EMF meters that provide frequency and amplitude information have been used, it is almost immediately possible to say with a high degree of certainty what was producing the observed electromagnetism and, in all cases so far, these have been recognised normal sources, mostly in the form of man-made fields from radio transmissions or appliances. One well-used statement by investigators in support of a measured EMF being paranormal is: "All the electrical appliances were turned off and we could find no hidden wiring, therefore, we were unable to explain the EMF spikes we measured."

This ignores the fact that in many instances the electromagnetic field that is being measured may be coming from a source that lies at some distance from the location.

In a number of locations, I have been able to measure electromagnetic fields inside the location when the electrical supply was switched off and when no appliances were being used. By using a meter that provided both the amplitude and frequency information it was possible to determine that the cause of the higher than anticipated electromagnetic fields were long wave radio transmissions by broadcasters including the BBC. The radio signal was picked up and re-transmitted by the wiring inside the building, which was acting as an antenna. There is actually no requirement for the building to have any additional wiring; the electrically conductive properties of the structure itself are often sufficient to create these localised electromagnetic fields. As an example, many people are no doubt aware that it is a simple matter to enhance the reception of a radio by placing a finger on, or touching the aerial. This knowledge about the true source of the observed EMF can only be obtained by using the frequency information. Unfortunately, the vast majority of investigators make no measurements of frequency relating to electromagnetic fields, the meters they are using are not capable of frequency measurement and as such the information they are working with is of little help when trying to understand the nature of the electromagnetic fields that are being observed.

There are a number of considerations that must be made when making any measurements in order to ensure that the subsequent data is as accurate and reliable as possible. Obviously the first of these is to become fully conversant with the operating instructions supplied by the manufacturer. These instructions should also provide the technical specifications of the device; the measuring range, operating frequency, and accuracy are important pieces of information. Be aware of any limitations placed on the use or positioning of the device. For example, if it is to be used near other items of equipment, this may affect the subsequent data. Another factor that needs to be considered is the actual distance between the source and the measuring point. For example a television set on standby may give a reading of less than 1mG measured at 30cm but over 50mG at the same distance when it is turned on. A bedside clock radio can give you a surprisingly high reading of around 100mG at 20-30cm.

Many types of EMF meter are described as being frequency weighted or frequency calibrated. These meters do not give a simple measurement of the field strength but instead the measurement is proportional to the frequency of the field. These types of meter measure the amount of energy the field is carrying and as the frequency of the electromagnetic field increases so does the energy it carries. The Alpha Labs TriField is just such a meter. An electromagnetic field of 3mG at a frequency of 60Hz will be correctly shown as 3mG, which is the true value. However, if the electromagnetic field frequency then increases to 120Hz, the same strength field will now be shown incorrectly as 6mG on the scale, around double the actual value. The added complication in such situations is that the meter does not indicate the frequency of the electromagnetic field, so the operator must either know beforehand the frequency of the field that is being measured and therefore what the source is, or they are simply left in the dark guessing about the accuracy of the displayed measurement.

If it is still the intention to use an EMF meter it is important to understand that the meter will register changes in the electromagnetic field values as it is moved around a location. Even if meter remains static in one position, any changes in the flow of electricity nearby will cause changes to register on the meter. This is quite normal and should be expected. Investigators may come across areas where the electromagnetism seems unusually high. Often wires can be hidden inside walls and other structures or the structure itself is electrically conductive. Domestic water pipes are also frequently used as part of the buildings Earth (Ground) protection and electrical currents flow through them causing electromagnetic fields to form around the pipe or wire. Electrically conductive structures including buildings, trees, and even people can also hold or even generate an electric charge; if this electric charge then subsequently flows to Earth it may well create a fluctuation in the measured electromagnetism. This affect may vary depending upon the weather or the humidity. As already mentioned, wiring, pipe-work, and electrically conductive structures can also act as an antenna picking up and re-broadcasting radio frequency electromagnetic fields from even quite distant transmitters. All of these factors will result in regions within a location where the measured ambient electromagnetism will be higher than expected. Natural changes in the Earth's electromagnetic field such as occurs during thunderstorms, increased solar activity, or even seismic activity, can also induce electricity to flow in conductive manmade and natural structures. This flow of electricity will produce electromagnetic fields that may be detected and measured by even a basic EMF meter. Investigators generally have multiple items of equipment in use throughout their investigation. This might include radios and mobile phones, together with cameras, sound recorders, and computers: all of these will produce fields around them and will affect the overall reliability of the electromagnetic measurements.

Problems measuring electromagnetism are legion and to hope that one can disentangle these normal fluctuations and assign them to a particular source using a cheap single axis EMF meter is generally a forlorn hope. Therefore, claims that some investigators are making that they can use such simple meters to detect the presence of an anomalous and potentially paranormal electromagnetism in such circumstances starts to look increasingly meaningless.

Very Special EMF Meters?

In recent years, a number of investigators have virtually ceased to make conventional electromagnetic field measurements and have instead switched to using their EMF meters as spirit communication or spirit interaction devices. They base their methods on the assumption that spirits or other discarnate entities can affect the meter's display in some manner and by this means answer questions put to them by the investigators. There are a number of EMF meters advertised and sold specifically for ghost investigating. Various claims are made to support their use, ranging from the direct measurement of spirit energy or the energy available for spirit manifestation to devices that can be utilised for indicating spirit interaction or even communication. The majority are off-the-shelf commercial devices such as the Safe Range EMF Meter, which according to its manufacturer, K-II Enterprises, of Syracuse, New York, is designed to: "Measure the electromagnetic field strength of every device in your home, workplace or school; outdoor power lines, underground lines and even when you travel and shop for appliances." As the manufacturer makes clear, it is intended and sold for use by those who may be concerned about exposure to electromagnetic fields: "Health concerns about the negative effects of electromagnetic field (EMF) from appliances, power lines, and home wiring have caused the U.S. Government to issue a warning to use 'Prudent Avoidance' to help reduce your exposure to this risk."

Whilst the Safe Range EMF meter name might not be immediately recognisable to many ghost investigators, the maker's name K-II will be. This same meter has become ubiquitous as a ghost-investigating tool. Sold simply as the 'K-II' or 'K2' those who offer the device for sale to ghost investigators make a number of additional claims, claims that cannot be substantiated except in the broadest anecdotal terms:

> The K2 EMF is used by Ghost Hunters to find indications of paranormal activity by looking for sudden erratic readings (spikes) of the lights on the K2 meter. A man-made electromagnetic field (EMF) creates a steady reading while the spirit world's energy is believed to be what creates the impulse reading on the K2 EMF meter. Researchers using the K-II EMF meter have been able to do what seems to be actual communication sessions with what is believed to be ghosts. The ghost is simply instructed to light up the lights on the meter in response to specific questions. For example, the ghost can be asked to respond with spiking up the lights of the K2 meter once for a No answer to a question and the light up the lights of the K2 meter twice for a yes answer to a question.
>
> (GHOST AUGUSTINE LTD)

In 2007, sensitive and investigator Chris Fleming used a K-II Safe Range EMF meter to apparently communicate with spirits during an episode of the US television series Ghost Hunters. Fleming's apparent success was quickly followed up by his public endorsement of the

K-II and it is now being offered for sale on a number of ghost-hunting equipment websites. As paranormal groups obtained their own K-II's they also began to report on social media and through their websites seemingly amazing examples of spirit communication using this meter. Following the success of the K-II it was found that many other types of simple EMF meter were also effective spirit communication devices. Following this discovery, more and more models of EMF that offered the potential for direct interaction and communication with the ghosts and spirits became available for sale.

K-II Enterprises Safe Range EMF meter

There are now several variations of the K-II (K2) available from different resellers, some have additional features that are after-market modifications such as a temperature probe or modified switches. These modifications are not provided or supported by the original manufacturer and immediately void any claim for the accuracy of measurement and calibration of the original equipment. On all K-II models, the information is displayed using a series of lights or sound with only a vague scale that relates the scale to the power density of the electromagnetic field being observed. Other than a measuring scale of 'more lights and less lights' or changes in tone, the information is essentially meaningless. Many of the claims of ghost interaction may appear impressive and those modifying, selling, and using them, often make the results obtained appear even more impressive. Ghost investigators love their gadgets and the more esoteric and high-tech they appear to be, the more investigators seem to love using them. However, in terms of providing data that is relevant and helpful to the investigation process and that will stand up to scrutiny, there can be no substitute for good quality measurements obtained using the correct item of measuring equipment in the correct manner and by someone who knows what they are doing.

Is it More Than Just Ghosts Inside the Machine?

The majority of cheaper EMF meters work using the simple principle of electromagnetic inductance, not dissimilar to that used in any electrical transformer. The sensor consists of a simple wire coil wound around an electrically conductive core. As the wire coil is moved through a static magnetic field or is exposed to a moving magnetic field, a voltage is generated within the coil, which can be measured and directly related to the levels of magnetism (or coil movement) that is present. The voltage produced within the coil by the external magnetic field is tiny and needs to be greatly amplified in order to drive the measuring circuit of the meter. Amplification leads to (electrical) noise being generated within the circuits which may also result in false readings being observed and manufacturers normally take care to design the amplification circuits to minimise this problem. Other sources of noise include the stray or erroneous electrical spikes from domestic, radio, and natural EMF sources such as weather related phenomena, all of which can cause false readings to be indicated by the meter, again manufacturers usually design the amplification and circuits to minimise this problem. However, it is interesting to note that many of the best EMF meters for spirit communications tend to be the budget models such as the K-II that have basic amplification circuitry and therefore correspondingly poorer noise suppression. Moreover, an examination of some K-II and similar meters offered for sale as spirit communication devices has found that the amplification circuits have been adjusted after the device has left the manufacturer and in such a way as to make the amplifier circuit highly unstable in operation and much more prone to the effects of electrical noise and interference. The modified meters are in effect now too sensitive and will therefore respond to small amounts of interference from any localised EMF source. They are also more reactive to weather related events such as storms. The user may then interpret these erroneous responses as having a spiritual cause. In other cases, it has been observed that the EMF is simply reacting to stimulation by the investigators radios and other equipment either wittingly or unwittingly. The fraudulent misuse of EMF devices has also certainly been observed. Another development of the EMF meter and spirit communication notion has led to the development and use of devices such as the Ovilus. Instead of a display that reads in terms of the amplitude of the electromagnetic field, the detected electromagnetism is used to drive a speech synthesis circuit. This is supposed to permit spirit communication with the investigator. From a vocabulary of a little over one thousand words, the communicating spirit then apparently manipulates the local electromagnetic field surrounding the device in order to select single words from the pre-set list. Quite why the spirit can't just directly manipulate the device's voice synthesiser instead of the surrounding electromagnetism isn't made clear by either the manufacturer or proponents of the Ovilus and other similar devices. Perhaps that is an accomplishment that the spirit realm has yet to master?

Ovilus 1

Following on from the Ovilus, there are now several other spirit communication devices based on the principle that spirits are able to manipulate the local electromagnetism, temperature, and other physical parameters in order to produce apparently evidential information including The Paranormal Puck. Most bizarre of all are the legion of smartphone and tablet computer 'apps' that are now being used for ghost hunting including the iOvilus which seemingly replicates the Ovilus. Various claims are made for the usefulness of these software applications, claims that are more often concerned with advertising hype than any actual capability. Apps such as The Ghost Radar, iOvilus, and Ghosthunter M2, must only be regarded as novelties with no demonstrable place in ghost or paranormal investigation, although their use is now becoming widespread in ghost investigations.

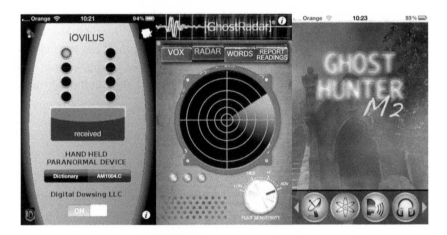

A Legion of Apps exist for Smart phones that claim to be real ghost hunting tools

To conclude this examination of EMF meters it might be worthwhile considering the views of a respected ghost investigation team on EMF meters and their use:

> EMF detector: One of the coolest ghost hunting tools is the EMF detector. Just like a compass it can detect strange electromagnetic fields. However, the EMF detector is able to pick up weaker fields than a compass can. When using this tool you are looking for a fluctuating energy field. Sometimes ghostly entities move around and you can attempt to follow them before they disappear. You should start snapping pictures when you experience this kind of activity on your EMF detector. When using this device you want to look for readings between a 2 and a 7. This is the range that most ghost hunters will agree a ghostly presence can register between.

Ionising or Nuclear Radiation?

Ionising radiation is also part of the electromagnetic spectrum. This is electromagnetic radiation of extremely high frequency that has sufficient energy to disrupt and break apart atomic particles creating ions, hence its name. Ionising radiation is almost always derived from nuclear decay and the release of radioactive particles such as alpha, beta, gamma, and x-ray's. There are a number of ghost investigation groups who now routinely use Geiger counters which are devices that measure ionising nuclear radiation. As is common in paranormal study, there are various claims relating to the usefulness and relevance of measuring ionising radiation when investigating ghosts. These include the suggestion that ghosts in some way emit ionising radiation that can be detected. One ghost hunting equipment supplier offers the suggestion that:

> A Geiger counter can be very useful in an investigation for monitoring changes in the background radiation of a location. Researchers have found that ambient radiation seems to be drained or increased in the presence of ghosts. Geiger counters have been shown to be effective in paranormal investigation since the 1970's and are recommended by ghost hunters such as Troy Taylor and Peter Underwood.

(THEGHOSTHUNTERSTORE.COM)

In reality, there are no research based studies that have examined links between ionising radiation and spontaneous experiences of ghosts or spirits so it is hard to understand why these meters are being used at all for ghost investigation. One researcher did measure nuclear radiation within a haunted English castle and, as a result, concluded that there may be a link between increased levels of ionising radiation and the reporting of anomalous experiences within a haunted bedroom. His conclusion proved to be seriously flawed as the Geiger counter was discovered by other researchers to be giving erroneous high measurements in the presence of a high man-made electromagnetic field, a fact confirmed by the device's manufacturer. Geiger counters are also a regular item of equipment for paranormal investigations that examine and study alleged UFO landing sights and crop circles. It is therefore probable that their use in ghost investigation simply resulted as a crossover from this area of paranormal research. Currently, no adequate case can be made for the use of these devices as useful tools for ghost investigation.

Radio Frequency Radiation

Very closely related to the EMF meters that are used by ghost investigators are radio frequency (RF) meters. In fact, in many respects they are virtually identical, in some instances even covering the same range of frequencies. The radio frequency spectrum is generally considered to be from 3kHz to 3GHz for most radio devices, although in reality the radio frequency spectrum extends from single hertz to hundreds of Gigahertz. For example, the noisy electrical interference that is often heard on car radios when passing beneath overhead power cables is radio interference with a frequency of 50Hz.

Standard ghost investigation EMF meters such as the CellSensor and EMF-1394 are calibrated for use between 20Hz and 2,000Hz (2kHz), much of which lies well inside the radio frequency spectrum. Beyond their calibrated range many EMF meters will, however, continue to respond to radio frequency sources. Investigators using handheld walkie-talkie radios have noticed how using radios in close proximity to EMF meters can make the reading of the meter jump about. It's therefore clear that EMF meters are generally highly susceptible to radio interference. Measuring radio frequency radiation is virtually the same process as electromagnetic field measuring but, there are some minor modifications that are required to the internal amplification circuits of RF meters as radio frequency energy levels tend be higher, but this is of little consequence to their use. Most radio frequency measurement devices tend to be broadband devices and are capable of measuring a range of frequencies (bands), indicating the total amount of energy within that band. For example, one common RF meter offers a measuring range between 1Mhz and 3Mhz with a resolution of 100kHz. That is actually a large chunk of the radio spectrum, some 2,000,000Hz, and it contains hundreds, and even thousands of individual radio broadcasters together with other radio frequency transmissions such as baby monitors, alarms, and remote telemetry devices. Radio frequency sources other than radio stations include the electrical systems of cars, and the switching of domestic and industrial appliances, and more distant sources such as the Sun and stars. As might be expected, this creates a huge problem for any investigator wishing to try and determine a source of any observed radio emission, although frequency band plans exist that detail known and authorised broadcasters and the frequencies they are allocated, which can be of some assistance. Dedicated radio frequency meters such as the Spectran HF-4060 offer a frequency detection range from 10,000,000Hz (10MHz) to 6,000,000,000Hz (6GHz). A key difference between EMF meters that measure low frequency electromagnetic fields and RF meters are the units of measurement that are used to express the energy. For EMF meters, this is typically expressed in SI units of magnetic flux density, the Tesla or more usually microTesla (uT) although many EMF meters still use the older unit of Gauss and milliGauss (mG). Radio frequency meters normally provide measurement in units of power density, Watts per cubic centimetre W/cm2 more often expressed in milliWatts per cubic centimetre (mW/cm2).

EVP researchers too, are interested in the radio spectrum and have for many years developed equipment that looks at specific and broad radio frequency ranges in the search for claimed spirit communicators or voices. Devices such as the Spiricom, Frank's Box, and other similar devices use radio frequency receivers to scan and monitor the radio spectrum in the search for these intriguing voices. EVP researchers have periodically focussed on different regions within the overall radio spectrum as being of particular interest such as 29MHz as described by John G. Fuller in his book '*The Ghost of 29 Megacycles*' which looks at the work of EVP researchers including Raymond Cass and others. Cass himself favoured 127Mhz and claimed significant EVP results from monitoring those frequencies. Some ghost investigators also believe and claim that spirits and ghosts exist within the radio or electromagnetic spectra but certainly the difficulties presented by making precise measurements within the radio frequency spectrum would make any evidence obtained by such means of questionable value.

Negative and Positive Ion Detectors

Air ions are air molecules that have either gained or lost electrons. When a molecule has a surplus of electrons, it develops a negative charge, becoming a negative ion (anion). When the molecule has too few electrons it has a positive charge and becomes a positive ion (cation). Ions may also consist of one or more atoms that have the same charge. Most positive natural ions come from nuclear radioactivity. Around half of the natural air ions come from radioactive minerals in the ground. Just less than half come from radon gas in the air and the small percentage remaining are produced by other sources such as cosmic radiation. Each time a radioactive atom decays near the air, it typically produces 50,000 - 500,000 air ion pairs as it travels a few centimetres. Indoors, ions typically exist for just a few seconds before touching a surface and losing their charge to Earth. Outside, Ions can survive for just a few seconds, sometimes much longer, perhaps several minutes or more. Evaporating water, lightning, and fire, also produces ions both positive and negative. Ions require an energy source for their production such as heat, flame, radioactivity, frictional rubbing, electricity and evaporation. Normal fair-weather outdoor ion concentrations are typically 200 to 800 negative and 250 to 1500 positive ions per cubic centimetre. Indoor levels are usually lower. Hot objects usually emit equal numbers of positive and negative ions. High direct current (DC) voltage (over 1000 Volts), especially when connected to pointed metal edges or needles, produces ions with the same polarity as the voltage source. This is the basis of domestic ionisers. Evaporating water produces negative ions in the air and as a consequence leaves a positive charge behind in the water that hasn't yet evaporated. Because a large concentration of positive ions can attract negative ions and vice versa, high concentrations of positive and negative ions are often found together. A cloud of ions of either charge is normally highly unstable and will tend to disintegrate. For this reason, high concentrations of exclusively positive or negative ions tend to be compact, and don't extend more than a few metres. Indoors, the concentration of ions can vary radically from place to place, even over a distance of less than a metre.

Exactly why ghost investigators are interested in measuring air ions and, in particular negative air ions, is perhaps difficult to understand. It might be related to the belief that ghosts and spirits require or use energy and air ions are seen as some form of invisible free energy floating around in thin air and this is a theory that has certainly been proposed by some ghost investigators. It may also relate to the work of researcher Dr Andrija Puharich who noted the effects of atmospheric ionisation on the performance of individuals in telepathy experiments. He observed that when there was an excess of negative ions the performance of some tasks was improved. James Houran and Rense Lange suggest in their book *Hauntings and Poltergeists; Multidisciplinary Perspectives* that many paranormal experiences may result from the effects of positive ions on the brain. Both the foregoing suggestions are of course unproven but have led to some novel experiments being conducted by ghost investigators. The Ion Flood Experiment is one example, in which a powerful domestic or industrial ioniser is used to flood a room or location with negative ions close to the ioniser and of course producing a concentration of positive ions further away from the device. The idea proposed by those using the Ion Flood method is that it either creates good conditions for the manifestation of ghosts or spirits or alternatively provides an excess of energy within the location that may be used by the spirits and allow them to cause noises or object movement. A further variation on this idea is that the positive ion clouds that are also produced in adjacent areas and which are apparently disliked by spirits and ghosts can be used to either drive them from a location or in some instances toward other equipment, a form of ghost trap or exorcism by electricity perhaps? Certainly, high concentrations of ions can have demonstrable effects on people. Negative ionisers are used to aid feelings of well-being and can assist with asthma and other breathing disorders, the charged ions attaching themselves to dust and pollen and causing it to be drawn toward oppositely charged surfaces and thus out of the air. High levels of positive ions are reported to lead to feelings of lethargy and are linked to increased reports of headaches and other minor ailments. It is therefore possible that, in some instances, reports of paranormal experiences may be attributed to exposure to high levels of negative or positive ion levels.

Several techniques for measuring the quantity and polarity of air ions are used but the one most commonly used by ghost investigators is the AlphaLabs Air Ion Counter which uses a device called a Gerdian tube through which air is drawn by a small fan. The charged ions are attracted to one of two charged electrodes, (one positive, the other negative) located within the tube. As the ions accumulate at the electrodes, negative ions to the positive electrode and vice versa, they generate a current which is related to the total number of ions and their charge. The device is not highly accurate, stated by the manufacturer as being only +/- 25% of the total field, but it does provide a reasonable indication of the total ion quantity and charge. The negative ion detector (NID) is another device that is often used by investigators. The NID uses a positive or neutrally charged probe or surface onto which the negative ions accumulate and alter the charge voltage of the probe. This change in electrical charge is then used to operate a simple detection circuit. The NID is not suitable for detailed measurements of ion quantities and is in reality measuring the static electrical charge of the probe (air). Most NID's use a simple buzzer or a light to provide a warning when the charge (and therefore the amount of negative ions) reaches a certain user pre-set level.

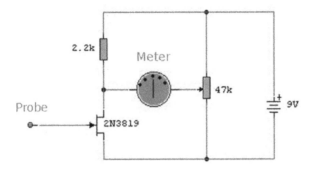

A simple circuit for a negative ion and static electricity detector

Static Electricity

Static electricity is usually created when materials rub against each other, like wool on plastic or the soles of shoes on carpet. The process of friction causes electrons to be pulled from the surface of one material and relocated on the surface of the other material, the negatively charged electrons building up a negative charge on materials where they accumulate. A positive charge develops on the material that has become stripped of its electrons. Materials and objects can become electrically charged by a number of mechanisms:

- Contact induced charge separation - the triboelectric effect. Materials having weakly bound electrons can easily lose or gain them. This can be most obviously be demonstrated in the basic school science trick of rubbing a balloon and sticking it to a wall, the negatively charged balloon being attracted to the positively charge wall.

- Pressure induced charge separation - the piezoelectric effect. Applying physical or mechanical pressure to some materials causes a separation of charge to occur. Some types of cigarette lighter use this principle; pressure being applied to a ceramic chip which becomes negatively charged and produces a spark as the charge leaps to the positively charged case igniting the gas.

- Heat induced charge separation - the pyroelectric effect. All pyroelectric materials are also piezoelectric. The application of heat to a material produces charge separation within the material.

- Charge induced charge separation - electrostatic induction. This happens whenever a charged object is brought close to an electrically neutral object and causes a separation of charge within the conductor. Charges of the same polarity are repelled and charges of the opposite polarity are attracted as the force, due to the interaction of electric charges, fall off rapidly with increasing distance. The effect is most pronounced when the neutral object is an electrical conductor as the charges can more freely move around. Earthing (grounding) part of an object with a charge-induced charge separation can permanently add or remove electrons and leave the object with a permanent charge. This process is integral to the workings of the Van de Graaf Generator.

It is the charge induced charge separation mechanism that is most commonly used by ghost investigators in devices used to apply additional energy to the location environment in order to supply energy for the use of ghosts and spirits. Devices such as Tasers, Van de Graaf generators, and other spark generating equipment are frequently encountered being used to support this unproven idea. These electrical charges can also produce noticeable physical effects too. Piloerection, the reflex that causes hairs to rise and goose bumps to form may be triggered by electrical charges acting upon the skin and the movement of charged electrical particles across the body may be detectable as subtle cooling or 'ion wind'.

The reasons for ghost investigators being interested in static electricity are difficult to trace but a number of theories exist within the ghost investigation community. Most are linked to claims by spiritualists that ghosts and spirits require some form of energy. There are a number of early séance room reports in which electricity-like sparks were observed or participants reported the smell of ozone, a by-product of electrostatic discharge. One respected team of ghost investigators offers the following explanation for their interest in static electricity and ions:

Electrostatic Generator: This tool is definitely for the serious ghost hunter. Because a spirit needs electrostatic charges to materialize (at least that's the theory), an electrostatic generator will help give ghostly entities that extra boost that they need to do so. This handy tool shoots ions into the nearby area, which will help to give strength to an already existing paranormal experience. This device is only good for indoor use. If you tried to use it outside, the ions would just shoot of too far away to be of any help.

A number of methods exist that can measure the electrical charge build-up on a surface. The design of most available electro-static detectors is very similar to the negative ion detector but a more complex circuit is used to measure the charge voltage that is induced within the detector. In all cases, the rationale for using these devices and the results that are claimed from their use in any investigation must be seriously questioned.

CHAPTER 9

MONITORING AND MEASURING THE ENVIRONMENT

There are a number of other elements within the environment that the investigator may also require to monitor or measure as part of a ghost investigation. The more obvious physical variables such as the local weather conditions, the humidity, and air pressure are sometimes routinely observed, as is sound, light levels and the movement of objects or even people. Many investigators also have instruments that can monitor more esoteric physical properties; geomagnetism and gravity fields are nowadays often observed in some form as part of the investigation process. It would be beyond the reach of this discussion to consider every item on the ghost investigator's equipment box but it is worth examining some of the more commonly encountered pieces of equipment and their value to the investigator. Sound is dealt with in depth elsewhere in this book, as is light measurement (mainly in the various forms of photography that exist).

Local and Regional Weather

The effects of the prevailing weather conditions upon a location should not be underestimated. At any location in which there is a combination of interior and exterior areas of interest, the effects of the weather might be immediately obvious and may play more of a role in the investigation than just determining if the investigator is going to get cold or wet! There are many documented instances where the reported apparition or other phenomena might be linked to variations within the weather. Hot, dry and humid conditions, the onset or recent passage of thunderstorms, mist, and even rain and snow have all been associated with reports of paranormal experiences. What is often overlooked is how the weather conditions can also affect the climate inside a building.

Obviously, if it is warm outside it is likely to be warmer inside too, although modern climate controlled housing and offices can upset this generalisation. The wind, varying in strength and intensity can alter the internal airflow leading to draughts. Draughts and air currents inside a location can create localised temperature variations and in some instances cause objects to move in an unexpected fashion. At one location in which I was involved, several witnesses described huge exterior doors that each weighed in excess of one ton, opening and closing seemingly without anyone being nearby. They attributed this movement to the action of a ghost that was reputed to haunt the building. Upon examination, it was found that the doors had an automatic system to assist opening that was fitted because of their weight and size. When pressure was applied by anyone in order to open the doors, the automatic system sensed the force and then took over, mechanically opening the doors. The door's mechanical assistance was set to operate when a quite gentle force was applied and action of a comparatively light breeze upon the large door surfaces was discovered to also activate this automatic opening system. The sensitivity of the automatic system was reduced slightly and the 'ghost' stopped opening the doors. The wind can also create unexpected acoustic events that may be transient and therefore hard to replicate or distinguish. Wind blowing over external vents and pipework, much like when a person blows over the open neck of a bottle, can cause sounds which may have a tonal quality, sometimes resembling music, singing, or speech. Blowing air through pipes and tubes is after all the basic principle of many musical instruments. The force of the wind, even when the apparent wind strength is low, can create large pressure forces on structures or individual building components causing them to move. This movement might actually be imperceptibly small and not noticeable but may be sufficient to cause noise as parts move against one another. In a quiet building it is quite surprising just how noticeable the resulting tiny squeaks and creaks can become and how frequently they are attributed to unexplainable causes.

The amount of moisture or precipitation in the air, can change the humidity inside a building. Water may also leak into the building affecting the structure, leading to shrinkage or expansion, which in turn may cause unexpected noises to be heard. Even the ghost investigators own equipment is not immune from the weather, bringing a camera or electronic device into a warmer building from the outside can quickly lead to condensation forming on the equipment on the outside, where it is visible, but also on the inside where it can seriously affect the operation of the equipment as condensed moisture can cause shorting of the microcircuits contained in many devices. Battery contacts and also the batteries themselves can be affected by this condensed moisture and may result in unexpected failures. Using equipment in any location where the air humidity is high, indoors, or outside can also create serious problems with moisture affecting the normal operation of electrical devices. Humid conditions can occur regardless of the prevailing temperature, there are as many mists and fogs in the winter as there are warm humid days in the summer. Many of these condensation related malfunctions and failures might just as quickly rectify themselves as the equipment dries out. Batteries are also temperature dependent, they don't perform as effectively when they are cold and this can lead to an item of equipment suddenly ceasing to operate. The majority of modern battery operated devices measure the battery's available charge and the inability of the battery to deliver its power effectively at low temperatures can cause a device to shut-down unexpectedly. Once the battery is warmed, its ability to deliver power is usually restored and the device will resume working normally once more. There are numerous accounts of investigators claiming that their equipment unexpectedly malfunctioned for no apparent reason yet operated perfectly a little while before and afterwards. Just as frequently, such events are then described as being unexplained and attributed as having a paranormal cause. In the majority of cases, it is highly probable that the cause is simply due to the prevailing environmental conditions.

These are just some of the weather created problems that face the investigator and it is an often overlooked but important consideration in many investigations. It might be difficult to sometimes see the small motions of building components or immediately locate the creaks and noises, but measuring the weather is generally an easy and straightforward process and one that every investigator should routinely undertake.

The Internet and the media abound with regional and local weather information that can be accessed so basic weather information for the area can be easily obtained throughout the investigation period. However, this weather information is normally obtained from a series of fixed locations. These weather-reporting stations are located in towns, cities, airports, and ports that might be some distance from the actual investigation site. Even small variations in distance can radically affect the prevailing local weather conditions, it might only be a gentle breeze in town but in the more exposed countryside nearby it can be quite windy. Such variations in local climate are extenuated by height and the nature of the surrounding terrain. Trees make excellent windbreaks and rural temperatures are generally much lower than the temperature in a nearby town, the bricks and concrete, the roads and pavements absorb and give off heat in a very different manner to vegetation. Even the layout of a location itself can have quite marked effects upon the microclimate surrounding the building. North facing walls get a lot less direct sunlight (unless you live south of the equator of course) and therefore do not get as warm as south facing structures. Breezes might be funnelled and channelled through passages and gaps leading to highly localised wind effects. These effects may alter dramatically from one visit to the next or even over a few hours as the prevailing conditions change. In order to address these problems and in order to monitor the microclimate of a location, some investigators use one of the many home weather stations that are available. If this is the case, then the investigator needs to be aware that the placement of the external sensors should be undertaken with care as quite marked differences in temperature, rainfall, and wind speed could exist on different sides of a building. If weather is to be observed, then it is important that any measurements and changes need to be properly documented so they can be related to any reported events and experiences.

Air Pressure

This is simply a measurement of the force that is exerted by the weight of air acting on a given point. The SI unit of measurement is the hectopascal, although there is still a tendency to use the millibar. Fortunately, it's an easy conversion between the two, as one hectopascal equals one millibar. Air pressure is measured using a barometer; if the device records the subsequent air pressure changes then it is known as a barograph. Mechanical and electronic barometers and barographs are both still commonly used in weather measurement.

Air pressure constantly varies over time. Changes in air temperature, altitude, and in the prevailing wind will all register as changes in air pressure. These changes may not be immediately obvious as many electronic barometers sample the pressure maybe only once or twice per hour. For weather forecasting this is generally sufficient but it fails the investigator using such a sampling frequency who will not see the small but constant changes in air pressure that are a feature of every single location, indoors and outside. More frequent measurement of air pressure can reveal these rapid fluctuations in local air pressure. Some barographs can sample the pressure once or more per second and using one of these devices will show the air pressure to be far from a slowly changing variable. These fluctuations may be small, sometimes less than 1/10th of a hectopascal but they are often sufficient to create draughts and when applied over a large surface such as a door might easily cause it to move. Depending on air temperature, air pressure falls by one hectopascal (one millibar) for every 25 feet of height gained, this means that the air pressure on the upper floors of a building will be slightly lower than the pressure on the lower floors and this will create some air motion in the air as it moves to try and equalise this pressure gradient. Prevailing wind conditions also affect the internal air pressure, sometimes leading to highly localised small but significant variations of the internal air pressure.

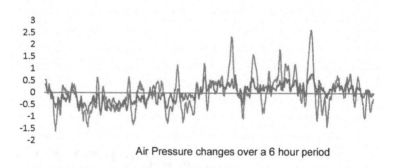

Air Pressure changes over a 6 hour period

Digital barograph output showing internal air pressure changes at fixed point on ground floor (hectopascals)

Humidity

Humidity is a measurement of the amount of water vapour in the air. Humidity may be expressed in several ways: -

- *Absolute humidity* is a measure of actual the amount of water within a given volume of air.

- *Specific humidity* is a measure of the ratio of water in the air.

- *Relative humidity* is a measure of the percentage of water in a given volume of air and is affected by the temperature of the air mass.

In terms of everyday humidity measurement, we typically use relative humidity (RH) which is always expressed as a percentage value of the actual amount of water vapour compared to the amount of water the air is capable of holding without it condensing at a given temperature. Relative humidity measurements must always be quoted together with the measured temperature in order to have any meaning. Relative humidity is measured using a Hygrometer, often combined with a thermometer in the same device. If the device records the relative humidity it is known as a hygrograph, if the device also records the temperature, it is a thermo-hygrograph. Both mechanical and electronic versions of these devices exist.

In some investigation situations it may be important to measure the relative humidity, as increased humidity will also increase the perceived apparent temperature to humans, this is known as the *Heat Index*. Therefore, in terms of usefulness to the ghost investigator, knowledge of the relative humidity might offer some insight into understanding reported perceived temperature changes. Related to humidity is the *Dew Point*. This is actually a function of temperature and is the temperature at which the water that is suspended in the air will condense, forming droplets on surfaces. Close to the dew point the air mists and fogs become more likely to form and to be seen. High humidity levels are an indication of high levels of suspended water vapour, which is known to lead to some types of photographic anomaly becoming more prevalent, specifically those anomalies classified as orbs. As the relative humidity approaches 100% and the air becomes saturated, water vapour may begin to condense out and form mist which has frequently been misreported as various visual phenomena and may, for example, be an explanation as to the frequent reports of white ladies and other ghostly forms seen close to rivers, streams, and standing water. Such occurrences are commonly seen when the water temperature is warmer than the surrounding air mass leading to locally high levels of relative humidity and subsequent condensation. Similar effects may be noticed in low-lying areas such as depressions in fields and dips in the road, the cooler air sinking into the depression; the cool air cannot sustain as much water vapour as the surrounding warmer air and condensation becomes much more likely to occur. Similar patterns of local humidity change can also occur indoors, again leading to the formation of sudden slight mists. Like air pressure, humidity can alter rapidly and the effects may be highly localised.

Air Movement

Movement of air takes places outdoors in the form of wind and indoors where it is known as a draught. The SI unit for measuring air speed (velocity) is metres per second (m/s) although there a number of other established units too, such as the knot (nautical miles per hour) and the Beaufort scale (expressed as numbered wind forces from 0 to 12). Air velocity is measured with an anemometer. If the device also records the air velocity, it is known as an anemograph. Mechanical, electronic, and electro-mechanical devices are commonly used in many applications. Some anemometers measure the air velocity directly whilst others use pressure or electrical changes within a sensor to determine the air velocity. The most familiar types of velocity meters use a small windmill, propeller, or a series of rotating cups. The spinning motion is directly translated into a measurement of the air speed. These are mechanical or electro-mechanical devices and the inherent friction within the rotating components means that they may be insensitive to low velocity air movements. Inertia within the rotating component may also mean that small variations in air velocity may fail to be measured. Measurement of lower air velocities can be made using a hot wire anemometer. This uses a very fine wire which is electrically heated. The wire is made from metal that changes its electrical resistance depending on its temperature. The air moving past the wire has a cooling effect on the wire and the electrical resistance of the wire is altered. Therefore, using a circuit that measures the electrical resistance of the wire, a relationship can be obtained between the resistance of the wire and the velocity of the passing air and the velocity of the air can thus be measured. This method is highly accurate and does not suffer from friction problems. Depending upon the sample rate even small rapid variations of air velocity can be measured by this method. Both of the above methods are found in use during ghost investigations as they are relatively inexpensive and are capable of producing accurate results. One important consideration is the units of measurement that the investigator selects. It must be the same for all measurements, indoor or outside. It may be difficult to relate an outside wind speed of just fewer than 6 knots to an interior draught of 3 metres per second. Likewise, choosing a unit such as the Beaufort scale is unlikely to be much help to the investigator as this scale is only a generalised indication of the wind, rather than a direct measurement of the actual speed.

Beaufort Scale	Wind Speed (mph)
0	Less than 1
1	1-3
2	4-7
3	8-12
4	13-18
5	19-24
6	25-31
7	32-38
8	39-46
9	47-54
10	55-63
11	64-72
12	More than 73

Moving air can cause objects to move or to be displaced. We are all familiar with the wind blowing leaves around or rattling doors but even air that is moving very slowly, at an almost imperceptibly slow speed, can produce sufficient pressure acting on an object to cause it to be moved. It is virtually never the case that the air inside a location is still. Small temperature and pressure variations or the movement of people and draughts caused by the weather all create small but nonetheless significant and measurable movements of the air. When someone walks through a room the air currents they create (rather like the turbulent wake of a boat) can take tens of minutes to diminish. In empty buildings and even on the calmest wind days the variations in temperature throughout the building are sufficient to create moving currents of air. These subtle motions of air, when they act upon a large surface area such as a door, can sometimes be sufficient to cause a movement of the door and, in a number of cases, these almost imperceptible air currents have been observed causing a door to swing to and fro.

There is another type of airflow that cannot be measured using an anemometer, this is an ion wind which is airflow induced by electrostatic charges. Individuals may feel it as a gentle movement of air, often related to a perceived and reported cooling effect and it cannot be detected by conventional equipment used to measure air motion. There have been several situations in which I was able to measure the electrostatic charges and demonstrate the ion wind as the true cause of perceived air movement that was being attributed to some unexplained paranormal cause as it was failing to register on a conventional anemometer.

Infrasound

Infrasound is generally considered to be audio-frequency energy that lies below the range of normal human hearing; typically 20Hz. Ambient infrasound within the environment is produced by both natural and man-made sources. Natural sources include weather-related effects (e.g. wind and storms) surf and wave action, volcanic eruptions, and upper atmospheric phenomena e.g., the jet stream and meteors. Man-made infrasound is associated with vehicles, aircraft, machinery, and the interactions of weather with buildings and other structures. In 1998, researchers Vic Tandy and Tony Lawrence published their paper *The Ghost in the Machine* in the *Journal of the Society for Psychical Research* that stated a case for infrasound as a causal factor in the production of certain subjective paranormal-like experiences in some people. Their work specifically pointed toward a frequency close to 19Hz as being key in creating such experiences, which included a sense of presence, depression, chills, sweating, and vague peripheral apparitions. Since then, infrasound has become an established explanation within paranormal research as a causal factor in the production of personal experiences that may be interpreted by the percipient as having a paranormal origin. Subsequently it has been shown that this assertion by Tandy of a single or narrow frequency range of infrasound being implicated in perceived paranormal experiences was incorrect but the role of more generalised infrasound frequencies in producing these experiences in conjunction with other factors has been clearly demonstrated.

Technically it is difficult to measure infrasound accurately as many systems for recording and measuring sounds are limited to operate within the audible frequency range. Specialist equipment does exist that can be used for detailed measurements but this is expensive. However, it is possible to make some measurements that may be helpful in indicating if infrasound is present at any location using basic sound level measuring equipment but this provides only an indication, not a definitive measurement. Infrasound is discussed in much greater detail in *Paracoustics, Sound and the Paranormal* (2015, White Crow Books).

Other Environment Monitoring

In their search for evidence, ghost investigators may also adopt or adapt equipment from others areas of environment monitoring, often proposing some theory or idea to support their use. One item of equipment that might be worthwhile considering however is the carbon monoxide (CO) detector. CO is a colourless, odourless, and tasteless gas, which is slightly lighter than air. It is highly toxic to humans and animals. Symptoms of mild acute poisoning include light-headedness, confusion, headaches, vertigo, and flu-like effects. Prolonged exposures can lead to significant toxicity of the central nervous system and heart, and even death. Chronic exposure to low levels of carbon monoxide can lead to disorientation, non-specific physical ailments, depression, confusion, and memory loss. Several of the symptoms of carbon monoxide poisoning are similar to reported personal experiences that have been attributed to a paranormal cause. Carbon monoxide measuring and monitoring may therefore be worth considering in some cases. CO detectors of various types and using several methods of detection are readily available, some can display the actual level of carbon monoxide in parts per million (ppm), whilst others simply indicate when the levels of CO reach dangerous levels.

Investigators have also taken an active interest in the measurement of ambient light levels. There seems to be no particular reason for this interest, as acknowledged by one of the many ghost-hunting equipment sales sites:

Absent of specific theories being tested by the ghost hunter, the light meter still helps us monitor another variable that could later be used to explain reported paranormal experiences. Learning as much about the environment that our investigations occur in, lends ghost hunters a greater possibility to notice patterns, or other explanations for any anomalies being investigated.

(WWW.GETGHOSTGEAR.COM)

One of the many and varied entities that are encountered by ghost investigators are the *Shadow people* and there are inevitably a number of rival theories about what these fleeting black figures and shapes might represent. Characteristically, they are almost always totally black, some say light absorbing. Shadow people have been occasionally reported for decades but the frequency at which they are being encountered seems to have increased at an exponential rate in recent years. However, this is not a discussion about shadow people but their preponderance is a stated reason why many ghost investigators have begun to use light meters. They rationalise that measuring changes within the lighting may permit them to detect these entities.

Light meters all work on the principle that light falling onto certain materials such as silicon will cause it to generate a voltage or permit an electric current to flow through it. Essentially, this is the same principle used in the image sensors of digital cameras. The German physicist Hertz discovered the photoelectric effect in the nineteenth century and today it is used in many different devices either as a power source or a detection sensor. Light meters do not just respond to the visible light spectra but just as readily react to light that is outside our range of normal human vision. Perhaps the most practical application for light metering is with barrier sensors. These use a simple photoelectric sensor that detects the interruption to a beam of light. When this interruption is detected a switch operates either an alarm or some other item of equipment. Such a technique is potentially useful for protecting an area within a location from intrusion or interference and is the modern equivalent of the string and sealing wax used by several earlier ghost investigators to ensure an area was free from human interference. Tony Cornell and Alan Gauld used photoelectric switches as part of the sensor switches that were employed in S.P.I.D.E.R., their spontaneous incident data recording system (see Chapter 1).

Environment Monitoring: Final Thoughts

It is clear that the environment at a haunted location plays a significant part in the experiences of witnesses. It is however true to say that a great deal more research remains to be undertaken before we are able to fully understand the links between the location environment and the reported and measured experiences and events. Some are easy and straightforward to understand; the wind blowing through and around buildings creates breezes, draughts, and temperature changes. Moving air has the ability to move and displace objects, both small and large. Others, such as ambient sound levels and electromagnetic fields, are still being tested but appear to be significant in some situations. Monitoring the environment is not wasted effort and the ghost investigator should certainly consider investing time and effort into this type of monitoring.

CHAPTER 10

ELECTRONIC VOICE PHENOMENON AND INSTRUMENTAL TRANSCOMMUNICATION

———————⟫●⟪———————

Electronic voice phenomenon (EVP) is basically voices and other utterances that appear on an audio recording without the operator being aware at the time the recording was taking place. In the majority of cases of EVP, the voice or voices only speak a few words. Some of the voices can appear to be very distinct, yet most are hardly coherent at all. Electronic voice phenomena is often said to have come to the fore in 1959 when the Swedish filmmaker Friedrich Jüergenson unwittingly captured voices on audiotape. After recording birdsong in a forest, Jüergenson discovered on playback that there was a distinct male voice remarking about birdsong at night. Jüergenson also claimed to have heard the voice of his deceased mother. After his discovery, Jüergenson claimed to record hundreds of spirit voices over the following four years and consequently published a book in 1964 entitled *Voices from the Universe*. His first book was followed by another called *Radio Contact with the Dead*. This was later translated into German and this caught the attention of Dr Konstantin Raudive a Latvian psychologist. Dr Raudive was at first sceptical of Jüergenson's claims but, after a number of experiments, he too claimed to have recorded hundreds of voices including that of his own deceased mother. Dr Raudive subsequently published his own results in *The Inaudible Becomes Audible*. Later this book was translated into English and extended becoming *Breakthrough; An Amazing Experiment in Electronic Communication with the Dead*. It is from Dr Raudive that we get the term 'Raudive Voices'. Since the late 1950's, many people around the World now claim to have recorded voices on audiotape and more recently digital media, and the use of EVP recording has become common practice for those investigating haunted locations.

Instrumental Transcommunication (ITC) is a more recent terminology that usually refers to messages claimed to be coming from a spiritual dimension by use of technical means including tape or digital recorders, televisions, radios, computers, telephones, and other technical devices, with the intention of getting meaningful information from the spirit realm by such means as voices, images, and text. Exponents of EVP and ITC claim that almost everybody who is really interested in the phenomenon can get positive results with practice and persistence.

Historical Attempts at Spirit Voice Communications using Electronic Methods

In the 1920's psychical researcher Hereward Carrington encountered what might be considered as being an early example of EVP during a studio radio session with an unnamed medium. Carrington and others who were present described hearing a disembodied voice asking, "Can you hear me?" which came from a microphone that had been left switched on in a closed room. The rest of the building was empty. No explanation could be found as to its source. In 1928, Thomas Edison was said to be working on equipment incorporating chemicals, including potassium permanganate, which he hoped would permit spirit communications. An interviewer from *Scientific American* magazine asked Thomas Edison about the possibility of contacting the dead. Edison responded:

> That nobody knows whether our personalities pass on to another existence or sphere but it is possible to construct an apparatus which will be so delicate that, if there are personalities in another existence or sphere who wish to get in touch with us in this existence or sphere,

this apparatus will at least give them a better opportunity to express themselves than the tilting tables and raps and Ouija boards and mediums and the other crude methods now purported to be the only means of communication.

Despite a number of claims to the contrary, there is no evidence that Edison ever actually designed or tried to construct such a device. During the early 1930's, strange unidentified voices were picked up by Swedish and Norwegian military radio monitoring stations. In March 1934, these voices ceased abruptly and they were attributed to stray Nazi transmissions. The voices were polyglot, containing several languages within a single message. However, after the war, when archives were searched, no evidence of German involvement was discovered. Also in the 1930's psychic Attila Von Szalay started to experiment with a record-cutter and player trying to capture paranormal voices on phonograph records, however, the results were disappointing. The publication *Psychic News* carried a series of reports discussing an event that took place at Wigmore Hall in London, also during the 1930's in the presence of around 600 people. During the séance, more than fifty disembodied voices were said to have spoken through a microphone placed at a distance from the medium and wired to loudspeakers in the hall. Technical staff from the company who provided and installed the public address system and who were present at the time also claimed to have heard the voices and stated that the voices must have definitely come from the microphone and that no human was close enough to have been within recording distance of the microphone during the sessions. Both technicians later signed a statement, published in *Psychic News*, saying that they had become Spiritualists as a result of their experiences on that occasion.

In 1949, a Spirit Electronic Communication Society was formed in Manchester, England. It was here that Mr Zwaan demonstrated a device, the 'Super Rays', later renamed the 'Zwaan Ray' in honour of the inventor in order to discover, using spirit guidance, a means of scientific communication with the dead. The Zwaan Ray set evolved into the 'Binnington' model developed in 1952 and then later into the 'Teledyne' model. It was claimed that direct spirit voice communication was eventually obtained by a medium with the help of this machine. During the 1950's, psychical researcher and psychologist Raymond Bayless joined Attila Von Szalay using a device that Bayless had devised and constructed. It consisted of a cabinet with a microphone resting inside a speaking trumpet, the microphone cord leading out of the cabinet, which connected to a tape recorder and a loud speaker. Almost immediately, they began to hear whispers originating from inside the cabinet and duly recorded them. In 1956, they produced an article documenting their research in the *Journal of the American Society for Psychical Research*. Von Szalay carried on taping for many years using an open microphone connected to a reel-to-reel recorder and he claimed to have achieved excellent results. At the end of the fifties, Friederich Jüergenson, a film producer and bird-watcher, was working on a project recording wild bird songs in the forest near to his home. Playing the recordings back he discovered that strange garbled fragments of seemingly human speech had apparently been picked up on the tape. Jüergenson said he had been completely alone when he made the recording. He said that he recognised one of the voices being that of his dead mother calling his name. Later, Jüergenson claimed that he had been trying to record spirit voices for some time but without success, and it was no accident whatsoever when he finally succeeded. Listening closely to the voices, Jüergenson found that they spoke in different languages, often changing language in mid-sentence. Also, the phrases often had incorrect structure or grammar and, in some cases, syllables were stretched or compressed in a way that made it quite hard to comprehend the messages. The strangest aspect of all was the uncanny way the voices seemed to respond to his comments. Jüergenson began to converse with the voices, recording his questions and afterwards searching the recording for answers. After four years of experimental recording, he announced his discovery at a press conference in 1963 and his book; *Roesterna Fraen Rymden (Voices from the Universe)* was published the following year. His conclusion was that the tape recordings were acting as a form of electronic communication link to the realm of the dead. Although not revealed until 1990 was possible further evidence for EVP that occurred in 1952, when two Italian Catholic priests Father Ernetti and Father Gemilli, were collaborating on a musical research project. Ernetti was a respected scientist, physicist, philosopher, and music lover, and Gemilli the President of the Papal Academy. In September 1952, the priests were recording a Gregorian chant but the wiring in their equipment kept breaking. Exasperated, Gemilli looked up and exclaimed aloud for his dead father to help. To his amazement his father's voice was heard saying, "Of course I shall help you. I'm always with you". They repeated the experiment, and the voice was again heard using the name that Gemilli's father had called him as a boy. Gemilli was astounded. No one knew the nickname his father had teased him with when he was a boy. After further experiments the two men sought an audience with Pope Pius XII. Gemilli told the Pontiff of his experience and was, to his very great surprise, immediately reassured. According to accounts of his meeting, The Pope is reported to have told Gemilli:

> You really need not worry about this. The existence of this voice is strictly a scientific fact and has nothing whatsoever to do with spiritism. The recorder is totally objective. It receives and records sound waves from wherever they come. This experiment may perhaps become the cornerstone for a building for scientific studies which will strengthen people's faith in a hereafter.

Inspired by Jüergenson's work, a small team of researchers assembled by Dr Konstantin Raudive, a psychologist and philosopher, began his own studies of EVP in the 1960's. He recorded thousands of disembodied voices, the majority of which communicated using a polyglot of languages. Raudive himself spoke more than ten languages. The polyglot messages used words in Latvian, German, French, and several other European languages. Raudive was frequently criticised and accused of misinterpreting his voices. His critics usually being unable to decipher what the voices on his recordings were actually saying. The critics often neglected the fact that Jüergenson too, had recorded similar polyglot messages. Raudive also received criticism for the fact that his messages mainly had a seemingly nonsensical content, sometimes including comments on the colour of the sweater he was wearing. Supporters of Raudive countered the critics by pointing out that if the voices originated from the dead, it should be remembered that they were once living people; the only difference being that they have experienced the change-of-state known as death, which need not necessarily make them any more wise or erudite. Raudive's team developed a technique that made use of a Germanium diode. The diode, which is in effect a broadband crystal-radio detector with a short antenna and a second wire directly connected into the microphone input of the recorder, provided white noise and apparently aided the voices in manifesting. They discovered that the voices gained in strength and number when background noises were prevalent. Although many of Raudive's critics claimed that what his team was actually recording were snatches of ordinary radio transmissions, it is perhaps strange that many of the Raudive voices made a point of mentioning his name as often as possible in the recordings. Several of Raudive's recordings appeared on a 7-inch record that was included in the early copies of *Breakthrough* (the translated English edition). Following his own death, Raudive's followers claimed that he became a regular spirit communicator via his own equipment. British Psychologist George Gilbert Bonner began using a reel-to-reel recorder and battery radio tuned between stations in order to produce white noise to act as a carrier for discarnate voices. Bonner began to conduct his experiments in 1972 after reading Raudive's book. He asked into his microphone: "Can anyone hear me and would anyone like to speak to me?" not expecting any response. He received the answer "Yes". Ultimately, Bonner claimed to have recorded more than 50,000 spirit voices up until 1997. Also inspired by Raudive's book was Raymond Cass, a hearing-aid practitioner in England, who began research into the EVP using a portable battery-operated radio tuned in to white noise on the VHF aircraft communications band. Cass claimed to have recorded thousands of clear discarnate voices over the years, speaking, and singing. He theorised that his proximity to a mass x-ray unit only thirty yards away from his office produced an emanation which was interacting with the selected aircraft band frequency and producing a transient condition enabling the voices to manifest. In August 1976, Cass, using a small multi-band radio tuned to the air-band together with a battery-operated recorder, claimed that he had recorded the hoarse voice of Dr Konstantin Raudive (who had died two years earlier) shouting in German "Here's Raudive...waiting at the bridge". During the 1970's, many EVP and ITC research groups were formed around the World. In 1982, Radio Luxembourg broadcast live what was claimed to be a two-way conversation with a dead person using an ultrasound device based upon the work of retired engineer and industrialist George Meek. The equipment was set up under the supervision of the radio station's engineers, connected to a set of speakers, and switched on. After a few seconds a clear voice was heard to say, "Otto Koenig makes wireless with the dead".

Following a lifetime's interest in the paranormal George Meek became fascinated by EVP. Meek was convinced that for electronic communication with the dead to become truly effective, then more sophisticated techniques and equipment would be needed. In order to achieve this, he decided to enlist the cooperation of the spirit communicators. Meek also wrote to the American magazine *The Psychic Observer*, following which he was put in touch with Bill O'Neil, an electronics engineer who was also a clairaudient and clairvoyant. Together with O'Neil, Meek established the Metascience Foundation, and claimed to have made contact with a man who had been dead for five years and who been a medical doctor in his life. "Doc Nick", as he became known, proposed that the team should use particular audio frequencies instead of the white noise traditionally used by EVP researchers. This, he said, would serve as an energy source against which the sounds produced by his vocal cords could be played. Apparently it worked, as shortly afterwards, a spirit calling himself Dr George Jeffries Mueller announced he had come to join the team after materialising one afternoon in O'Neil's living room. Mueller said he was a university professor and NASA scientist who had died in 1967. Meek and O'Neill said that Mueller gave them numerous facts with which to verify his identity including his security number and intimate details of his life and scholastic achievements. Mueller began communicating regularly, helping to design a new piece of electromagnetic equipment that would convert spirit voices into audible voices. In October 1977, his first words were recorded on the new system the spirit and living team jointly developed and which Meek called a 'Spiricom'. Tapes of conversations with Mueller were released to the public and made fascinating listening. Mueller could be heard joking with Meek and O'Neil and discussing his favourite foods and the view of time from the perspective of the spirit world. Mueller provided unlisted telephone numbers and asked that Meek should call the number and confirm the identity of the subscriber, which Meek states they were able to do successfully. It was claimed that Mueller also gave O'Neil precise directions with which to help build experimental video equipment. George Meek never patented the Spiricom in the hope that science would carry on his work and take it to the next stages. In 1982 he held a press conference in Washington, USA, and revealed Spiricom's secrets. Before Mueller ceased communicating with Meek and O'Neil, the team had been working to develop spirit communications using video techniques, but with little success. In 1986, Klaus Schreiber, a Swiss electronics engineer claimed to have obtained pictures of the dead on television by means of an apparatus he called a 'Vidicom'. This consisted of a specially adapted television, switched on, but not attached to an aerial and with a video camera in front of it forming an opto-electrical feedback system to capture images on the screen. He stated that using this method he had made audio-video contact with his two deceased wives. Perhaps the best-known experimenters receiving audio-video communication are Maggie and Jules Harsch-Fischbach of Luxembourg. They developed and successfully operated two electronic systems in 1985, which they claimed could produce results that could be reliably duplicated. In 1987, they received their first television picture sequences and a year later, they claimed to have established sustained computer contact. Messages were being left on unattended computer screens, and photographs of dead friends and co-workers were uploaded onto their computers that were not connected to any external network. A further case of ITC using a computer took place in Doddleston, England, between 1984 and 1986. The homeowner, Ken Webster received messages from a man named Thomas Harden, who he claimed he was writing to from the year 1545, during the reign of Henry VIII. The language of his messages appeared to be authentic but this has since been disputed by a number of linguistics experts. Webster received more than two hundred and fifty messages, whilst at the same time reporting poltergeist phenomena in the family home. In addition to the messages from Thomas Harden in the sixteenth century was a series of messages from a group calling themselves '2109' and apparently communicating from the future. After the communications at Doddleston ceased, it was reported that the 2109 group began communicating with the Harsch-Fischbach group in Luxembourg. Webster detailed his experiences in a book published in 1989, *The Vertical Plane*.

Modern EVP and ITC experimenters are broadly separated into two groups. There are numerous dedicated groups around the world who continue to follow and develop upon the research of Raudive, Meek, and others. The Luxembourg team under the direction of the Harsch-Fischbach's also claim to be regularly communicating with the 2109 group.

Ghost investigators have become intrigued with EVP and the easy access to small portable recorders has led to them being used extensively in haunted locations. It is also claimed by a number of ghost investigators, that EVP is believed to be occurring at very low frequencies, within the infrasound region and well below that which the human ear is capable of hearing. The technical complexities of actually recording sound at these sub-audible frequencies tends to be overlooked and the actual ability of the equipment that is used to record these infrasonic EVP's is generally incorrectly stated. The usually strict protocols evolved by EVP researchers over the years have been largely cast aside by ghost investigators who seem to prefer simply calling upon the spirits to communicate via a simple handheld recorder as they sit or wander around the location. Little control of either the location or the recordings is applied and post investigation analysis is usually completely lacking or is seriously flawed.

EVP Some Key Dates

1852 - American Spiritualist, Jonathan Koon, claimed to have devised a machine for communicating with spirits. The plans of which have never been discovered.

1888 - Inventor, Nicola Tesla, suggested radio could be used to communicate with the dead

1893 - Priest, Father Landell de Moura, an early radio pioneer described the possibility of radio communication with the dead and was said to have built a prototype spirit radio device but no plans or notes have ever been found.

1925 - Brazilian, Oscar D Argonnel, publishes his book *Voices from Beyond by Telephone* describing contacts from other dimensional beings using the telephone.

1923 to 1928 – Brazilian, Cornelio Pires, worked on equipment intended to communicate with spirits.

1960 to 1970 Writer and Parapsychology researcher, D. Scott Rogo, and Raymond Bayless publish the book *Phone Calls from the Dead* after extensive literature research.

EVP Methods

Early encounters with spirit voices tended to be almost accidental as was the case with Jüergenson and Carrington. The voices appeared spontaneously, often seemingly interacting with or trying to respond to the conversations of the living. Researchers quickly discovered that they could obtain responses to questions they asked and these responses were often cryptic and usually relied upon the researcher's own interpretation of the replies. The simplest technique involved setting up a microphone and a recorder, then asking for the spirit voices to respond to the questioning researcher. Normally, replies were only discovered when the recording was played back, although in some instances, such as at the Wigmore Hall séances the voices apparently responded in real-time. Raudive was perhaps the first to make a deliberate use of noise to aid the voice communications. That is not to say that before Raudive the recordings were noise-free, the technology available inherently produced noise, whether from within the equipment or in the form of ambient noise from the surroundings. Raudive appreciated that this noise seemed to be needed by the voices in order for them to produce better responses. He often used a radio that was de-tuned to frequencies between the broadcasting stations. The static hiss it produced apparently aided the production of the voices but left room for critics to claim that, in reality, he was simply recording snatches of real radio broadcasts as the radio tuning frequency wandered slightly or picked up harmonic frequencies (multiples or divisions of frequencies) from the original transmission. To counter such criticism, he experimented using a Germanium diode connected directly to the microphone input of the tape recorder, replacing the microphone and the radio receiver. The diode was a simple device that acted as a primitive radio frequency receiver capable only of picking up a broad spectrum of radio frequency energy and passing it as a wide audio frequency hiss, usually referred to as white noise. This resulted in a dramatic improvement in the quality of recorded voices. Other researchers, continued to pursue methods that used artificial or natural noise sources. Some continued using de-tuned and modified radios or specially constructed white-noise generators, whilst others used wind or water, from life or from recordings to provide the noise source to help the voices manifest. Some researchers went to considerable trouble to ensure that the voices were not simply the product of radio and other interference; acoustic and electrical shielding was used as part of increasingly stricter controls. Radio and sound engineers together with physicists were brought in to assist. The voices continued to be recorded regardless and led to many of the critics and the specialists becoming converted to the idea that the voices had a supernormal origin. Thousands and tens of thousands of recordings were amassed by the various researchers using a variety of methods, mostly derived from the work of the Raudive group.

Basic Methods

The simplest method for conducting EVP experiments is to simply set up a microphone and a recorder. Experimenters recommend and favour an external microphone rather than using any built-in microphone. The recorder is started and the experimenter asks aloud a series of questions with pauses of suitable length in between for any responses to be recorded. At the end of the experimental session the recording is played back and any responses can be examined. Experimental sessions are normally short, typically between five and fifteen minutes. Many experimenters discovered that results were rarely forthcoming at first but that repeated sessions over a period of many weeks or even months would eventually produce voice responses to their questioning. Other researchers added a simple de-tuned radio or white noise generator to the set-up, the output of which was broadcast via a loudspeaker to be recorded along with the experimenter's questions using a microphone. Again, it was observed that it typically took many sessions before voices began to appear on the recordings.

Some EVP researchers have also made recordings at sites of reported hauntings or other paranormal activity. These should not be confused with straightforward audio recordings made during an investigation which may also contain seemingly paranormal voices, for example, those made of the during the Enfield poltergeist case which apparently came directly from one of the children involved. Many ghost investigators also use EVP recording as part of their investigation. They have developed a less stringent method using simple handheld cassette or digital recorders, which are either just placed or held whilst any questions are asked. Keen to explore these voice communications further, researchers developed new technologies and approaches which led to the introduction of specialist EVP apparatus. The diode device used by Raudive has already been mentioned but one of the most influential devices for EVP use was the Spiricom series.

George Meek operating the first Spiricom device

Spiricom

Together with Bill O'Neil, the retired industrialist, George Meek, developed the Spiricom device in 1979, which consisted of a series of 13 tone generators, producing a range of tones that spanned the range of the typical adult male voice i.e., from 130Hz-710Hz. The output from the tone generators was then transmitted at frequencies of around 29MHz to an adjacent radio receiver. The resultant audio was fed to a loudspeaker and together with the questions of the experimenter was recorded to tape via a microphone.

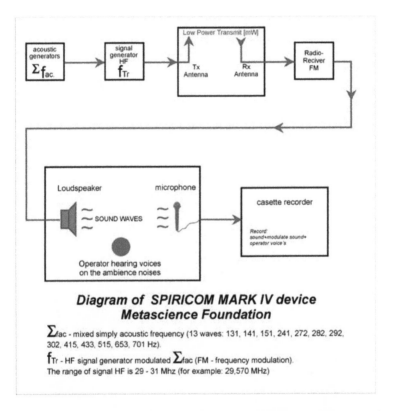

Diagram of SPIRICOM MARK IV device
Metascience Foundation

Σf_{ac} - mixed simply acoustic frequency (13 waves: 131, 141, 151, 241, 272, 282, 292, 302, 415, 433, 515, 653, 701 Hz).

f_{Tr} - HF signal generator modulated Σf_{ac} (FM - frequency modulation).
The range of signal HF is 29 - 31 Mhz (for example: 29,570 MHz)

Spiricom voices have a typically synthetic almost robotic quality. Over the years Meek and O'Neil made additional modifications and improvements to Spiricom and made the details of the device openly and freely available to other researchers. There are also a number of software Spiricom emulator programmes available via the Internet and auction sites.

The Frank's Box

In 2002, American EVP researcher Frank Sumption developed a device that he claimed had been developed with assistance from the spirit realm and was said to be able to facilitate real-time communications with spirit voices. Originally it comprised a white noise generator and an AM radio that continuously tuned through the frequency band. The combined audio outputs from the two components were output via a loudspeaker contained inside a small chamber that also contained a microphone connected to a recorder. The units built by Sumption became known as 'Ghost Boxes' and have been continually developed over a number of years by Sumption who has also made circuits and plans for the devices openly available online via a number of Internet sites. Sumption's Ghost Box spawned a series of other designs, all generically referred to as 'Frank's Boxes'. Many of these are much less complex in their design and functioning, many relying solely upon a continually scanning tuning circuit and often built using a modified cheap digital AM / FM radio receiver. They are available to buy on a number of Internet stores and auction sites. The manner in which these devices operate is actually far removed from Sumption's original Ghost Box. They produce short staccato snatches of radio broadcasts and noise, which is listened to or recorded by the experimenter. They are relatively inexpensive, although much more expensive than the donor radios which typically cost less than £10 prior to the simple modification and this has made them popular with ghost investigators, particularly after they were shown in use on several television ghost investigation shows in the USA and UK. In the past five years, there has been an increase in the number of EVP gadgets being offered to ghost investigators. The MiniBox, Steve's Box, the Shack Hack, and others, continue to be based on some form of continuously scanning radio receiver. Devices such as the 'EVP listener' use a simple electromagnetic coil that replaces the microphone, originally used for placing on telephone handsets for recording the conversation by means of electromagnetic induction, they will readily produce responses in proximity to any nearby electromagnetic field. This close association with electromagnetism has no doubt helped their popularity with the ghost investigators.

Many current EVP experimenters still use the simple methods of microphone recording with and without the use of an additional background radio or white noise source with much claimed success. Others are working with Spiricom derivatives. Researchers at the German

Association for Transcommunication Research (VTF) developed the radio 'Sweeping' method in 1991, which was subsequently described in their journal:

> The technical term 'sweeping', which is well known in electronics, means to automatically move the tuning between two fixed frequencies back and forth. The distance between these frequencies is called "sweep amplitude", the speed of the back and forth movement is called sweep frequency, and both of them are usually adjustable within certain limits.
>
> Sweeping a radio receiver now is done by moving the scale pointer back and forth over a defined (small) frequency band.
>
> An example: The receiver is tuned to Radio Vatican (1530 kHz). By using a sweep amplitude of ± 10 kHz, the tuning of the receiver would move back and forth between 1520 and 1540 kHz i.e., over Radio Mainflingen and Radio Kosice. This happens with a speed of 4 Hz, which is adjusted to four times a second. Now assume that these three radio stations all transmit voice transmissions at the same time. You would hear a mixture of Italian, Slovakian, and German, and all these languages would alternately blend into each other.
>
> In this mixture, EVP are formed very often – voices independent from the background, the mode of speaking peculiarly linked to the sweep rhythm. The voices arise through the actual sweep movement, and it's a misunderstanding to believe that it's possible to produce a "sweep cassette" for subsequent application. This can be done just as little as one can spare somebody gymnastics by watching a gymnastics video.
>
> Now how is it done technically? What you need are two very simple constructions:
>
> 1. A receiver with a sweep connector i.e., an input that allows varying the tuning by applying a voltage.
>
> 2. A sweep generator. This is a device, which provides a slowly increasing and decreasing voltage and thereby can alter the receiver tuning by a certain amount and with a certain speed (sweep amplitude and sweep frequency).

To do an EVP recording, you first find a radio station or a mixture of stations; preferably all voice transmissions, with the sweep amplitude turned to the minimum. Next you slowly increase the sweep amplitude, and maybe alter the sweep frequency. The whole thing requires some experience, but after a few attempts it will work very easily.

(VTF-POST ISSUE 2/91 P.63)

It may be noticed that this technique is remarkably similar to and predates the development of Sumption's Ghost-Box and the Frank's Boxes by over ten years.

Simple EVP Experiments

Recording the voices seems to be remarkably easy and generally does not require any special equipment or costly and purpose built EVP / ITC devices. The following list should suffice for anyone interested in investigating this interesting phenomenon further:

- Cassette tape recorder - full size cassettes are preferred to ensure best quality.
- A digital audio recorder that records uncompressed sound files such as .wmv is a good alternative, try to avoid mp3 audio as it is compressed and may lose detail.
- A reasonable quality external microphone, the built-in microphone of many recorders is prone to picking up machine noise from the recorder.
- If you are using a cassette recorder then ensure only new tapes are used.

EVP researchers also specify that a great deal of patience is required. Many saying that it requires weeks, even months of regular sessions before any voices are heard and many more before good quality voices are regularly recorded. The initial sessions should be regular i.e., taking place at the same time every day or week and last for around thirty minutes. They advise limiting the questions to around ten per session and leaving thirty-second intervals between each question to permit any response to be made. Questions really should be simple at the start e.g., "Is there anyone who wishes to communicate with?" "Will you tell us who you are?" etc. The recording is then played back following the session and any responses noted.

Researchers may also wish to add some form of ambient noise, this could be in the form of a radio that is tuned in-between stations thus producing white noise, the typical inter-station hiss on AM is a good source. Computer programmes are available that can generate white noise which can be played aloud using either the computer's own or external speakers. For those who wish to experiment using the Germanium diode method that Raudive claimed was highly effective, the diodes are readily available from online and specialist electronics components suppliers. A suitable cable will also be required to attach the diode to the microphone input of the recorder, which can be easily obtained by cannibalising a cheap mono microphone that already has the correct size jack plug for the recorder. Cut the microphone off leaving the plug attached to the length of cable and solder the inner conductors of the cable to the wire tails of the diode, one to each, the orientation doesn't matter.

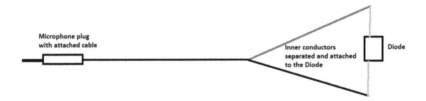

Once assembled, the diode can be plugged into the recorder's microphone socket. However, using the diode in this manner means the researcher won't be able to record their own questions, as the diode cannot pick up normal sounds. The questions can be noted down in a book, together with an indication of the point in the recording session when they were asked. By connecting the diode to the recorder using an audio input splitter adaptor or audio input mixer it is also possible to plug in a normal microphone too and record the questions and any responses.

The Voices

EVP researchers have recognised certain characteristics of the voices that differentiate genuine EVP voices from standard radio broadcasts. These characteristics have been observed by experimenters from the earliest days of EVP study right through to the present day and are consistently reported regardless of the geographical location of the experimental recording. Raudive, writing in *'Breakthrough'* observed:

I will summarise briefly the characteristics [of the voices] I have mentioned:

1. The voice-entities speak very rapidly, in a mixture of languages, sometimes as many as five or six in one sentence.
2. They speak in a definite rhythm, which seems to be forced upon them by means of communication they employ.
3. The rhythmic mode of speech imposes a shortened, telegram-style phrase or sentence.
4. Presumably arising from these restrictions, grammatical rules are frequently abandoned and neologisms abound.

These characteristic features of the language of the voices and their speech content are the outstanding paranormal aspects of the phenomenon and the guide-lines to further research, and in my opinion this is, at least for the time being the best approach to our endeavours to get closer to its essence.

(BREAKTHROUGH CH.1 P.31-32.)

British Audiologists and EVP experimenter Raymond Cass noted: -

Firstly, the voices used a polyglot mode of speech using the elements of two or more languages in fast, terse, highly compressed 'blips'. Unusual neologisms, idiosyncratic grammar and syntax, try the patience of linguistic purists. The voices, however, are not robotic...they are, are on the contrary, lyrical, musical, entrancing and sometimes siren like.

(THE RAYMOND CASS REPORT. CH.16 P244)

The voices tended to cooperate with the researchers and frequently offered help and suggestions in developing the equipment and techniques in order to assist further development of the communications. By and large the voices were friendly and rarely threatening and seemed to welcome the opportunities to communicate with the experimenters. The actual content of the communications were generally relevant to the conversations and the questions of the researchers. Dedicated EVP and ITC experimenters continue to recognise these characteristics, but it is interesting to observe that those who engage in making

EVP recordings as an aspect of their ghost investigations normally report voices that are uncooperative, threatening, aggressive, or abusive. Moreover, the voices they report tend to lack many of the speech and linguistic characteristics previously noted by EVP researchers. EVP's recorded by ghost investigators tend to be much more akin to the normal patterns of human speech in speed and intonation and are also frequently chopped into single words or partial phrases that are incomplete. This is at odds with the EVP researchers who recognise another key characteristic of EVP that has been consistently noted since the days of Jüergenson and Raudive as the VTF in their guide to recognising electronic voices as opposed to radio interference point out, "EVP messages are complete and are not truncated at the beginning or end. If EVP were (radio) crosstalk, they would often begin in the middle of a word or cease before the word or phrase was completed".

Critics and sceptics often claim that EVP's are simply the product of various types of radio and electrical interference or are the product of audio pareidolia, in which random sounds from the radio, white noise, or ambient sounds are perceived as being significant by the listener. This is certainly a potentially valid explanation for many of the recordings that are presented as EVP's but it fails to recognise the care and diligence of the many dedicated EVP researchers who go to great lengths to construct equipment and techniques that can be shown to remove or reduce to an insignificant amount any electrical or radio frequency interference. Sophisticated EVP listening methods involving numerous blind listening tests i.e, without any prior information or transcript being provided, together with the controlled and limited use of audio enhancement also carefully employed by EVP researchers. There have been very few in-depth studies conducted by parapsychologists examining EVP, perhaps the most comprehensive being in 1974 by Perrot-Warwick funded parapsychologist David Ellis. His extensive survey of EVP up to that time led him to conclude: "EVP was merely the projection of the minds of the experimenters onto random noise or even mechanical noise of the tape recorder with a generous amount of self-delusion".

Stanley Gooch, a member of the Society for Psychical Research, briefly looked at the voice phenomena and stated that in his opinion: "Everyone had been listening to taxi, police, and other public service broadcast transmissions".

This apparent lack of interest by parapsychology is at odds with the opinion of numerous physicists and science academics that have been personally closely involved with EVP research. Technical and radio engineers from several radio and electronics manufacturers who have been closely involved in helping to develop EVP techniques and equipment have also publicly stated their belief that the voices recorded under controlled circumstances defy logical and plausible explanation. *Breakthrough* contains more than 80 pages of testimony in the appendices from such experts attesting to the inexplicable nature of the voice recordings.

Current EVP Research

There are a number of groups around the world who remain dedicated to EVP and ITC research. Claims of extraordinary encounters with voices abound together with discussions as to their origin and meaning. Ghost investigators also maintain an extremely active interest in EVP or as some now seem to prefer to call it; Real Time Spirit Communications (RTSC). The Internet is awash with sites showcasing EVP / ITC / RTSC results, equipment, and merchandise. A Google search conducted in May 2015 using the search term "electronic voice phenomenon" produced over 400,000 unique results. The same search term entered into YouTube turned up more than 20,000 results. Many of the early EVP recordings from Jüergenson, Raudive, Meek, and others, are available to either listen to or download alongside thousands of EVP recordings made by other researchers and ghost investigators. Listening to and understanding these EVP recordings is difficult and without some form of assistance most people will simply not understand what they are supposed to be hearing. Fortunately, the vast majority of these recordings, historic or contemporary, also recognise the necessity of providing the listener with a transcript of what apparently is being said by the discarnate, a technique that works best if you tell the listener beforehand what it is they should be expecting to hear.

EVP research has produced some interesting and challenging results and there are many who continue to study and explore the possibility that the deceased may be able to communicate using some electronic means with the living but the evidence that is offered is yet to be substantiated. EVP / ITC / RTSC research in all its forms has never been more popular than it is at present and it is a trend that shows little sign of diminishing. Ghost investigators now routinely use some form of EVP device as a keystone of their investigations. Most have moved away from the traditional recorder based techniques in favour of using one of the numerous radio receiver type devices.

Is sitting in a darkened room around a noisy and distorted radio asking for the resident ghost to say its name or that of the investigator a demonstration of spirit interaction, or is it merely a demonstration of the desire within investigators for some shred of proof to prop up their beliefs and claims?

CHAPTER 11

SOUND RECORDING AND
SOUND EQUIPMENT

Unusual or unexpected sounds are amongst the most commonly reported phenomena that people associate with ghostly activity. Recording sound allows the investigator to determine a number of important points of information, for example, was the sound real or imagined (hallucinated)? Does the recorded sound support the account from the witness? The study of electronic voice phenomena (EVP) is also an area of research in which sound recording is an important consideration. The human ability to remember and subsequently describe sound is extremely poor. Hi-Fi enthusiasts have known for years that any comparison between similar music systems must be done simultaneously as a delay of even several minutes can result in a decreased ability for the listener to accurately recall the qualities of the sound being compared. Sound perception is extremely subjective and varies greatly between individuals depending upon factors such as hearing acuity, age, and the frequency response of the ear. Likewise, the description of the sound a person hears will be coloured by many factors both physiological and psychological.

Sound

The vibration of matter causes sound. When the cone of a loudspeaker vibrates, the air adjacent to it is pushed to and fro. This creates a series of pressure waves and rarefactions in the air as the loudspeaker pushes and pulls the adjacent air molecules. A sound wave can be described in terms of as having a wavelength (frequency) and amplitude (power or loudness)

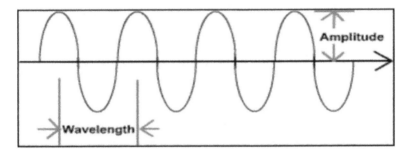

Sound waves are in effect small and rapid changes in air pressure. A microphone may be considered as being simply a highly sensitive barometer in which these tiny variations in air pressure cause some type of diaphragm to move. The movement of the diaphragm is then used to create an electrical signal. There are a variety of ways this can be done but the dynamic microphone is the simplest. The electrical signal produced by the microphone is then used by the recorder to store a representation of the sound wave. This is done by using either an analogue or digital technique.

Analogue Recording

Analogue recording has been used since Edison patented the first sound recorder in 1878. The recording is a direct representation of the signal coming from the microphone. The signal from the microphone is tiny, typically just a few millivolts, and it must be amplified in order that the recorder can use it. The process of amplification causes unwanted electrical noise; further electrical noise will come from components within the recorder such as the motor and also from any nearby electrical device that is poorly shielded. Techniques, such as Dolby® recording, which uses a combination of selective frequency cutting and amplification, may be employed to reduce the impact of the noise. Analogue recordings contain all the information coming from the microphone but the electrical noise is also recorded. With every successive copy that is made, the ratio between the noise and the original desired information is altered with the information becoming progressively more obscured by the noise.

Analogue recorders have almost entirely been replaced by digital recording devices and these days the only analogue recorders likely to be found in the ghost investigator's kit are the standard cassette or micro-cassette recorders that some investigators still use. It would be a rare sight now to see a ghost investigator using a reel-to reel tape recorder but, regardless of the format, analogue machines can still offer an effective way to record sound. Many portable recorders have their own built in microphones that can produce reasonable quality recordings for something like a personal memo or an interview with a witness. The quality of the recording can usually be greatly improved by fitting an external microphone. Not only is the external microphone itself generally better quality but also this method has the added benefit of reducing mechanical noise from the recorder, although sometimes at a cost of slightly increased electrical noise being picked up via the microphone cable. Using an external microphone allows the most suitable microphone to be selected for different recording situations. For example, omni-directional microphones are designed for general coverage whilst zoom, shotgun, or cardioid types are best when trying to selectively record sounds from a particular area without picking up too much from other sources.

Analogue machines do have some drawbacks, they are prone to noise and hiss on the recording that may mask or distort the sound that the investigator is seeking to record, particularly if that is a quiet sound. The relationship between the desired recording and the noise that is inherent in the device is called the signal to noise ratio (SNR) and many analogue recorders make use of specialised electronic circuits to remove this hiss and noise; such as those developed by the Dolby labs. Unfortunately, analogue noise reduction works by selectively boosting and cutting the levels of some of the recorded frequencies. This of course, alters the nature of the sound being recorded and potentially reduces the usefulness of the subsequent evidence being obtained. Noise reduction and other similar enhancements offered by the equipment manufacturers must therefore be used with great care by the investigator and, if noise reduction has been used, its use must be noted and considered in any subsequent analysis or interpretation of the recording.

The cassette tapes that are used have a very limited life and it may not be possible to completely erase earlier recordings, potentially making it likely to hear previous recordings underneath a newer one, this can, and has, fooled many unwary investigators into thinking they have recorded some great EVP's. Accordingly, the investigator should use each cassette only once on any investigation. However, once used to record an investigation, a tape may be re-used for less critical recordings such as witness interviews a few more times.

The smaller micro-cassette tape format means that the signal to noise ratio is generally higher than in standard size cassettes and the smaller recording head that is used can create further potential problems. Irrespective of format, precise alignment between the tape and the recording head are important in all analogue recording devices and any physical distortion or misalignment of the tape as it passes the head will cause additional audio problems leading some investigators into thinking they are hearing an anomalous event.

Analogue machines offer the investigator some potential advantages too. Many digital recorders need to compress the amount of information that is recorded in order to make effective use of the space available in the memory. One common digital technique for compressing the data involves removing parts of the audio information for any frequencies above and below the range humans can hear. Therefore, in devices that utilise this type of data compression technique some of the audio information is lost forever. This problem does not exist with analogue recorders as they do not use audio data compression so the information recorded onto the tape may have a greater range of frequency information (within the already mentioned restrictions of SNR) and therefore it may be a better choice in some investigation situations.

Digital Recording

Digital recording techniques sample the electrical signal from the microphone tens or even hundreds of thousands of times every second. This is done using an A/D (Analogue to Digital) converter. The digital output is then recorded as a stream of data in the same way that a computer writes information to its memory. Digital techniques make use of error checking and other methods that remove much of the unwanted electrical and mechanical noise that analogue recording can suffer from. This generally results in an improved signal to noise ratio and a higher fidelity for the recorded sound.

Depending on technique, digital sound recording can generate huge amounts of data and this can use the available recording memory at an astonishing rate. For instance, in some high quality audio recorders this can be several Megabytes or more every second. This is obviously not very practical, as in order to provide a usable recording time a recorder would need a vast amount of memory. The huge files that are generated can also become unwieldy and can make subsequent use and storage a significant problem in terms of the required processing power and hardware. Modern computers and cheaper memory media reduce the impact of these drawbacks somewhat but most digital recorders still rely on some form of data compression. Digital audio compression can use a number of different techniques to reduce the amount of memory needed to record the audio but all of the methods degrade the sound in some way. For example, the almost universal .mp3 format discards sound frequencies that occur outside the normal audible range and other methods include reducing the number of times the audio signal is sampled, or only storing information to the memory when there are changes to the audio signal, such as alterations to frequency and amplitude. Digital recorders can make use of different recording media such as tape, discs (including CD's, DVD's and Mini-Discs), or more often these days a removable memory card. Some professional models use a hard drive (HD) similar to those fitted to laptops and personal computers. Regardless of the recording media that is used, the same basic principles may be applied to any digital recorder when it comes to choosing and using them. Most digital recorders offer the user the option of changing the file format for the audio data and altering the total recording time for the available memory. Some digital recorders allow the user to change other recording parameters such as the data sample rate, a lower sample rate allows more data to be stored on the media but with a loss of overall fidelity for the recorded sound. As already mentioned, before being written to the memory, the data is normally compressed in some way in order to reduce the amount of data to manageable levels. The compression rate is also something that the user can adjust in some models.

Many digital recorders are advertised as having a recording time of many hours, a figure that is achieved by either progressively lowering the sample rate or increasing the amount of data compression or both together. The result of these long recording times (without increasing the amount of storage memory) is nearly always a reduction in the quality of the audio and an increase in the noise levels. Sometimes, the audio quality can be reduced to the point of making the recording almost useless for later analysis, although this may not be initially noticed when simply listening to the playback through the supplied basic ear buds or headphones. If a longer recording time is required and the recording quality is not to be sacrificed, then the only option is to increase the amount of memory available. The standard audio sample rate for compact disc (CD) audio is 44.1 kHz (44,100 samples per second). Many modern digital audio recorders can exceed this and sample rates of more than 200 kHz are possible on some machines fitted with small hard drives or large amounts of solid state memory. Such sampling rates can be used to make very high quality recordings although at the expense of shorter recording times.

Although many digital recorders have built-in microphones, investigators should consider models that are fitted with an external microphone socket rather than relying on the built in microphone. Many digital recorders are small and light and can run on batteries for several hours; if a longer recording time is required most may be plugged into the mains via an adaptor. The solid-state digital recording media can be safely erased and therefore be re-used almost indefinitely. Digital recording can sometimes suffer when previous recordings bleed through onto subsequent recordings but reformatting the media between uses instead of merely erasing previous recording eliminates this problem. Re-use of the recording media means digital is a cost effective method; SD-cards, for example, can be re-used thousands of times so they are very economical to use. In recent years there has been a huge price reduction in studio and broadcast quality digital recorders. These machines are capable of recording using an uncompressed audio format such as .WAV, and .BWF (Broadcast Wave File) in addition to the more usual compressed .mp3 format. When coupled with a high quality microphone, the quality of the recording from one of these devices is excellent and there is virtually no noise to mask the quietest sounds. Some investigators continue to use small dictation recorders. These are generally inexpensive and may seem to be an attractive option but the sound quality is generally poor and very heavily compressed. Such models should be avoided and they have no place in the investigators kit except perhaps for witness interviews or audio note taking. Until quite recently there were no digital recorders that were fitted with high quality built-in microphones.

Manufacturers such as Zoom, Tascam, and Marantz have all released digital audio recorders with excellent in-built stereo microphones in addition to also having sockets for plugging in external microphones. With the increasing capabilities of smart phones and tablet computers it has even become possible to use these devices as high quality portable audio recorders (see Chapter 20, Smart Ghost Hunting).

Modern digital recorders have become so good that the high quality recordings will often show up any weaknesses of the microphone so the main consideration in obtaining the best quality recording becomes the choice of microphone that is used. As mentioned, some recorders have excellent microphones built-in, but these are still susceptible to handling noise and sometimes electrical noise from the recorder. Prices for external microphones range from just a few pounds for something that really isn't going to improve the recording to many hundreds or even thousands of pounds. Generally, it is best to avoid dynamic microphones as they need high input levels to work efficiently and are not really suitable for recording quieter sounds. Electrets, sometimes called condenser microphones, are more sensitive and are therefore potentially a better option for room recordings. Depending upon price and specification, condenser microphones offer better sound quality too. All condenser microphones require some form of power, either from an internal battery or taken from the recorder. This is not a serious issue, as most devices designed to work with such microphones usually provide a means to power them (phantom power) but it is wise to check that any microphone is compatible with the recorder.

Included in this section must also be video camcorders and many of the available models now use digitally recorded audio. The quality of the sound recorded by even basic digital camcorders can often equal or sometimes better some audio-only recorders. The built-in microphones used on some camcorder models may also be of a better quality than those found in basic sound recorders. Many high specification camcorder models also permit the use of external microphones. All of the limitations of digital recording still apply, but the usefulness of having a synchronous video recording can be invaluable to the investigator.

Microphones

Regardless of the type of recorder that is used or the file format selected, ultimately it is the microphone that turns the sound waves into an electrical signal for recording and plays a crucial role in the overall recording quality. The operating frequency range of the microphone is dependent upon a range of factors, such as its type, design and cost. Essentially there are two distinct types of microphone that are commonly used in ghost investigating, dynamic and the condenser.

Dynamic microphones use a thin diaphragm that vibrates and moves in response to passing sound waves. These small vibrations cause a small coil attached to the diaphragm to generate a minute voltage. The amount of voltage that is produced alters in a direct proportion to the movement of the diaphragm and therefore is directly related to the passing sound waves. As voltage is generated within the microphone, it does not require any additional power in order to operate but because the voltage is so small, amplification is needed in order to make the microphone's output signal usable with recording equipment. Signal amplification can lead to higher levels of electrical noise. Dynamic microphones also normally require higher sound levels to operate effectively and for this reason they are often chosen by singers or for recordings made in loud acoustic environments. Frequency response is often limited to an optimised range of frequencies for example 100Hz – 10kHz for vocal use.

Condenser microphones use an electrically conductive diaphragm, which forms one side of an electronic capacitance circuit. As the diaphragm vibrates it causes changes within the capacitance of microphone and changes the signal voltage being sent to the recorder. Condenser microphones need some form of power supply, either from an internal battery or from the recorder. The output voltage from a condenser microphone is higher than from a dynamic microphone and so they generally require less signal amplification, producing less inherent electrical noise, thereby allowing quieter sounds to be recorded. Generally, the frequency response of a condenser microphone is also broader and flatter than that of a dynamic microphone. However, the delicate components needed for high quality audio reproduction can be expensive to manufacture and they are susceptible to moisture and can be easily damaged.

Regardless of the type of microphone and even if a high quality recorder and microphone is used, poor positioning and handling of the equipment can ruin any sound recording. Recorders that use a built-in microphone are very susceptible to vibrations being picked up through the recorder's body. This may take the form of handling noise or vibrations transmitted through contact with the surface the recorder has been placed upon. Placing the recorder or microphone close to electrical equipment may also result in electromagnetic interference.

Further Considerations When Recording Sound

Investigators need to consider sound very carefully in all investigations, as it is a frequently reported experience in many cases. If a sound is heard and the same sound is recorded by a machine, then it is clearly not the result of any form of hallucination or imagination but it does not mean it is paranormal however unusual the sound may at first seem. Locations can and do have unusual acoustic properties, sounds may appear to come from unexpected sources or perhaps change in nature so that they sound strange. Infrasound, which is sound considered as being below our normal hearing threshold (about 20Hz), or ultrasound that is above our upper hearing threshold (about 16,000Hz), are also factors that may need to be considered. Aside from any direct effects on the body of the witness, it may also cause parts of a location's structure, or objects within it, to vibrate and produce sounds that are within audible hearing range. The evidential usefulness of any recorded sounds obtained during an investigation should not be overstated in the subsequent presentation of the findings. A recording may appear to have good evidential qualities but in reality that may not be the case. As an example, a recording of footsteps in an empty corridor may seem to be impressive but, in reality, the recording on its own cannot demonstrate that the corridor was actually empty at the time of the recording so the value of the evidence is diminished. Sound recorders can allow the investigator to do more than simply record sounds at a location; it is also possible with computer assistance and accurate positioning of microphones to triangulate and determine the position that a sound was coming from. The method is relatively straightforward but does need some care and practise to undertake. At least three (and ideally at least five) identical microphones must be placed at very carefully noted positions. This knowledge of microphone placement is crucial. When the recordings are played back using a computer and suitable software, it is possible to measure the difference in the time that it takes a sound to reach each microphone using the computer. The minute differences, often in the order of milliseconds, can then be used to indicate the direction from which the sound was coming from. By then comparing the different directions indicated from the known microphone locations it is possible to triangulate the source of the sound. In some locations, such as those with long corridors or locations with unusual acoustic properties, this method may, however, only provide a rough indication as to the location of the sound event.

Some Sound Terminology

A. *Decibel (dB)* is the unit used to measure the intensity of a sound. The smallest audible sound (near total silence) is 0 dB. A sound 10 times more powerful is 10 dB. A sound 100 times more powerful than near total silence is 20 dB. A sound 1,000 times more powerful than near total silence is 30 dB.

B. *Sound Pressure Level (SPL)* In a sound wave there are extremely small periodic variations in atmospheric pressure to which our ears and also microphones respond. The minimum pressure fluctuation to which the ear can respond is less than one-billionth (10^{-9}) of atmospheric pressure.

Because of the wide range of pressure stimuli, it is convenient to measure sound pressures using the decibel scale i.e., a sound has a pressure of x dB (SPL)

Volume: In acoustics this is related to the:

1. Amplitude

2. Sound Pressure Level

3. Frequency

Loudness: Is the quality of a sound that is the primary psychological correlate of physical strength (amplitude). The loudness control on some consumer recording equipment merely alters the frequency response curve to correspond roughly with the characteristic of the ear. Loudness compensation is intended to make the recorded music sound more natural when played at a lower sound pressure level.

Paranormal Sounds?

Sounds have frequently been a feature of paranormal reports. Things that go bump in the night have traditionally featured in many ghost stories, true and otherwise. The first attempts at using sound to develop some understanding of what was taking place at a haunted house or place was in the form of communicative raps and knocks, a method that is often considered to be the creation of the Fox sisters in the 1840's, whose exploits led directly to the founding of the Spiritualist movement and religion. The sister's technique of asking for a communicating spirit to answer questions by a series of knocks, typically one knock for yes and two knocks for no, was in fact being used almost a century before in London. In 1762, investigators questioning the Cock Lane ghost, (also known as Scratching Fanny) made use of an identical method of rapped responses. By the time of the Fox Sisters, this technique was well understood and practised by psychical investigators. Clearly the option to record these communications did not exist for these early ghost investigators and Spiritualists but following the invention of the phonograph in 1878 it became possible to record sound as part of the investigation process. Possible it may have been, but practical considerations meant that recordings were rarely actually undertaken. In 1899, the results of an investigation at an alleged haunted house in Scotland were published. 'B' House became notorious for the loud explosive bangs, thumps, and footsteps that investigators experienced. The investigators, some of whom were members of the Society for Psychical Research (SPR), proposed that a phonograph should be used to record the numerously reported sounds. Sadly, this plan was thwarted by a legal dispute with the house's owner. In 1915 and 1916, the engineer and psychical researcher Dr W.J. Crawford did make extensive use of a phonograph to record the direct voices produced by medium Kathleen Goligher at her family's séance circle in Belfast. It is believed that these recordings have been preserved and may be made publicly available at some future date. Sound recording equipment tended to be cumbersome and although some investigators, including Harry Price who carried out a live radio broadcast from a haunted house in 1936, did use sound recording in some circumstances, its use in haunted locations was not yet widespread or common. Sound recording in spontaneous investigations may properly be thought to have begun with the investigation of The Enfield Poltergeist in 1977 and 1978. Members of the investigation team used cassette and reel-to-reel recorders to make extensive sound recordings of the various phenomena that took place. These recordings, a number of which have been broadcast in television and radio documentaries about the case appear to be a record, not only of the sounds of objects being moved or thrown about, but also the alleged voice of the poltergeist answering the questions of the investigators and apparently speaking by using the vocal cords of a young girl.

With the advent of portable sound recording apparatus; first the reel-to-reel tape, followed in the 1970's by the much more portable cassette recorder ghost investigators took sound recording equipment to many more haunted locations. Some notable recordings include those made inside Borley Church in 1974 and which were subsequently broadcast by the BBC as part of a documentary series *The Ghost Hunters* in 1975.

The widespread use of easily portable sound recording equipment means that now almost every ghost investigator carries at least one sound recorder when they conduct their investigations. Digital recording and the Internet have resulted in many such recordings being placed online although many are frequently mislabelled as EVP's. Despite the technology that is employed, it seems surprising that so many of these claimed recordings of paranormal events and sounds are of poor quality and have little, if any, use evidentially. However, when the techniques used for sound recording are examined it may not be that much of a surprise to discover why so many poor quality recordings are made. In this digital era, many investigators pay comparatively little attention to the selection of the recorder, the choice of microphone, and the placement of their equipment. Sound recorders tend to be either carried or placed around a location with little apparent thought to the technical requirements of making a successful recording. Extraneous sounds, often made by the investigators themselves, can mask potential paranormal sounds and, in some cases, may result in being interpreted as the claimed paranormal sounds. The overuse of sound editing software in the name of analysis may also result in alteration of the recording that often renders the presented audio as nearly unlistenable and worthless as evidence. Sound has been a feature of almost every reported haunting down the centuries and sound recording is an important asset to the ghost investigator in the search for information and evidence. But it is only with due care and attention to the selection, use, and placement of equipment together with equal care being given to the post investigation handling and interpretation of the recordings, that sound recording will be a useful and helpful asset to the investigator.

CHAPTER 12

INVESTIGATION SOUND RECORDING

The type and model of recorder chosen is often dictated by the budget. It may be tempting to get several less expensive models rather than fewer more costly machines but this almost certainly a mistake. There is an old saying 'You get what you pay for' and it is generally good advice. More expensive recorders normally offer a better range of options for adjusting the recorder to suit the particular requirements of different locations and circumstances. For instance, a less expensive recorder designed for dictation and audio note taking may not be the best choice for trying to record the sound in a larger room due to limitations with the gain controls and possibly an inability to connect an external microphone. Cheaper machines are likely to be less well built and make use of cheaper components. As result they tend to be less reliable and liable to produce more electronic noise on the subsequent recording. There are some recorders that are advertised and sold on the basis that they are optimised for paranormal use; in some instances particular models of recorder have become highly sought after (and highly expensive) because of their perceived reputation as being better than other machines for recording paranormal sounds. Such claims and reputations are entirely false and misleading. A sound recorder is just that, a device for recording sound, the methods and means by which they achieve this are well understood. Whenever they have been examined, recorders that are said to have been optimised for paranormal use are, without exception, found to be either entirely standard or have had some amateur modifications carried out. Commonly encountered modifications usually involve turning the microphone amplification or recording gain up to levels whereby the electrical signal from the microphone is distorted and the recording becomes overloaded with noise.

An important consideration when selecting a recorder is how the subsequent recordings will be used, the same consideration will also affect the way that the recorder needs to be set-up. For instance, if it is intended to do nothing more than listen to the recorded audio, then there is nothing to be gained by setting a very high sample rate and bit depth. The standard for CD audio (i.e. a sample rate of 44.1 kHz and 16 bit) will more than suffice for any listening only task. If the recording forms part of some measurement or post-recording analysis then higher sampling rates and a greater bit depth may be advantageous. It is worth mentioning that in a recorder that makes use of a fixed amount of memory then higher settings for the sample rate and / or bit-depth will inevitably result in a lot more data being written to the memory, this will decrease the available recording time. Of course, if the recorder uses removable memory in the form of a memory card or disc, then this consideration does not apply. When selecting a recorder it is wise to select models that offer the ability to use one of the uncompressed recording formats rather than a format that uses compression. Compressed recording formats such as the universal adopted .mp3 may be perfectly adequate for general listening, but information from the original sound is irretrievably lost in the compression process. Our ears may not notice this loss too much but, if it is a requirement to make any form of post recording analysis or measurement, this is a significant issue. Consideration should also be given to the means and methods of powering the recorder; batteries may be preferable in some circumstances but they will limit the time that the device is capable of operating. Mains power will allow extended recording periods limited only by the capacity of the storage media.

The majority of recorders have an automatic gain, which sets the overall level of the electrical signal coming from the microphone to what the manufacturer considers to be an optimum setting for general use. Gain is also called recording level. Manual recording level may be a user selected option on some recorders but other machines may lack any form of manual gain control and are completely reliant upon the automatic gain circuit within the recorder. Automatic gain is almost certainly a disadvantage when trying to use the recorder in an investigation scenario. In quiet locations or when there is very little sound, the recorder will increase the gain. Should louder sounds be encountered, then the amount of amplification is automatically reduced to lower the signal level from the microphone and prevent distortion. Automatic systems have an inherent flaw; they need time to respond. Even with the best recorders this will result in some sound being misrepresented on the recording. In a quiet environment, any sudden loud transient sound such as a bang or thump may appear to be distorted and much louder on the subsequent recording than it actually was. Conversely, in a noisy environment, quieter sounds may not be recorded at all. Therefore, it is always better to be able to set the recording level manually. A professional soundman on a film or television shoot and the sound engineer in a studio would never use automatic gain. Ultimately, the recorder is there to capture the signal coming from the microphone. The microphone is undoubtedly the most important individual component of any recording set-up. Many people consider that all microphones are pretty much the same, but there are substantial differences between a microphone bought for a few pounds and one costing several thousands of pounds. Those differences will directly affect the quality of the recorded audio. There are very few circumstances where spending thousands of pounds on a microphone will be advantageous but there are many circumstances where spending just a few pounds more on a microphone are extremely disadvantageous. As a general guide, the cost of the microphone should at least equal the cost of the recorder. Microphones are normally optimised for a range of frequencies specifically chosen by the manufacturer for its intended use. Some microphones are designed primarily for human speech, others for musical instruments or for industrial applications such as the measurement of noise levels around airports. Reputable microphone manufacturers provide information about their products in the form of a frequency and amplitude response graph for each model and this information should be considered before acquisition. It may also be worthwhile considering hiring various types and models prior to purchase in order to test their suitability or for one-off investigation tasks. Microphones can also be designed to be more responsive to one direction or they may be omni-directional, responding to sound from all directions more or less equally. Although most microphones are monophonic, meaning a separate microphone is normally required for both left and right stereo channels of a recorder, there are some which are designed for stereo recording and have two microphone capsules one for each of the stereo tracks combined within a single microphone body.

It is not just the microphone that needs to be considered, some thought needs to be given to how the signal is carried from the microphone to the recorder. The signal coming from a microphone is tiny, often just a few millivolts, and this needs to be amplified by the recorder in order to drive the recording circuits effectively. One method in which electrical noise can interfere with a recording is when it is picked up through the cable and connectors. Professional systems use a three-wire connection which eliminates some of this electromagnetic noise from nearby electrical systems such as power supplies, appliances, and motors. This is achieved by sending the signal down two of the wires, each wire carrying the same signal voltage but with the phase of each signal reversed with respect to the other and effectively cancelling out much of the electromagnetic interference. The third wire is a shield and is normally connected to a foil or braided metal shield that surrounds the inner signal wires and is connected to an earth or ground inside the recorder. These methods are generally referred to as balanced systems whereas a standard two-wire microphone and connection is known as an unbalanced system and is much more prone to induced electromagnetic interference being picked up through the cables and connectors. Some microphone types such as condensers require power to be supplied to the microphone capsule, this may be in the form of an internal battery within the microphone body or as 'phantom power' with the power coming from an external source such as the recorder via the microphone cable.

Whichever type of recorder is used, analogue, digital, professional or domestic grade, whenever possible avoid handholding any sound recording device in order to minimise handling noise picked up through the body of the device itself. This step is especially important when using a recorder that is using a built-in microphone. If the recorder has the facility, it is always preferable to use an external microphone for recordings as it reduces the likelihood of noise, either electrical or mechanical, being picked up and recorded. Be aware when using an external microphone to also avoid handling noise by ensuring that it is always used with a suitable microphone stand, but remain aware that vibrations may still be transmitted through the stand to the microphone and thus picked up. Vibration reducing microphone stands are available which will reduce, but do not totally eliminate physical vibrations of the microphone. In situations when the investigator is using a small handheld portable recorder such as a cassette or digital recorder with only a built-in microphone, a simple technique to reduce handling noise and other vibrations from being picked-up is to simply place the recorder on a piece of sponge or foam rubber (a simple bath sponge is perfect and very cheap to acquire). This will also work when placed beneath microphone stands that lack a suitable vibration reducing microphone mount.

The actual placement of the microphone itself is important to the final quality of the recording. From personal observation, it appears that many people simply place the recorder or microphone down with little regard to how placement or the type of microphone they are using will affect their recording. A position close to a wall or in the corner of a room will greatly increase the amount of reverberation and echo that will be picked up, particularly if the microphone they are using is an omni-directional design. Reverberation will add additional acoustic noise to the recording and may make the sounds less distinct and intelligible. Positioning a microphone close to a surface or in a corner may also adversely affect the frequency response of the microphone and the subsequent recording. Omni-directional microphones perform best when they are placed toward the centre of a room, away from surfaces and obstructions to the sound path. If the recording is to be made in a long space such as a corridor then a directional design is preferred, again such a choice minimises reverberation and echo and, due to the way in which acoustic standing waves may also form in such places, it is also sometimes better to position the microphone around a third of the way from the end wall on the longest side of the space.

The worst possible scenario for ensuring good quality recording is to just place the recorder or microphone onto a floor, table, or hard surface without any real thought or consideration of the consequences for the subsequent recording.

CHAPTER 13

SOUND RECORDING, WHAT NEXT?

Assuming there is something of interest on a recording, perhaps an intriguing sound or an unexpected noise, is there anything that can be done with it to help the investigation? The recording may be unclear, noisy, or simply downright confusing but it does represent a record of an actual acoustic event, regardless of any problems; technical or otherwise that the recording may have. As such it is objective information about the event and needs to be considered as potentially significant to the overall investigation and treated accordingly.

The first step is obviously to listen to the sound recording, but the investigator should try to avoid succumbing to the temptation of listening to it straight away during the investigation, except perhaps to briefly check that the event was actually recorded. Playing back during the investigation may cause the investigator or others hearing the playback to make assumptions that could affect the remainder of the visit. Sleep on it is good advice.

Listening Test

Whenever possible the initial listening test should be done using the original recording device in order to reduce any effects caused by using a playback machine or by the transfer process. This mainly applies to analogue recordings but it is still a valid consideration with digital recordings too. A good step for trying to understand what the recording might contain is to play it to several people. Ideally, these should not be people who have been on the investigation or have knowledge of the location. Non-ghost investigating friends and family often make good candidates. To avoid listeners being forced to sit through overly long recordings, the recording might need to be shortened or parts that are not of interest edited out. If editing is necessary, ensure that a sufficient amount of lead-in and lead-out on the recording remains; at least ten seconds pre and post section of interest is a good general guide. It might also be a good idea to make a thirty second recording of a control section containing nothing of any significance, its purpose being to allow the listeners time to tune-in or acclimatise their hearing to the recording.

Provide no information to the listener about the content of the recording and avoid statements such as: "Listen to the voice in this recording" or "Can you hear the footsteps in this bit?" Conduct each individual session separately. Avoid group listening sessions as it becomes more difficult to prevent one of the group members saying aloud their opinion and priming the others. Immediately after the listening session ends, ask the listener to write down their comments and thoughts. Do not wait, even for a few minutes, as the human memory for sound is notoriously short and unreliable. Ensure that the listeners don't discuss the recording between themselves until they have all listened and written down their comments.

Analysis

True audio analysis is a highly specialised skill that requires extensive training in order to be properly undertaken. It is not simply a matter of playing around with the recorded sound using home audio software such as Audacity or some other piece of sound editing software, although many investigators use such techniques and continue to call what they do analysis. Software can be used in some instances with CARE and PRACTISE. Its use in these circumstances should not be to analyse but to assist and to help the investigator. Knowledge about the principles of sound and a good knowledge of what the software is capable of doing are needed to carry out this type of work. For example, it is often stated that some presented sound anomaly "was not produced by any animal or other known source". This is a very bold statement to make as it implies that the investigator has considered and tested every possible animal and the range of sounds that they make in addition to every other potential sound causing activity. Do they have a database of every animal sound for comparison? And every other potential noise source too? How did they reach that conclusion? In reality, these claims are pretty meaningless and more accurately mean that the investigator simply did not immediately recognise the sound or was unable to relate it to some obvious cause.

Often a recording will be indistinct, noisy, or difficult to understand. Software can be used to help the process of understanding. Remember that whilst any software changes applied to the recording may aid the process of understanding, it will alter the recording and may change the way that it is interpreted. If it is decided that altering the recording by using software might help, it is essential that every change is documented and recorded. Start with a working duplicate copy and make a single change and once this is done save this change using a meaningful new file name i.e., *soundgain.1.wav*. For every subsequent change, save the change using a new file name i.e., *soundgain.2.wav*. This will build up an archive of the stages that have been used. In addition to the sound files sequential labelling, maintain a written log to document each step of the process, linking the notes to the appropriate sound file. Document the change made at every single stage linked to an appropriate file i.e., *"soundgain.1.wav – gain increased by 5%" "soundgain.2.wav – gain increased by 5%"* etc. Don't overlook noting the software that is used, including the actual software version and any software tools or plugins that are used. This technique is how forensic audio analysts work and this technique will ensure that the recording will have the highest possible value in supporting any investigation results and conclusions.

As already stated, sound analysis requires specialised knowledge of sound including the software and the effects of any changes that are made. This knowledge is acquired with training, use, and understanding. Software can be complicated to use and is often difficult to understand. Software can also be used to objectively measure some parameters of the recording such as the amplitude and frequency of the component sounds. This information can be used to make direct comparisons with known sounds and may be able to prove similarity. Ultimately, the final interpretation of the recording will most likely be a subjective interpretation based upon the operator's knowledge and experience, information about the recording, and a range of other factors including the recording equipment together with the techniques and methods for obtaining the recording.

Once the listening tests and any analysis is completed and the investigator is still sure that he or she has recorded something truly anomalous, potentially even paranormal, what can be done with it? Many investigators write a brief account of how amazingly evidential their recording is and stick it onto their website, possibly they will post it onto their YouTube channel too. Too often, little actual consideration is given to the value of a simple recording. It may reasonably be argued that any recording on its own is of little evidential value. A recording of a sound is just that, a recording of a sound. It demonstrates nothing except that an acoustic event took place and that it was recorded. This at least confirms that it wasn't simply imagined by those claiming to have heard the sound, assuming that it was the same sound event that they heard. The debate over the validity of sound recordings made during paranormal investigations remains on-going but, by the proper application of the right equipment and correct post recording treatment of any recordings that are made, the investigator should be able to demonstrate that they are aware of some of the issues and have acted to address them responsibly.

Ultimately, interpreting a recording is almost invariably subjective. That means that the final decision about what the recording actually represents comes down to a human being, complete with all the potential problems of the human factor. Personal belief, expectation, suggestion, and desire all play a part in this, together with physical factors too. It is rare that two people will hear in exactly the same way. The listener's age also affects the acuity of our ears, high frequency hearing decreases with age, even the amount of earwax can affect what we are able to hear.

CHAPTER 14

OBTAINING STILL IMAGES

Tools of the Trade

Almost since the invention of photography over one hundred and fifty years ago there have been many images that claim to show definitive proof of ghosts, anomalous moving objects and other such paranormal phenomena. Some have been quite compelling, whilst others have had numerous criticisms levelled against them. As a ghost investigator it is important to make the most of every opportunity to capture useful evidence that may support the investigation findings or demonstrate the true nature of the phenomenon.

Perhaps the most sought after evidence by all investigators of paranormal phenomena is the visual evidence. A picture speaks a thousand words as the saying goes. Images can take the form of still pictures from both film and, more recently, digital cameras and also video footage from both analogue and digital camcorders. This is not an in depth technical description of the various means of producing still and moving images, there are many resources available to those interested in such things. It is a discussion of the relative advantages and disadvantages the various methods offer to those who wish to make use of photography in support of their own investigations. Some technical information is necessary and will be provided where it is relevant to the discussion. In all cases where the ghost investigator seeks to use image recording as a tool they are advised to fully consider all of the available options, their relative advantages and disadvantages, and decide for themselves what best suits their specific requirements.

Choosing and using the right type of imaging device is an important first step.

Selecting the best position for the camera will also maximise the chance of capturing something useful. Interpreting the subsequent images is the final stage of the process and is perhaps the one that is most likely to cause problems for the investigator.

Choosing the Camera

Many (if not all) investigators use a camera of some type during an investigation; often the choice of what camera is used is made on the basis of whatever is available. Most people have access to a camera or perhaps a video camera-recorder (camcorder). Usually, these will have been bought on the basis of the needs of the family for the recording of holidays and other family occasions. Increasingly, investigators may decide to purchase a camera or camcorder to support their investigations. The choice is usually made on the basis of one or two features or abilities that the investigator considers may be helpful in obtaining proof or evidence of ghosts. Usually, the first and foremost consideration relates to the camera's ability to work in low light, this is especially true when selecting a video camcorder. Irrespective of the actual need for darkness, it is most often the case that ghost investigations are conducted after dark where the use of additional lighting is required to obtain a properly exposed and focussed image. Therefore, it is for this predominant set of conditions we must consider when assessing the abilities of the various types of camera and camcorder.

RTFM... Read The Flipping Manual

Ghost investigators are human and it is almost a normal human trait to assume that instruction manuals are simply part of the packaging. Manuals are something to be briefly glanced through, then put away and forgotten; after all how difficult is it to take a photograph? Modern cameras have a wealth of additional features and most of them are pretty pointless when it comes to ghost investigating but some of them, such as manual control of exposure and focus can offer real advantages and benefits. In every case the investigator should dig out that forgotten instruction manual and fully familiarise themselves with the capabilities of the camera or camcorder. Take plenty of test shots and use the different modes, test out the features. With camcorders and digital still cameras this is made easier by the fact that the recording media is re-usable and therefore the only cost is time. Time is a wise investment and this stage should not be overlooked even if the investigator considers that he or she can take a pretty decent photograph. By definition ghosts and hauntings are spontaneous events; they are unpredictable and there can be no worse situation than when the investigator is left fumbling around, blindly jabbing at the camera's buttons and fiddling with the controls until the moment has passed and they have completely failed to capture the moment a ghost appears before them. Investigators need to be as familiar with the essential controls and functions of their camera, indeed any piece of equipment that they are using, as they with the controls of their car. Operating the camera should become second nature and this can only come through practise and total familiarity with the controls and their layout.

The stills camera is the most likely type of camera equipment the ghost investigator either owns or has access to. A stills camera is one that is primarily designed to take still pictures rather than moving images, although nowadays many cameras will do both equally as well. They are available in two forms; the film camera that predominantly uses a 35mm film cassette and the digital stills camera, which in recent years has vastly overtaken film models, and is now the type most commonly found in the investigators kit. More recently, there has been a huge increase in mobile phones that provide a digital camera built into them, many of which are capable of taking excellent quality pictures, even in challenging conditions.

Film Cameras

Film cameras have been around for well over 150 years and the technology is mature and well understood. Despite the domination of digital photography, film cameras still have a role in ghost investigation and are worth considering in some detail. Many of the most significant ghost photographs have been taken using film, although it could be argued that this is simply due to the longevity of the film media compared to the much more recent use of digital photography. Film uses Silver based chemicals contained within the film which chemically alter when exposed to light. Following exposure, additional chemical processes are required in order to produce the final picture we are familiar with. In practise most people simply hand the film to a high street lab for the development and printing of the images.

Film is available in a range of speeds, this is an indication of its sensitivity to light. Speed or sensitivity is normally quoted as a numeric ISO (International Standards Organisation) rating, the higher the number, the more sensitive the film is and the less light is required to produce an effective image. Slow speed film, normally considered to be ISO 100 and below needs bright daylight or good lighting to produce the best quality images. Fast films, from ISO 400 and above need correspondingly less light for an effective image to be produced.

It might be thought that simply using the fastest film available will suffice but there are some additional factors that need to be considered. The increased light sensitivity requires a different chemical mix in the film and the resulting images will have an increased graininess and correspondingly less definition, colours may also be less accurately defined. Select a very high speed film with an ISO rating of 1600 or even 3200 and the image becomes rather like looking through a fine mesh, very soft and with little definition in the objects. Fast films may also require specialist processing and developing that can significantly increase the costs.

Film is available in colour and monochrome (black and white) varieties. Monochrome can offer some advantages such as it has the ability to take pictures with a higher contrast ratio than colour. Related to monochrome film is infrared film. Psychical researchers have used and experimented with this type of film for almost one hundred years. It is highly specialist, expensive to buy and expensive to develop and due to its nature cannot easily be used in many cameras. Furthermore, it needs careful storage and handling. Overall, in most investigation situations colour film in the ISO range of 400 and 800 offers perhaps the best compromise between the need to capture low light images and has reasonable definition in the subsequent pictures.

There are still a small number of investigators who use instant film for some experiments. Pioneers of the format, Polaroid, ceased production of their instant cameras in 2008 but still manufacture instant film for several of their models. Fujifilm also continue to manufacture both instant cameras and film.

Film - Pros and Cons

Film does not have an infinite lifespan; it is after all a chemical concoction and deteriorates after a period of time or in conditions that are detrimental to the chemistry such as heat or high humidity. Poor storage, leaving the film inside the camera for long periods, or a failure to have it promptly developed after use will all cause anomalies in the final image. Over the years, many of the pictures which have been presented as evidence for ghosts and spirits being captured on camera have turned out to be, on closer examination, the result of poor film storage and handling. However, it is at the development stage where a majority of problems can occur that may lead to the production of anomalies. Poor temperature control at the processing stage, watermarks, and mishandling all are well known causes of reported paranormal images.

Cheap, generically branded film that is sold in many shops and supermarkets may be tempting as these films can often be considerably cheaper than a branded film. Generally speaking, these generic branded films should be avoided, as the economy can be false. Generic and store brand film tends to use older film technology and the final images can be softer, less defined, and have poorer colour rendition than the corresponding branded version for the same ISO rated film. If a lot of pictures are required, perhaps for a record of the locations visited, then generic film may be worth considering but try different brands and experiment to ensure that the final image quality is suitable. Film still retains one key advantage over digital camera images, this is the negative; the original piece of film upon which the image has been recorded and from which prints and all subsequent copies can be made. The negative can be used to show that the final picture has not been tampered with after the film has left the camera. Processing faults or faults within the film itself, which are a frequent cause of many photographic anomalies, are also easier to detect by using the negative.

Film cameras used to be available in a wide variety of types and film formats. Many of these have now become scarce or have been discontinued entirely due to the popularity of digital photography. There are some large format films and cameras that use roll or sheet film but it is now really only 35mm cameras that are worth considering for investigation use. These use 35mm film cassettes and are available in two main varieties, the compact camera and the single lens reflex (SLR) camera. Film camera use has become much less common in the past decade; therefore it is hardly worth considering film cameras in great detail. In function and operation they are almost precisely the same as their current digital counterparts and, for the most part, exactly the same considerations will apply when using either a 35mm film compact or a digital compact, likewise, when using 35mm film SLR or a digital SLR (DSLR).

Digital Photography

Digital cameras are a comparatively recent innovation gaining widespread use from the late 1990's. Early models were horrendously expensive and produced images with low resolution and poor colour rendition. Battery life was also a serious issue as was the cost of the memory media needed to store the images. With the advent of improved technology, some of it developed originally for mobile phone use, digital cameras now provide low cost and good quality images that have the extra advantage of being immediately viewable via the on-camera screen, computer (or personal device), and television. Once the camera and sufficient memory is purchased then there are usually no further costs involved for the user. In terms of investigation use, printing of the final picture is rarely undertaken; most are used on websites or social media pages. Computer disk drives and solid-state memory cards now provide almost perfect long-term storage options. For those that require printed pictures, photo printing is straightforward and inexpensive.

Digital Film

Not a mistake, this is the description now commonly used by some memory card makers to describe the memory cards upon which the actual image data is stored after taking. Actually, this terminology is misleading as the memory card is perhaps better compared to a photo album. The best digital analogy for the film is actually the imaging chip or sensor, as this is where the lens directs the light, exactly as light is directed onto the film in a 35mm camera.

Instead of film, a digital camera uses a silicon chip to turn the light into electronic information. There are two types of silicon chip in use, the Charge Coupled Device (CCD) and the Complimentary Metal Oxide Semiconductor. (CMOS). In the past CMOS sensors were typically of low resolution and normally only to be found in webcams, mobile phone cameras, and in the cheapest digital camera models. This has now changed with the development of high-resolution CMOS sensor designs. The CMOS works slightly differently than the CCD; this difference means the CMOS can transfer its data to the camera processor faster and camera makers such as Nikon, Canon, and Sony have all begun using CMOS in place of CCD sensors in most of their models.

Both types of sensor do the same job however and there is no further consider the technical differences between the two sensor types here. For those who are curious, there is a wealth of technical information and discussions about sensor technology available online.

The ability of the imaging sensor to resolve detail within the scene being photographed is a function of two variables; the number of individual light gathering points (pixels) on the surface of the sensor and the physical dimensions of the sensor. Most manufacturers simply quote the number of light gathering pixels when promoting the specifications of a camera model (1 Mega-pixel, typically being one million individual pixels). While it is generally true that the more pixels a sensor has then the greater amount of information it is able to resolve within any scene, as with many things there is always a downside. For any given physical size of sensor, simply cramming more pixels into the same space inevitably means each pixel has to be physically smaller. Many bridge and compact models have an individual pixel dimension of less than 3 microns (0.003mm). Smaller pixels are inherently less sensitive to light than those of similar technical specification but of a larger size; some DSLR's have pixel dimensions of 5-7 microns or more for example. In bright daylight scenes this may not be a serious issue as there is plenty of light available, but indoors or at night, imaging sensors with smaller pixels quickly begin to show their weakness. In low light conditions, additional amplification (signal-gain) is required to obtain usable data from the sensor regardless of the pixel size and even more amplification is needed for sensors that have smaller pixels. Whenever more amplification is required, there will be a corresponding increase in the amount of electronic noise that will be present. This will inevitably result in more degradation in the final image. Electronic noise also produces anomalies in the image itself, which may be interpreted as being paranormal by the unwary investigator. Some manufacturers limit the ISO sensitivity range of their sensors to prevent the noise becoming problematic. Manufacturers also use in-camera software (noise-reduction) processing to reduce the image problems caused by the electronic noise, with varying degrees of success. For the same number of pixels, physically larger sensors allow the inherently better sensitivity to low light levels to be exploited and the manufacturer can offer a greater range of ISO equivalents – in some cases ISO numbers exceeding 6400 are possible without excessive electronic noise being a serious problem. By combining the increased light sensitivity of the larger sensor, together with improved pixel technology pixels and better noise reduction software, the likes of Canon and Nikon have allowed ISO sensitivity ratings of over 100,000 and higher to be achieved, which means usable pictures may be taken in extremely low light levels. Larger individual pixels also permit a greater tonal range to be captured from the scene and this results in a more accurate scene rendition, even at lower light levels. An additional bonus of physically larger sensors is that the design forces the manufacturer to provide a physically larger lens diameter too and such lenses generally have better optics, thus further improving the overall image.

Of course, as camera makers develop the electronics within the cameras over successive models they are able to better control the noise and low light weakness of the smaller sensors. This is done using additional electronics and processing after the chip and improvements in the design of the pixel elements too; the placing of a microscopically small lens over each pixel element improves light gathering for example. Large imaging sensors are not without problems either. These are essentially the same problems that apply to their smaller relatives. As makers vie with each other to cram even more pixels onto the sensor, the pixels have to shrink in size. As an example, manufacturers such as Canon, Nikon and Sony have used the small pixel technology to produce 35mm or "full-size" sensors, the resolution of which can begin to exceed that of 35mm film i.e., around 40 Mega-pixels. However, it is important to remember that using a digital camera with a more typical 12 to 25 Mega-pixels the end result will contain less than half of the original information in the scene when compared to a similar sized film image. At normal viewing resolutions such as on a computer screen or in a print, our eyes normally do not notice this lost information. However, zoom into the image and increasingly the fine detail will be missing. This missing and lost detail may be an issue in some situations where that information may hold vital clues and may mean the difference between something remaining unknown and possibly anomalous and an identified object. The individual pixels on the sensor cannot resolve colour so the light first needs to be passed through a filter that allows colours to be detected. This filter has led to some comments that digital images all present false colour information. To an extent this is true but it is also the case that 35mm film uses a filter within the structure of the film in order to resolve colour in a scene. When considering the operating specifications of any digital camera, the form factor (its physical design) should be considered such as the overall size of the camera, the lens, and the usability of the camera. Small cameras are portable and often easy to use but they have smaller sensors and so perform less well in lower light. Larger cameras generally perform better in low light but are less portable. Larger cameras do have more space to provide better user controls such as separate buttons or switches for different settings, this generally makes the camera easier to operate without resorting to the need to dig down through numerous menu options to adjust the camera settings.

For many investigators, one of the most attractive reasons for using a digital camera for ghost investigation is perhaps the ability of the sensor to see into the infrared (IR) part of the light spectrum. It should be pointed out that all imaging sensors have about the same degree of sensitivity to infrared light but most manufacturers choose to apply filters to remove it as it can seriously affect the colour rendering of a scene under normal lighting conditions. Sony have in the past made a feature out of this extra sensitivity that allows pictures to be taken in conditions where there are very low visible light levels, aided by the use of a small camera mounted Infrared light source. Although this infrared enhanced shooting mode is mainly found in their video cameras, in the past, one or two Sony still cameras have exploited this ability. The handful of stills cameras that used this NightShot ® option allowed infrared still photographs to be taken in locations where there was almost no ambient visible light and of course many of their digital video cameras have used this technology to take night-vision still pictures. Many paranormal investigators claim that paranormal manifestations are more visible under IR light or that the ghost or spirit emits light within the IR part of the spectrum that can be seen by the sensor. This idea is highly contentious and as yet unproven but it does mean that locations can be photographed under conditions of extremely low light, which may aide the investigation process.

183

The Digital Darkroom

Film cameras simply expose the film to the light. The film is then removed for developing and printing in order to reveal the final picture. But within every digital camera there is a built-in developing lab that produces a finished image almost instantaneously. The information about the light hitting the sensor is transferred directly to a microcomputer within the camera and it is this that turns the raw data from the sensor into a final image, rather like the developing and printing that used to take place in the darkroom. This process can cause some additional problems for the unwary as the user is reliant upon the camera manufacturer to programme the internal computer thereby effectively undertaking this step of the digital process. Some digital models do allow the user to store the image information in the form of a RAW file. As the name implies, this is basically the raw data from the image sensor which can be examined and adjusted using a computer in order for the final image to be seen. Here again, we have to be aware that the final image will be the result of a subjective and creative process on the part of the user who will produce a picture that appears as they wish to see it. Of course many of these same criticisms and dilemmas can be levelled at film photography and the darkroom process, and the settings of commercial developing and printing machines are largely subjective or, at best, at the discretion of the manufacturer or operator.

Another setting that users should take notice of with every digital camera is the amount of image compression that is applied to the final image when it is written to the memory card. Most camera makers allow the user to select this setting although some may label this option as "image quality". In order to fit a sufficient number of finished images onto a memory card the data needs to be compressed and this does mean even more lost information when compared to the original scene. By choosing to use either a lower compression setting or a higher picture quality option, the photographer will get fewer images onto the memory card but each will be of a higher quality. Most cameras store the final image as a compressed .jpg (jpeg) file but some models allow the user to select an uncompressed file format such as a .tiff (TIFF) instead. Using uncompressed file formats means fewer images can be stored on the memory card but a lot more original information is retained in the final image and that may be important for any subsequent determination of what an anomaly actually is. Increasingly, many cameras now allow files to be stored as 'RAW' file data. Using the RAW option allows most of the available information from the sensor to be retained, although this method does require the use of a computer in order to process the final image.

Cameras are sometimes supplied with a small amount of built-in memory that is barely adequate in terms of storage abilities, allowing only a few of the highest quality images to be stored on it. Memory cards are now inexpensive, especially compared to their cost just a few years ago. A large capacity memory card, such as 32Gb, 64Gb, or higher will permit the investigator to take and store more images at the highest possible quality levels.

Digital Camera Types

Broadly speaking there are four main digital camera types that may be considered, the Compact camera, Bridge camera (Hybrid), Digital SLR camera (DSLR), and mobile phone camera.

Compact Camera

Entry-level models can be bought very inexpensively these days. The lens on these basic cameras is often fixed focus. However, they will generally do a reasonable job of photographing anything from about one metre in front of the camera to infinity. The aperture is also normally fixed or has only a limited range of options and the exposure control is normally carried out automatically. Perhaps to be expected, these cameras produce the least good images with the highest incidence of picture problems. Unless the investigator is on a really tight budget and is aware of the potential drawbacks then these cameras really ought to be avoided, as they are simply not up to the task of gathering any useful evidence. Perhaps their only use is as a visual sketchbook allowing the investigator to make a quick photographic aide-de-memoir of something, such as the layout of a location for example.

In the mid-range, the user is almost spoilt for choice with a vast range of cameras having between 10 and 20+ Mega-pixels supported by a wide range of settings and options that allow the user to tailor the camera's abilities to their specific needs. One of the key problems with some of these advanced designs is the complexity and range of picture taking options that are provided. Many users simply do not properly read the manual and take the trouble to learn how to best use the numerous features and options. Instead, they turn the camera on and shoot away allowing the fully automated controls to take care of the picture settings. This method will mostly produce good pictures but frequently does not allow the best possible image to be obtained. It is therefore a good idea to read the manual and experiment with the different settings. This is easy to do with a digital camera as it involves only time and that time will be very well spent. As already mentioned, an important consideration is the sensitivity of the sensor to light. Quoted for ease in ISO units (the same as film) the lower the number the better the final picture will normally be as the camera requires less electronic amplification of the (gain) to be needed. A faster setting (higher ISO number) will allow pictures to be taken in situations where there is less available light but will subsequently lower the quality of the image.

There is a trend amongst camera manufacturers to produce very small cameras, around the size of a credit card in some cases. These designs inevitably use a smaller lens and a small image sensor and such a combination will reduce overall picture quality however expensive the camera may be. However, in some circumstances the user may be prepared to accept a trade-off between an easily portable camera that fits neatly into their pocket and is always available and the slight loss of final image quality. Compact models also tend to have the flash closer to the lens axis, allowing the flash illumination to be reflected from objects onto the sensor more readily. This is a known cause which many paranormal investigators refer to as Orbs (see Chapter 19). The incidence of red-eye effect is also higher is this type of camera, perfect for making the other investigation team members look demonic should no real demons be encountered whilst investigating.

Bridge or Hybrid Camera

This type of camera is a comparatively recent development. They are a mid-point between the compact and the DSLR, taking some of the best features from each and therefore may seem like the ideal camera for the investigator. They are, however, a compromise and they do have a number of drawbacks, although the makers are constantly evolving them to make improvements with every succeeding model. Bridge cameras usually have a high pixel count and often a large zoom range. The built-in flash also tends to be more powerful and pops up to a good height above the lens reducing some of the problems mentioned earlier, such as red-eye and orbs. Bridge models are rich in features and modes including full manual settings and this means they can be tailored for specific types of picture taking requirements which may suit the ghost investigator. One day it can be used on a site reconnaissance visit and later can take excellent images in a darkened room. The zoom lens allows wide-angle shots that takes in whole scenes and also permits close-ups of more distant features. Bridge cameras are normally larger and may resemble DSLR's. For some, this may mean that they are difficult to carry around all the time but the effort is usually offset by the provision of improved image quality over compact models. The larger body often allows the manufacturer to fit a larger viewing screen or a viewfinder (sometimes both) for setting-up and viewing final images and the screen may also be able to be rotated and tilted to allow better camera positioning when setting up the shot.

Best of all, the image sensor is normally physically larger than in many compact models which means a potential improvement in image quality and several recent bridge models now use the same image sensor as the more expensive DSLR cameras. The fact that the lens is permanently attached to the body may also be an extra bonus for the ghost investigator. Dust on the image sensor is a potential major cause of problems for DSLR users. The bridge design means less dust can penetrate and settle on the imaging sensor thereby reducing some image anomalies that might be interpreted as being of paranormal origin. The viewfinder is normally in the form of an electronic viewfinder or EVF. Some of these EVF's may be a little more difficult to use with some subjects but as most users tend to use the LCD screen this is not a major drawback and EVF's do offer some advantages in bright light when an LCD screen might be harder to see. Bridge cameras may be among the best all round solution for the ghost investigator and although they are a compromise they can represent an amalgam of the best options from the easy to use compact models and the more advanced capabilities of the DSLR's. Used with care and with the proper amount of time taken to learn and experiment with all the features that bridge cameras have available, then these cameras should be high on the list of useful tools for the ghost investigator.

Digital Single Lens Reflex Camera

These cameras are not unlike 35mm SLR's, the main difference being that instead of film, a large image sensor is used instead. Most models use a mirror and prism arrangement to bounce the light coming through the lens up to a viewfinder, the mirror moving out of the way and a shutter opening to expose the image sensor to the light at the time the picture is taken. There are more recent innovations that do away with the moving mirror but to all intents and purposes we can consider all the variations here. There are two main advantages of DSLR cameras; they use a larger image sensor and they generally have much better controls and ergonomics. Another key advantage is that they allow the user to change the lens to suit their specific picture taking requirements. They are normally part of a system with various lenses, flashguns, and lots of specialist accessories available, further allowing their use to be specifically tailored to the user's needs. It is this system concept that may offer some users a further advantage; many DSLR's are backwards compatible with previous 35mm SLR systems and this means that users with existing lenses and accessories have no need for further investment. This backwards compatibility can also benefit those investigators who wish to explore both film and digital techniques as the same lenses can often be used with both types of camera.

A major problem for DSLR owners is dust gathering on the image sensor itself. Every time a lens is changed some dust inevitably gets inside the camera body and some of it will eventually get onto the surface of the image sensor. Dust also gets inside 35mm film SLR's too but this is not a major issue as the film is wound through the camera and prevents the amount of dust building to excessive levels. Even small dust and pollen particles can be larger than the individual pixels on the sensor surface and so blocks the light falling onto individual pixels that become obscured in this way. This results in dark or bright spots on the final image together with other anomalies. The only satisfactory method of dealing with this dust build up is to have the image sensor surface cleaned. This is a task that most people prefer to have professionally carried out as it is an extremely delicate operation and can permanently damage the sensor if not done properly. Several camera makers now offer sensor-cleaning settings within the camera, for example, Canon uses a special filter in front of the sensor that vibrates 35,000 times per second to shake the dust onto a sticky collector pad thereby reducing the amount of dust remaining on the sensor. These in-camera anti-dust solutions are not 100% effective and dust can still be a headache for DSLR users.

Mobile Phone Camera

Cameras have been a common feature in mobile phones for a number of years. Initially these were low-resolution devices and with simple optics. As such they were perfectly adequate for picture messages to friends and family and the occasional small format print. In recent years smart phones such as Apple's iPhone and others have begun to offer cameras that are capable of taking pictures that can certainly rival and in many cases outperform the quality of pictures taken on lower specification digital cameras. Improvements to sensor technology and better optics combined with much better software and processing power has meant that in many instances the smart phone camera has actually begun to replace the digital camera in everyday use. With each successive generation of smart phones these camera systems improve and they are perfectly capable of producing excellent quality pictures and video in challenging situations. Although some smart phones offer manual controls these are often very much almost an afterthought and in reality camera phones are designed for fully automated use, the device's software dealing with almost every aspect of the picture taking.

All of the considerations regarding digital cameras apply, particularly in relation to the physical size of the sensor and the optical systems, which of necessity are much smaller than in other digital cameras. That aside, the portability of smart phone cameras and their simplicity of use are potential advantages when an investigator is faced with the situation of needing a camera quickly. One major consideration that must be mentioned here is that all smart devices can make use of small software programmes generally referred to as 'Apps' (Applications). These can be used to modify the operation and function of the built-in camera and can permit the user to tailor the camera for specific situations, such as low light levels or permit a rapid sequence of pictures to be taken. BUT... Apps are readily available that allow the user to edit or change the final picture and even insert or remove items from the picture in almost real-time. There have been many examples of ghost pictures being presented which were taken using one of these apps and in many cases the immediacy of the presented picture has led some to believe that they are genuine. Using a smart phone camera can make sense in many investigation situations but their use needs to be carefully considered in light of these problems.

Digital Conclusions

Digital photography offers the ghost investigator a means of taking an almost unlimited number of photographs without additional cost after the initial outlay on equipment and memory cards has been made. Once the memory card is full it can be downloaded to a laptop or one of many portable hard disk devices that are available, allowing more pictures to be taken. Pictures can also be reviewed immediately on the camera's screen.

Digital images may have a lower resolution than similar pictures taken with any 35mm film camera, even the most basic models. The image also has less information within it, which may be critical for some situations. Digital images are also prone to problems of electronic noise caused by the further electronic manipulation needed within the camera in order to produce a viewable image. Individual pixels may become faulty leading to anomalies within the image that may fool the unwary investigator. Dust may also cause problems in some models and may lead to anomalies appearing in the images produced if not effectively dealt with.

A frequently overlooked problem with digital cameras is their need for power; they all require batteries and heavy use (particularly when using lots of flash) may cause them to them to quickly run flat. Rechargeable batteries are one solution to this and, whilst battery technology is constantly improving, batteries have their own inherent problems. Temperature plays an important role in how long the battery lasts and, the colder it is, the shorter time it will last. Temperature sensitivity of the batteries can result in the functioning of the camera being affected and this is frequently cited as being paranormal: "My battery was fully charged but when I tried to take some pictures it refused to work but later, when I tried again, it was working perfectly, it must be paranormal!" is a frequently encountered statement. In reality, the batteries were probably simply too cold for the chemical reaction to properly take place and so there was insufficient power for the camera to operate. When the camera is returned to the bag or pocket where it warms sufficiently to permit the battery to function, the camera starts to work again. Some types of rechargeable batteries, notably the older Nickel-Cadmium (NiCad) types may also have another trick to play on the unsuspecting investigator; they are designed to deliver their output voltage in a more stable way than non-rechargeable batteries. In a non-rechargeable cell, the chemical reaction steadily slows down over time as the battery is used, causing the output voltage to drop steadily until finally reaching a point when the 'Low Battery' warning flashes. At this point the user may still have up to twenty per cent of the battery life still available and can keep on shooting for a while longer before the battery must be changed. However a rechargeable battery delivers a constant voltage throughout the period of use until the chemical reaction is exhausted, the battery will then fail quickly, often without the user noticing the low battery warning. It is therefore always a good idea to carry a second set of batteries.

Perhaps the final issue with digital photography is one that applies to all camera types, the manipulation of images. Digital picture editing has become an extremely simple and straightforward task and sceptics say that with digital images fakes are easy to produce, even more so as software develops to permit easier picture editing. Digital photography lacks the negative that film uses and which acts to some extent as a safeguard against manipulated images. This can be partially got around by developing good protocols for handling the data both in the camera and afterwards in the computer. Modern cameras write secondary information. This data contains a wealth of additional and useful information about the camera, the settings used at the time the picture was taken, together with the date and time (provided they have been correctly set beforehand). Most photo software allows the user to read this additional information but unfortunately some software also allows it to be re-written thus minimising the effectiveness of this method to reduce fraud.

Many of the issues with digital photography can be accepted as a compromise against the advantages, such as the immediacy of the final image and very low cost per image. Digital photography has now become the dominant form of photography. Ghost investigators and sceptics need to accept digital photography and work towards minimising some of the problems currently associated with this form of picture taking.

CHAPTER 15

VIDEO PHOTOGRAPHY

Video cameras are perhaps the most frequently used tools of the amateur paranormal investigator and many use one of the Sony models that offer the ability to record images in zero visible light conditions, NightShot® mode. This makes use of the inherent ability of the sensor to see infrared light almost as well as the visible portions of the light spectrum.

In effect, all camcorders, regardless of whether they use analogue or digital tape, DVD, a hard disc, or internal solid state memory, are just a digital stills camera that takes a continuous series of pictures. All camcorders made within the last 20 years use a sensor, in the form of either a CCD or CMOS type device and so the first step for the reader should be to go back to the previous sections dealing with digital still cameras and re-read it. However, there are some subtle differences with the sensors and the way the image information is dealt with that do need to be considered. Sensors in digital still cameras are used to produce a picture that may be viewed on a computer, a television, or printed in a range of sizes. The main function of a camcorder is to produce a high quality-moving image. Actually, it is best to describe the final product as a series of still images. In the UK, a television picture is actually a series of 25 or more still frames per second, so the similarities in the initial stage of the image making process are easy to see and indeed most camcorders have the ability to act as digital still cameras too, recording the still images to either the main recording media (tape, etc.) or an additional memory card.

Camcorders generally do not need to have a lot of pixels in order to produce perfectly watchable pictures. With some recent exceptions, most still use less than 3 Mega-pixels, although the sensor used may have many more to accommodate the requirement for high-resolution stills to be taken. Some manufacturers offer greater pixel numbers; although the specifications need to be carefully looked at prior to making any purchase, some models have sensors of 8, 10, or 12 Mega pixels but the figure refers to the total number of pixels that are available for use in taking digital stills. The number of pixels used for the video images remains typically around 2 or 3 Mega-pixels even for high definition (HD) use. The key reason that camcorders do not need so many pixels per sensor is primarily because television screens cannot display very high resolution pictures, even full High Definition video still has a much lower resolution than a printed picture requires. For a number of years broadcast resolution video cameras have used three sensors to maximise the quality of the video images. This allows each sensor to be optimised for a single primary light colour i.e., Red, Green and Blue (RGB). This reduces colour smearing and makes the final pictures appear sharper and better defined. Three sensor designs are now a feature of many consumer camcorders although their advantage is largely lost at lower light levels and also it is rare to find night-vision abilities on such models as they are designed mainly to optimise daylight use or use with powerful video lights.

Large image sensors do have some advantages in video photography. As with digital still cameras, they usually perform better in low light situations as there is a larger available light gathering area, but unfortunately it is never that simple. Most camcorder manufacturers use developments in sensor design to squeeze more pixels into a physically smaller device, which most people prefer to use. A number of recent designs, even those models with night-vision, perform markedly worse than previous physically larger models under the same conditions as the smaller individual pixels mean less light sensitivity. Another feature that most camcorders provide is some form of image stabilisation. In many models this is done optically, by a moving lens or prism system. In other models, image stabilisation is done electronically; the imaging sensor having more pixels than are required to make-up the final picture. These extra pixels are used to reduce the effects of movement of the camera when hand holding. This is an effective system particularly when one is using the camcorder at higher zoom lengths. No stabilisation method will remove all camera motion but having this ability can make a big difference to the final picture quality. A word of caution about these image stabilisation systems regardless of type. Whenever the camcorder is used mounted to a tripod or other form of solid support, even a table top, then any image stabiliser must be turned off. If left on, it can cause the image to appear to move, both sideways and also up and down, as the image stabiliser operation can cause movement within the image. This can, and has, caused many unwary investigators to believe that either their camera was being played with by some unseen force or that some other strange paranormal effect was happening.

Analogue or Digital?

There are two main methods of turning the information from the sensor into the finished moving footage for display on a television, generally known as analogue and digital. All the early models of video camera and camcorder used analogue tape as the recording medium. In analogue systems the information from the sensor is sent as a series of voltages to be written magnetically onto the tape in virtually the same manner as an audiocassette recorder works. This method can permit a lot of electronic noise from the amplification circuits and the tape drive motors to also be recorded. A further drawback is that the tape surface has inherent imperfections within it and these further reduce the quality of the recorded signal. Such systems are termed low-band video and include VHS (both full size and compact VHS-C) along with the smaller 8mm tape format. The camcorder manufacturers used developments from commercial broadcast systems to offer the high-band systems S-VHS / S-VHS-C and Hi8. All these formats separated the signal into two individual components prior to recording, one for the chrominance (colour) the other for the luminance (brightness) component of the picture. This gives less colour smearing and a sharper overall picture although it does need to have a television or computer fitted with dedicated inputs and circuits to handle the picture information in this format. The tape has to be of improved quality too but surface imperfections may still degrade the picture. Analogue recording has another drawback; it is difficult for the user to make high quality copies as in each successive copy generation the voltage signal is reduced.

If copies are ever needed then they should always be made using the original tape to ensure picture quality isn't excessively reduced. Second or third generation copies are usually easy to spot as the colours look washed out and the overall quality of the picture is fuzzy and ill-defined. These recordings are of little use to the paranormal investigator.

Hi-band systems can produce excellent quality pictures and camcorders using such systems are available on Internet auction sites at bargain prices from users who have upgraded to digital models. Provided they are used with high quality tapes purpose made for high-band recording, and the user is aware of the limiting factors, then these models remain a first class video tool for paranormal investigation work.

Digital camcorders have been around for about fifteen years as consumer products. The first models had a massive price tag, well over £1000, but today digital camcorders can be found for very much less and produce footage that early camcorders could not achieve. Digital camcorders sample the information from the image sensor thousands of times every second and this data is sent as a continuous stream of digital data to the recording media. To further reduce picture flaws, the data from the chip is error checked by a microprocessor to ensure that the final data stream is error free before being written to the media. Digital video generates a vast amount of data and therefore some way of compressing the data is needed in order to allow a useable amount of recording time. Essentially, only one picture frame in every twenty-five (1 per second) is fully written to the recording media, this is called a Key Frame. The next twenty-four image frames (sub frames) only have information about the changes to the key frame, meaning that those parts of the image that do not change are not recorded. Key frame compression also reduces memory and recording problems too; if a flaw occurs on a sub frame data section of the recording then it may not affect the final image excessively.

There are a number of recording formats and the most common, solid state or internal hard discs, have now become the standard models that are sold. These have advantages for the paranormal investigator but they also have some distinct problems of their own too. Those models with internal solid-state memory may offer restricted recording times. Some camcorders are fitted with larger internal hard drives or higher capacity solid-state internal memory. These allow very long continuous recordings to be made and eliminate the need to change tapes or discs. Tape formats and DVD formats still exist and are widely available on the second-hand market, for both formats the respective recording media is still easily available. There are some drawbacks to these recording methods, chiefly relating to the tape disc handling and storage and the need to transfer the final footage to a computer.

Digital video, as with digital still photography, needs to be carefully considered in terms of its potential evidential value. Software and in-camera editing means that images can be easily altered either unwittingly or deliberately leading to the creation of false anomalies that some may then consider to be paranormal. Removable media camcorders can allow copies of the original footage to be made whilst retaining the original video file. Sceptics may never be fully convinced, but having the original recording is always a good additional safeguard. With these write to memory systems, the footage must be transferred to either a computer or copied to a DVD, etc. This is now a copy of the original and it becomes more difficult to demonstrate that no additional steps have taken place.

Some Useful Features

Camcorders often have a wide range of features built-in by the manufacturer to make the products more saleable to the consumer. Most are little more than gimmicks and are of little use to the ghost investigator, but one or two are of real benefit and if used correctly can increase the usefulness of the potential video evidence. It is these that we will look at here.

Night Vision and Low Light Systems

Perhaps the best known and most sought after camcorder feature by ghost investigators is an ability to take high quality video footage in conditions of little or even no visible light. Pioneered by Sony, who continue to offer it in some models, NightShot® utilises the inherent sensitivity of all imaging sensors to infrared light. Infrared, if left unfiltered, seriously affects the colour rendition of normally illuminated scenes and so the infrared light is normally filtered out both optically and electronically. Sony made the infrared filtering selectable by the user and at the same time fitted infrared light emitting diodes (LED's) to the camera to provide additional illumination in situations where there was no visible light available. This is a different technique from that used by true night-vision devices which use a technique of amplifying the tiny amounts of light entering the device by means of a phosphor coated tube and photo-multiplier. Originally designed for nature watching or video work in very low light situations Sony has, over the years, incorporated NightShot into many of their consumer camcorder models. NightShot use in paranormal investigations quickly followed the release of the early models, soon becoming one of the most frequently used tools of the modern ghost investigator and a staple of ghost hunting television shows.

These low light infrared systems do permit usable video footage to be obtained in very low light and no (visible) light situations but despite many claims to the contrary, they do not appear to have any special ability to see ghosts or spirits. Inevitably, a lot of theories and ideas to explain their usefulness have sprung up over recent years; most of it nonsense by individuals who base their theories on a poor understanding of the technology they are using or else some pseudo-scientific information that they have picked up along the way. In short, infrared night vision cameras do allow the investigator to record a greater portion of the total light spectrum and allows pictures to be recorded in conditions of no visible light. This has obvious advantage to investigations, for example, observing fraud being performed that may otherwise have gone unnoticed in the dark. It is a simple fact that, to date, there is no evidence that ghosts or spirits emit infrared light or are more visible under infrared lighting conditions, although as one might expect there are some who will no doubt challenge that statement. Ghost investigators are generally considering something that is a true unknown and some may believe that it makes sense to look for evidence of it in as many different ways as we have available. It is however worth noting that witnesses who report visual apparitions as a rule are not using night vision devices and with a few very rare medical exceptions, people do not see very far into the infrared or ultraviolet light spectra. Night vision is an excellent tool for the paranormal investigator but its use confers no special advantage or magical ability to the user. In the past infrared enhanced night vision camcorders were readily obtainable and affordable; the mode was often included in many of Sony's cheaper consumer models. Currently, the mode is only available on a very small number of models, all of which are at the upper end of the product range and therefore expensive. Panasonic also offer a very similar infrared night vision capability in models. These camcorders require the use of an attached external infrared illuminator and like Sony, Panasonic now only includes this mode in their more expensive models. The widespread removal of infrared night vision from many camcorder models has resulted in many ghost investigators who wish to use this technology being forced to seek out discontinued and second hand camcorders or switching to using security camera systems that provide an infrared capability. It is also worth noting that there are several camera manufacturers who somewhat misleadingly have labelled low light modes as being "night vision" on several of their camcorders. These should not be confused with the infrared NightShot system offered by Sony or the similar system used by Panasonic. These other techniques generally work by increasing the gain and slowing the shutter speed in order to make recordings under very low ambient light levels. The results of these increased exposure techniques are of little benefit to paranormal investigators. While they do increase by several orders of magnitude the ability of the camcorder to make images in very low light situations, any movement, either by the camera or by objects in the scene is badly motion blurred and has extremely low definition as a result. Even when the movement is of a known subject, such as a member of the investigation team for example, it is often impossible to identify them on the resulting video footage due to the motion blurring these modes create.

Interval Recording and Motion Detection

This is simply the ability to use the camcorder to make recordings over an extended period of time. Images are recorded for a given period, normally around a second, and then recorded to the media. After a pre-set interval (normally user selectable), a further recording period begins. In this way it is possible for time-lapse animation footage to be obtained. This may be useful where movement of objects within a scene might be suspected but is slow or subtle and may otherwise go unnoticed. For example, filmmakers may use this technique to show flowers opening or clouds rushing across a sky. In some haunting cases, objects such as furniture are described as moving or being moved and using this method will reveal on playback of the recording the movement of any objects as if speeded up and most current models offer this ability. Interval recording can allow recording periods of up to twelve hours to be made using a single one hour tape or memory card and, provided mains power is used, there is no further need to return to the camera.

An important point to note here is that this mode, whilst potentially very useful, is open to relatively easy hoaxing. In the interval between the timed recordings being made it is perfectly possible for someone to move objects without the camera recording their interference. As such, this technique should be applied with additional safeguards such as ensuring the location is fully secured throughout the recording session. Many camcorders and security camera systems provide motion detection. Put simply, the camera continually views the scene sending the data to be scanned by software that looks for differences within successive frames of the scene being observed. Once any change is detected, such as a person entering the room or an object within the scene moving, the software switches on the video recording system. The sensitivity of these systems may be user selectable. The sensitivity to change can be adjusted so that even small objects or small amounts of movement can trigger video recording. In some systems the software can also be set-up to ignore or concentrate on specific areas or targets within the scene. A drawback with motion detection is that the camera has to be continually switched on, making it less suitable for battery-powered operation. As with interval recording methods, it can be relatively easy to hoax the motion detection systems on some camera models but with care it can provide a useful additional capability in some investigation situations.

Progressive Scan Video

Video recording systems rely on fooling the eye by providing a rapid series of still images in turn on the screen. This technique is further enhanced by actually shooting and showing two sequential images on the screen at the same time, a technique known as interleaving as used in 1080i HD video recording. Each alternate horizontal line of pixels shows one of the pair of images. By doing this the motion flicker is reduced and a more convincing smooth flow of motion is obtained. The drawback with this technique is that if the footage contains potential evidence and it becomes necessary to grab a still frame of the anomaly or freeze the television picture there may be blurring or distortion of the picture which is in reality two pictures woven together electronically. Some image editing software packages allow the option to de-interleave the image but this is a compromise option and often results in not very satisfactory stills being available for viewing and interpretation. Many camcorders still record the images using an interleaved technique; first, all the odd numbered horizontal lines of pixels are sampled, followed by the even numbered horizontal lines, thereby effectively recording two images simultaneously. This has the added disadvantage that only half the vertical resolution of the chip is used for any single image thereby reducing the data stream and the processing power that is required to handle it.

A technique borrowed from high-end video cameras is the ability to use the whole chip to make a single image scan, repeating the process 25 times or more per second. This offers better colour saturation and image definition as there are now many more pixels being used for each separate image. The downside is that any movement may appear slightly jerky or a little awkward to the viewer. But for those who are using video cameras to attempt to capture some anomaly and then analyse it afterwards using a computer, this progressive scanning technique allows much better stills to be obtained that are sharper and more defined. Such a feature can be a valuable tool to the paranormal investigator.

Still Pictures

Many digital camcorders provide some method of permitting the user to take still pictures and these may be recorded to either the main media (tape, disc or memory) or to a separate memory card. As previously mentioned, in some Sony models this capability can also be combined with the camcorder's low light mode giving the investigator an effective night vision still camera. To take a still image there is usually a dedicated photo button on the camcorder; effectively meaning it can be used just like any other digital stills camera, in some models this can also be used even whilst taking video footage. This is a useful tool for the investigator who does not wish to carry around a camera and a camcorder. Potentially, even more useful, some camcorders allow stills to be taken from previously recorded video footage as it is played back. The stills capability of some camcorders does make it easy for those investigators who wish to obtain some stills to import them into a computer for further examination or for use on websites and within investigation reports. There is of course a downside to all this, as mentioned earlier. The number of pixels required on a video sensor does not need to be very high and this may result in low resolution still pictures when compared to those taken on dedicated digital still cameras that typically have many more pixels. Some camcorders do offer larger sensors with up to 12 Mega pixels, some even offer other photographic tools such as a built-in flash or the ability to add powerful external flashguns to the camcorder, but such capabilities are not really a substitute for using a proper digital camera. Nonetheless, still taking ability should not be overlooked as a valuable tool for the ghost investigator, providing they are aware of the limitations and work within them.

High Definition (HD) Video

Almost every camcorder and many still cameras offer high definition (HD) video recording these days and this capability is even commonly found on mobile phones. HD is everywhere and it does provide a better picture quality than standard video formats. However, HD may not be quite as impressive as first appears. There are several standards for HD video i.e., 720i or 720p and 1080i or 1080p (sometimes called full HD). The number in the designation refers to the number of vertical lines within each picture frame and the letter suffix indicates if the method of producing the picture uses interleafed (i) or progressive scanning (p). High definition video also has much lower picture resolution than most cheap compact digital still cameras; a full HD frame contains just 1920 x 1080 lines which is the equivalent of just over 2 Mega-pixels - 2,073,600 to be exact.

Photography and Video Overall Conclusions

Paranormal investigation is primarily all about gathering information. Visual information can be amongst the most compelling and useful we can provide. The sounds recorded on audiocassette may be of ghostly footsteps along a deserted corridor but, without the images to prove it was an empty corridor, it is of poor evidential value. Picture and video evidence is admittedly easy to fake and there are countless examples of such trickery around but this has been the case almost since the invention of photography and video. With the ownership of digital cameras now commonplace, it is almost childlike simplicity to create ghost photographs in a couple of minutes on the home computer or smart device. This needs to be recognised and addressed by the investigator and with some consideration it is possible to design methods and protocols to at least reduce such accusations. Regardless of whatever method is used to obtain the images, be they moving or still, the investigator needs to be fully aware of the abilities and weaknesses of their chosen tool. A thorough read of the instruction manual and knowledge of all the controls and what they do is an essential first step. There are many books and websites that explain in detail the mechanisms and features of film, digital, and video cameras and the wise investigator should use these to increase their knowledge.

The human eye has over 120 million light receptors, approximately equivalent to over 80 Megapixels, film cameras have an equivalent of around half this amount, and digital images contain, on average, less than twenty per cent of the overall available information contained in any scene. It is therefore easy to understand that a lot of potentially valuable information has been lost whenever we view a photograph or look at video footage. However, both film and digital sensor do have the ability to record information that cannot be seen by the human eye. Both methods see light differently than humans do and the use of variable shutter speeds can allow motion to be frozen or blurred. When used sensibly and with caution, any camera can be a very valuable addition to the paranormal investigators arsenal. Careful selection of the camera and even more care taken with its use may greatly assist an investigation. Failure to do so will increase the risk that the resulting images and footage will only serve to confuse and mislead.

CHAPTER 16

TECHNIQUES FOR VIDEO AND PHOTOGRAPHY

D ifferent types of camera and video camcorder have already been considered and their respective merits and weaknesses discussed but it is also worth considering some of the photographic accessories that are commonly used. It is insufficient to simply take a camera and use it without some thought being given to the techniques and tools required to obtain the best possible images, regardless of which type of camera is selected. An in-depth consideration of photographic techniques would fill an entire volume and investigators are strongly advised to carry out further reading and to experiment with their own equipment.

Tripods and Other Supports

There are many situations where it may be necessary for the investigator to handhold their camera or camcorder. The simple rule here is to hold the camera as steadily as possible. This becomes critical in low lighting situations when the camera requires longer exposure times. Many digital cameras, especially compact models and mobile phone cameras, lack a viewfinder and rely on a large screen to view the scene and compose the picture. This almost encourages the user to hold the camera at arm's length and greatly increases the risk of camera movement during picture taking. With smaller cameras, many people have a tendency to hold them in one hand making camera movement during exposure even more likely. It is situation that can be commonly observed during ghost investigations, the investigators snapping away with almost no thought being given to the way that they are holding and supporting the camera. It is therefore hardly surprising that so many pictures that purport to show anomalies are, upon closer examination, found to be merely the result of camera movement when the picture was taken.

During ghost investigations it is often necessary or desirous to make video recordings over long periods of time. Therefore, some means of supporting the camcorder is essential for successfully obtaining good quality images. Tripods are the most common form of camera support used and many investigators will simply buy the cheapest model they can find without giving this common item very much thought. A good tripod is one of the more important items in the investigators kit and the right model will make a substantial improvement to the quality and therefore the usefulness of any video footage.

The first consideration when buying a tripod is its weight; ideally this should be the heaviest model possible. Weight adds stability and reduces unwanted movement or vibrations of the camera. Some tripods have a small hook underneath to allow the user to hang their camera bag or some other weight to add to the tripod mass but it is also a simple matter to drape a camera bag over the tripod to increase its weight. Consider the construction of the tripod legs; ideally these should have strong locks on the leg extensions to provide their slow collapse and additional bracing between the legs to the centre pole provides better stability. Extend the legs to their maximum length and check how high the camera platform is from the floor. Most tripod models have a central pole that can be raised, but it is always better to get as much of the overall height by using the legs as the single centre pole is inherently less stable and so should be kept as short as possible to minimise camera movement and vibration. The tripod legs should have rubber feet to prevent slipping and of course preventing damage to floors and carpets at locations. Some models provide optional spiked metal feet that may have some advantages on stone or concrete flooring at locations where damage to the floor is not an issue.

Tripods come with two distinct types of head, the part to which the camera is attached. Heads that are designed primarily for use with stills cameras have three axes of motion, *Pan*, (side to side) *Tilt*, (up and down) and *Rotate* which allows the camera to be turned through 90 degrees from landscape to portrait format. Dedicated video camera heads often only have two axes of motion, *Pan* and *Tilt*. Rotating a video camera only causes the final image to be turned on its side, great for special effects and music videos but not much use to paranormal investigators. In reality it doesn't matter too much which type of head is used as the camera will normally be locked into one position, however, there may be a requirement to pan the camcorder around in order to cover a second area or to follow some movement. In these situations, a dedicated video head can offer some advantages. Video heads are designed to allow panning to take place without jerkiness. One other type of tripod head is the ball and socket, which allows the camera to be moved through a continuous range of positions in all three axes. Many tripods also have some form of removable mounting plate that allow the camera to be removed quickly from the tripod. This is a useful feature that allows the investigator to easily change the camera between hand-held and tripod mounted use and when it is necessary to access the camera to in order to change the batteries or the memory media. It is usually possible to purchase additional mounting plates for each tripod allowing the same tripod to be quickly swopped between different cameras.

Basic tripods are inexpensive but in reality these models are best avoided. They are often flimsily made and can cause the camera to react to even small amounts of vibration, which may produce images that can appear to be anomalous. The weight of the camera might also cause movement of the tripod head or joints. However, even a cheap tripod is generally better than simply putting the camera down onto a table, chair, or even the floor. Cheaper tripods may be useful when supporting a lightweight CCTV camera now favoured by many investigators. Another type of tripod that is available is the table top model. Most often, these are simply three small legs, perhaps with a small extension available and a small ball and socket head. They are designed for small cameras and really are not suitable for camcorders or larger cameras. They can be used in emergency situations but it is important to check beforehand that the camera will be stable and that the tripod can safely carry the weight of the camera. Look for those models that offer the widest spread of the legs and avoid the lightweight plastic models that are sometimes found cheaply on the high street.

In addition to tripods, camera clamps can also be a useful addition. These generally have a basic camera mount attached to some form of clamping mechanism. Many manufacturers offer models that are reasonably priced and can be fitted with a good quality three axis head. Clamps are excellent in situations where it is not possible to place a full size tripod or where it is important to securely mount the camera onto some item of furniture or a structure at the location in order to obtain a viewpoint impossible with an ordinary tripod. Of course, the investigator must be aware of the potential for these devices to cause damage to the items they are attached to.

Other types of camera support that are available such as beanbags and suction cup mounts can also be a valuable addition and will always be better than just simply putting the camera down on a surface somewhere. Having a range of camera support options available increases the likelihood of finding the most suitable for specific needs. One final and very important consideration is to ensure that there is at least one tripod or mount available for every camera and camcorder.

Lenses and Lights

Just about every video camcorder has a zoom lens these days. Many digital and 35mm stills cameras also come with some form of zoom lens as standard too. Mobile phone cameras and the latest body mounted 'action-cams' still tend to have a fixed lens but may offer a digital zoom option.

A zoom lens allows the user to pre-select the area that will be photographed and it is rare that the zoom will be used during the actual image taking process. DSLR's and the similar Compact System Cameras (CSC's) together with a number of very expensive video cameras permit the lens to be changed but compact and hybrid models use a permanently fitted zoom lens that is designed to provide adequate general coverage. The telephoto setting is not usually needed for the majority of ghost investigations, but there may be some situations when it is necessary or advantageous. Telephoto settings can be used to isolate one part of a scene for example or when it is not possible to place the camera sufficiently close to the area of interest. The digital zoom option provided on many cameras, camcorders, and in particular mobile phone cameras should be ignored as this simply electronically enlarges the central portion of the image, seriously reducing the image quality. Most camera manufacturers and camera accessory makers offer a range of secondary lenses that simply screw onto the front of the existing lens using the filter thread. Typically, these may be a 2x telephoto adaptor and a 0.6x wide-angle adaptor, which gives a wider coverage. Of the two types, the 0.6x wide angle is by probably the most useful for ghost investigation. The standard lens is rarely sufficiently wide enough to permit an area to be fully observed, a common problem in small rooms where it may not be possible to get the camera far enough back to allow the full scene to be adequately covered. Fitting a wide-angle adaptor to the lens will increase the amount of the scene that can be observed and recorded and can allow entire objects such as items of furniture or doorways to be seen, when it may not be otherwise possible. The wide-angle adaptor is an extremely useful addition and is simple to use, only usually needing to be screwed to the front of the lens in order to work. Basic models are inexpensive but buying one made by the camera manufacturer that has been specifically designed to work with the camera will produce better quality images. Some wide-angle adaptors also have additional lens elements designed to reduce some of the noticeable curving that occurs, particularly toward the edge of the image. Some caution is needed when using any accessory lens, however, their use adds additional lens elements and increases the risk of lens reflections and refractions. They may also block some of the other features of the camcorder such as camera mounted or built-in lights, creating areas of shadow and poor illumination. They may also cause the camera to become front-heavy and unstable on its support.

Regardless of any discussion regarding the pros and cons, it remains the case that the majority of ghost investigations take place in conditions of near darkness. In such circumstances, it is essential to have some extra lighting available in order to successfully obtain a good quality image. Stills cameras generally have a built-in flash or the facility to attach a flashgun. If the camera only has a built-in flash and no means of adding a more powerful unit, it is possible to increase the flash range by using a light activated slave flash. Slave flash is available in two forms, either as a slave cell that can be used to fire any attached flashgun, or in the form of a dedicated slave flash, normally designed for use with compact cameras. The light from built-in flash triggers a light activated switch within the slave unit that then fires the secondary flash. Several slave flashes can be used together and positioned, wherever needed, allowing large areas to be successfully illuminated. Some camcorders also have both built-in flash units and the ability to use an add-on flash. These operate only with the still picture-taking facility of the camcorder but can be used with secondary and slave units in the same way as stills cameras. For video footage, lights are readily available and, depending upon the make and model, can either be directly attached to the camera using the camera's battery or can be attached to an external bracket and use their own battery or mains electrical power. They are available in a range of power settings from small 3-watt units up to units giving more than 1000 watts of light. There is no limit to the number of external video lights that can be used, so it is a straightforward matter to fully illuminate any size space.

Although virtually discontinued by the manufacturer, still the most commonly used type of camcorder for ghost investigations are those Sony models that offer the NightShot® mode. These have built-in infrared LED's on the front of the camcorder that provide sufficient infrared light and allow a nearby scene to be recorded adequately in conditions of very low or no ambient visible lighting. There are several makers who offer additional IR lighting options to improve the usefulness of infrared night vision equipped cameras. Some models have the ability to interface directly with the camera. This type of accessory light can be simply attached to the camera and uses the camera battery to power the light. For camcorders without a suitable interface, accessory lights are available that can be attached to the camera via the tripod socket, powered from a separate battery. A further option to consider is customised video lighting. In situations where the requirement is for powerful visible lighting, then halogen work lights which are sold in many DIY stores are perfectly adequate. These are generally sold complete with a stand or tripod, they are inexpensive and available in single or twin light units. They do have some things that need to be considered; they produce a lot of heat and so need to be used with care, and adjustment to the camcorder's white balance settings may also be required although most of the modern automatic white balance settings will cope well enough. Work lights have started to become available that use an array of powerful light emitting diodes that require less power, and some have the option to use a built-in rechargeable battery.

Infrared lighting is a bit more specialised but can still be achievable on a budget. The first option is to consider security lighting, although this can be expensive, but there are dealers who specialise in second hand and surplus stock at reduced cost. It is wise to check the power requirements of security lighting; some units operate on 24 or even 48 volts and require the use of special transformers. It is also important to check the wavelength of the lighting; infrared security lights are available in a range of wavelengths from around 700nm to over 1000nm. Consumer night vision camcorders are optimised for lighting of around 750nm and infrared light above this wavelength cannot be properly seen by the camcorder. A second option worth considering is to fit normal visible wavelength lights with infrared pass filters. These filters are available from a number of online retailers in the form of plastic sheets that can be simply cut to fit and then attached in front of the light. This option does need to be carefully considered as some lights generate a lot of heat that may melt the filter or damage the light. This method is not suitable for fitting to halogen work lights as they generate an excessive amount of heat but work lights that use LED's typically produce much less heat and may be suitable. The total amount of light produced by a lamp is reduced when any filter is fitted but the technique can still provide a useful increase in the range and usability. Glass infrared filters are also available and these can be found in sizes that are compatible with some lights and even some models of torch such as the Maglite® range. Again, check the wavelength of the filter regardless of what it is made from and be prepared to experiment.

For those who are comfortable with a soldering iron, then the option of building suitable camera lights may be attractive. Electronic component dealers offer infrared and visible light LED's for just a few pounds each, together with all the additional parts needed to make a custom lighting set-up. By grouping numbers of these LED's together in an array it is possible to manufacturer lights that are specifically tailored to the requirements of the camera, the investigation, or even to a specific location. For a small camera mountable light, generally between 6 and 10 LED's will be sufficient to make a light that will provide illumination for between 3 and 5 metres from the camera. Adding more LED's will increase the amount of illumination but won't add much to the distance. More powerful LED's are available that cost more and will provide illumination at an increased distance. Power can be supplied either from a mains supply or by using a battery. Finally, there are a number of specialist lighting manufacturers who can supply off the shelf or custom designed lighting units that are suitable for investigation uses. Some domestic and commercial security alarm companies may also offer similar lighting solutions.

Technique

Regardless of whether the investigator uses a stills camera or a video camcorder, having a good technique is the most important part of maximising the chances for obtaining evidentially useful images. Simply owning the best camera in the world is no guarantee that it will provide images that are helpful to an investigator. The first rule has to be, support the camera, either learn to handhold it properly in order to minimise camera movement, or use a tripod or some form of solid support for the camera. Too many potentially useful images and footage are rendered useless because the camera was moving around at the time of taking thus causing motion blurring to the image. If using a camera or camcorder that uses any form of image stabilisation (digital or optical) make sure it is turned off when using the camera on a tripod or other support. Image stabilisers can cause movement within the image as they attempt to stabilise the picture in a non-moving camera. They are designed to work in situations when the camera is being handheld and many manufacturers provide a warning in the instruction manual against their use in such situations.

Set the Date and Time Correctly

All digital stills and video cameras allow the date and time to be recorded electronically with the image, even if it is not displayed. The date and time are important items of information. If they are incorrectly set then it will seriously jeopardise the credibility and the evidential value of the images. Date and time recording is a feature of many electronic devices and it is vital that they are set correctly. In situations where several recorded items of information may be coincident with one another, such as a recording from a sound recorder and a picture from a stills camera, it would be impossible to demonstrate that they took place at the same time if the date and time have not been correctly set. This same caveat applies equally to the investigators notes and watches used to note the time must all be accurately set to the same time as that of all recording devices.

Be Familiar with the Camera and How to Operate it.

Remember RTFM? Know what each mode and function does. Keep the manual in the camera bag so that it can be referred to whenever necessary. Set the camera to the appropriate mode and required settings for the situation in which it is being used. Modern cameras have fully automatic settings that will normally produce good quality images without further intervention but, sometimes, in order to obtain the best quality images, the investigator may need to make additional selection of appropriate controls. Generally, it is best to avoid automatic slow shutter modes as although they will make the overall image brighter in dim conditions, this is at the expense of blurring any movement within the image. Auto focus may also cause problems, particularly in low light levels or when different wavelengths of lighting are in use at the same time. Such situations may cause the camera to suddenly lose focus or begin to hunt around for a point of focus. In these situations, if possible, switch the camera to focus manually on an area or object of particular interest. On some models zooming in fully, focussing, then zooming out to obtain the required viewpoint, can be the most accurate way to achieve this but with some cameras the lens may shift focus as it is zoomed thus rendering this method useless. Experiment with the camera and read the manual (RTFM).

Positioning the Camera

Placement of the camera is an important part of the image making process. This is especially true with video cameras that use auxiliary lighting or have night vision ability. It can be extremely helpful to view a scene from several camera angles at the same time. Many investigators simply aim cameras across a room or space. If the cameras are using additional lighting then what normally happens is one camera simply dazzles the other and this leads to a degraded overexposed image and sometimes a completely useless piece of footage as both cameras are effectively blinded by the lighting on the other. It is much better to position cameras at forty-five degrees to one another whilst locating the cameras on the same side of the room or space so that their lights do not interfere with one another. Careful placement and checking of the image through the viewfinder will enable the investigator to still obtain excellent coverage of the area. When using multiple cameras these same principles still apply. With still cameras this may not be such an issue unless they are set-up so that the two flashguns fire at the same time, perhaps using some form of motion triggering. The placement of additional lighting also needs to be carefully considered for exactly the same reasons and careful positioning is important to prevent blinding cameras by shining the light directly toward the lens.

Generally speaking, cameras are mounted into the corners of a space to maximise the angle of view from the lens and this is a good rule of thumb. It is also good practise to mount the camera as high as possible which can further increase the viewing angle across a room or space. Tripods rarely extend sufficiently to allow very high positioning of a camera and in such circumstances a workable solution may be to use a heavy-duty microphone stand fitted with a camera clamp mount. The stand needs to be sufficiently robust enough to safely hold the weight of the chosen camera and minimise any movement due to vibrations or passers-by. It is an effective solution in some situations and works best with lightweight cameras. Microphone stands, especially those that have an expending boom arm, can often reach heights of over seven feet from the floor. The same method can also be useful in situations where space is too restricted to allow a normal tripod to be used or where the camera needs to be placed in awkward places.

Viewpoint

Randomly placing cameras around a location will rarely produce anything worthwhile and it is worth restating that the reason for using any camera should be on the basis of a witness previously reporting a visual experience. Therefore, consider the witness information and try to match the viewpoint and perspective of that of witnesses in any given area. Obviously, it is also necessary to ensure that the key areas of interest can be clearly viewed by the cameras and carefully checking the scene through the viewfinder is an important step whenever positioning any camera.

Camera Care

A camera might be considered as an essential tool for every investigator so it is surprising how often I see investigators treating their cameras with little regard or thought. Every camera, regardless of the cost needs to have a clean optical system in order to produce the best results, proper care and maintenance is therefore an important consideration but lenses can often be seen covered in finger-marks. Often, investigators will pack away their equipment following the investigation and not open the boxes again until a few hours before the next one. I rarely ever see a lens cloth or cleaning kit anywhere in these investigation kits. Batteries need to be freshly charged and inserted before every investigation, something all investigators are generally aware of. However, investigators are less aware that different battery types require different regimes in order to maintain good battery performance. In situations where it may be an extended period between uses, it might for instance be necessary to remove the batteries or to allow them to partially discharge, or perhaps to ensure that they are not stored away fully discharged. The user manual for each camera will always include a section on caring for the camera and the batteries should be used as a basis for implementing a good care regime for the camera.

CHAPTER 17

IMAGES: WHAT NEXT?

Once a picture or video has been taken, the obvious first step is to look at the picture or view the footage to see if anything of interest has been captured. However, this step has several pitfalls that need to be addressed in order to prevent important information being missed or too much significance being given to apparent anomalies within the picture.

The first consideration is that of the viewer, the person who is looking at the pictures or video footage. It is highly probable that they are aware they are looking at pictures that have been taken either at a haunted location or during an investigation and, accordingly, they will become more likely to look for anything within the pictures that they do not expect to be there. Pictures that are taken without prior knowledge of a location's reputation rarely have the same level or degree of scrutiny applied to them. Many photographs and video films have artefacts and anomalies simply as a result of the processes involved in their making or introduced by either the camera or the environment. If the viewer is aware of the haunted reputation of the location or was part of the investigation team then they will have a higher desire to seek out anything unusual. The viewer's expectation and personal beliefs will also affect the way in which they assess the information within a picture or video.

Looking through hundreds of pictures or countless hours of video footage is a pretty mind-numbing task and is beyond the capability of most people to undertake effectively. Breaking up the task into smaller periods with suitable rest periods is a much more effective method and ensures that the viewer does not lose concentration and potentially miss something that is significant. It might be better to split the task between several people, or it might be worth considering another approach entirely. By carefully considering the information from witnesses beforehand and targeting the resources in a more focussed manner it is likely that the number of pictures or the hours of video footage can be significantly reduced to a much more manageable amount. Is there truly anything to be gained by placing a number of cameras around a location in areas where no witness has ever reported seeing anything unusual?

Sometimes the picture or video footage was not taken by the investigator or during an investigation. Often, pictures are sent to investigators for their scrutiny and opinion. In these instances, the first step is to consider and ask why the picture or video was taken in the first place? Does the picture show something that would normally be photographed, for example, a family member or a holiday scene, or does it seem to show something that one would not normally expect to be photographed? By and large, most people routinely do not take pictures of things such as the empty corner of a room or an item of furniture that has no artistic or historic merit. By asking basic questions about the situation in which the picture or video was taken, it will provide important additional information that can be useful in determining the nature of the presented anomaly. Additional important questions to consider are why the person considers the picture to be significant? Do they believe it shows something anomalous? Why are they requesting your opinion?

The answers to these questions can provide a great deal of valuable information for the investigator. It will offer insight into the thoughts and wishes of the photographer and will allow consideration to be made about the expectations and beliefs of the photographer and it also may reveal much about the anomaly itself. For instance, it has previously been noted how easy it is for anomalies to be created using apps or photo editing. It may therefore simply be the case that the photographer has created the anomaly for a number of personal reasons and merely wishes the investigator to add some degree of credibility. It might be the case that the photographer has already decided that the image is of a genuine ghost or other anomaly and wish this to be confirmed. The photographer might be seeking to use the photograph for personal gain in some way and again hopes to add to its authenticity by having someone examine it further. In other instances, it might be that the person is genuinely perplexed and surprised by the picture or footage they have taken and are requesting assistance to understand it. With digital imagery, there is also a great deal of information that can be gained by examining the information that is contained within the data attached to the picture or video. This contains basic information such as the date and time that the picture or forage was taken and details about the camera and the settings used. By comparing this data with the account of the photographer, discrepancies can sometimes be found between the two. Notwithstanding the fact that many people never bother to set the date and time correctly, it can reveal the shutter speed, if flash has been used, the focal length, the lens aperture, and a great deal more. In modern cameras and especially mobile phones it can also reveal the precise location where a photograph or video was taken, even the direction in which the camera was being pointed as many cameras now have highly accurate GPS tracking and built-in compasses that store information into the picture or video file.

It is only after any image has gone through the above stages that the investigator need concern themselves with using any software that may assist them with determining the nature of any apparent anomaly.

Most people do not have specialist image enhancement software or the special skills needed to apply the various techniques of image and video analysis correctly. Instead they are most likely to use one of the many image-editing programmes that are available including the photo editing software contained within the Windows and OS-X operating systems. The original image is likely to already be in digital format direct from the camera or it may need to be scanned and digitised by using a scanner. Video too will need to be imported into the computer prior to any examination being carried out. One important point here is to ensure that any subsequent work is only carried out on a copy and never on the original file itself. The original file should be stored; ideally this should be on the original media such as the memory card that was used in the camera. In many instances this is not possible and the media may not be removable, or it may already have been copied off prior to the investigator receiving it. In these cases, the investigator should treat the first copy they have as being the original, hopefully any process of making that copy will also have preserved the important file data, the (.Exif file). In instances where this is not available or when the image has been digitised from a print by use of a scanner, the investigator will be forced to proceed without any additional file information.

Image editing software has several potentially useful tools available but the user must exercise great care as many of these tools work by altering the image, sometimes irrevocably. For this reason, the user must always make a copy of the original. This ensures that any changes they make can always be referred to the original image or video. Initially the user should simply confine himself or herself to looking at the picture or watching the video and resist the temptation to alter anything. It is also helpful to ask others to view it too. If others are asked, then it is important to avoid telling them what it is they are supposed to be looking for. It is an easy mistake to inadvertently change someone's opinion by priming them beforehand; "Can you see the figure?" Look at the strange movement on the bed". After they have examined the picture or footage, ask them to note down their thoughts and compare them to your own. Do they agree with what you saw? Did they entirely miss the anomaly? This is an important step and should not be overlooked. The fact that the other person agrees with your opinion, sees what you see, or disagrees entirely is not evidence of the paranormality or otherwise of any anomaly but it does provide some helpful information that can be considered.

If it is decided that altering the image might be helpful in revealing more information about the anomaly, then the investigator should confine their activities changing only the most basic image values and then only by the smallest degree. Too many are tempted to simply drag control sliders around in the hope that the truth about the anomaly will suddenly reveal itself. It is important to bear in mind that no matter how objective and unbiased an investigator may consider himself or herself to be it is almost inevitable that to a greater or lesser degree they will try to make the anomaly conform to their own expectations. If they believe it represents or resembles a human form or figure, then there is strong likelihood that they will end up adjusting the image until it closely resembles that notion. It should be preferred that two people independently and separately review every picture or image, this won't prevent an individual's tendency to make anomalies conform to expectation, but to a degree it may reduce the effects.

Assuming that any alterations to the image or footage are needed then one value only should be changed, by a small degree. The result should be saved as a new image file using a file labelling system that is meaningful, i.e., *contrast1.jpg*, at the same time a written note should be made with information about the actual change made *"contrast1.jpg - contrast increased by 10%"*, etc. Continue in this manner for every change that is made naming the files sequentially and linking the files to the notes. This method allows every change made to be fully accountable. This technique is how a forensic image analyst works and using this method will ensure that the images or footage will have the highest possible value in supporting the investigation results and conclusions. Other photo editing controls, such as those relating to individual colour channels, i.e., red, green, and blue (RGB) should only be used with great care as the user risks changing the appearance and the way it may be perceived. Editing options that radically alter an image such as those that clone or remove parts of the image should be avoided altogether. It is all too common to see an image presented as evidential and which has been altered or enhanced in order to demonstrate the reality of a claim that is being made or to support a belief or assumption made prior to any process of examination. Almost without exception, any examination relating to images will be a subjective process. Software, however complex or specialised, will only assist the investigator towards an interpretation of what is seen. The final decision is almost invariably a human decision and of course that means it usually remains open to further questioning. It is not within the scope of this chapter to discuss methods or techniques of image analysis in depth or detail, but to raise awareness that to do anything other than the most basic adjustment of the brightness or contrast is a highly specialist technique that requires additional training and software. Many investigators may claim that they have analysed an image and shown it to be beyond explanation and therefore proof of the paranormal. Unless they are able to explain and demonstrate their protocols, methods, the individual steps that have been taken, together with the qualifications of the person undertaking the image examination, then the claim should be considered as being unreliable. Many images and videos are presented, almost daily, on social media but is there any real value of a picture in which the anomaly needs to be highlighted by placing a red circle around it to draw the viewer's attention?

Can Ghosts be Photographed?

In the 1860's the American photographer William Mumler set up his psychic photograph studio, providing many of his numerous clients with seemingly convincing photographic proof of deceased loved ones appearing alongside the living in the portraits he took. The craze for spirit photography rapidly spread. In London, Frederick Hudson set up in business offering this service, quickly followed by Richard Boursnell and, in Paris, Edouard Buguet had many rich and aristocratic clients. For the most part, these early psychic photographs were simply double exposures but later, more elaborate techniques were used to produce convincing fakes. One by one the psychic photographers were shown to be fraudulent. Harry Price was one of several dedicated psychical investigators whose work exposed the frauds; Price devotes many pages to the methods and techniques used by the fraudulent photographers in his book *Confessions of a Ghost Hunter*. Other researchers were perhaps more inclined to believe that ghosts and spirits could be photographed. Sir Arthur Conan-Doyle, creator of Sherlock Holmes, was fooled several times. For example, in 1909, the image of a monk was convincingly captured in a photograph taken during an overnight ghost vigil at Brockley Manor, near Bristol. The partial but undeniably recognisable figure was for many years presented in talks and lectures by Conan-Doyle as convincing proof. In 1929, he presented the picture during a lecture in Kenya only to be confronted by a member of the audience who explained that it had been a student prank that used a prepared double exposure and that he himself had been the student who had dressed up as the monk. Despite the reality of the hoax being revealed, the photograph of the ghostly monk of Brockley Manor is frequently reproduced together with the claim that it shows a genuine ghost.

There are however a number of photographs purporting to show ghosts that have not been satisfactorily explained. For example, a photograph taken in 1891 in the library of Combermere Abbey, Cheshire, seemingly shows the partial apparition of a figure said to be the deceased Lord Combermere seated in his favourite chair. The picture has never been fully explained but it has often been suggested to be the result of either a double or long exposure.

The ghost of Lord Combermere?

Perhaps the most famous ghost photograph of all was taken on 19th September 1936, at Raynham Hall in Norfolk by photographer Captain Provand who was taking photographs at the hall as part of a commission for *Country Life* Magazine. The photograph that is said to show a ghostly figure known as 'The Brown Lady' has to date never been fully explained despite several attempts to cast doubt upon its authenticity.

The Brown Lady of Raynham Hall

Thousands of photographs have been presented over the years claiming to show genuine apparitions and, whilst many appear convincing, only a comparatively small number have ever been properly examined and have withstood scrutiny and found to be free from obvious fraud or photographic error.

Evidence of ghosts obtainable by photographic means may be possible but, so far, and despite many thousands of photographs being offered as evidence and claiming to show ghosts, there remains a lack convincing proof.

Photography does have an important part to play in the overall investigative process however. Ghosts and spirits may be camera shy and elusive but the apparently abnormal movement of objects has been documented using photography such as in the work of the Scole group. The group, who gained their name from the Norfolk village in which they met, began working together in 1993 and over the following four years produced effects that they claimed were the result of spirit forces directly affecting physical objects. Poltergeist manifestations have also been documented with cameras, such as at Manheim in Germany and in the famous Enfield case, where instances of the abnormal movement of objects and indeed people have been recorded. Photography has also been a valuable tool for revealing fraud, the spirit of Katie King and medium Helen Duncan both succumbing to careful and sometimes surreptitious use of the investigator's camera and ghost investigation photography continues to produce contentious claims. More recently there have been pictures and videos that claim to show ghosts, shadow people, and of course the Orb phenomena. Orbs continue to be hotly debated by ghost investigators despite them having been shown to be simply the result of airborne particles and moisture. As photographic technology advances and new photographic equipment is developed it might be the case that other claimed paranormal anomalies will be shown to be mundane in their origin or it might just happen that a truly convincing photograph of a ghost will be produced.

CHAPTER 18

LET THERE BE LIGHT

Increasingly, ghost investigators have started to use modified cameras that are claimed to visualise those portions of the light spectrum, which are normally invisible to the human eye in their search for evidence of the paranormal. Initially, this was made possible by manufacturers such as Sony and Panasonic who fit their cameras and video cameras with an infrared night vision mode that uses the inherent sensitivity of the sensor to respond to light outside the visible spectrum thereby permitting pictures to be taken in apparent almost total darkness. Investigators have now turned their attentions toward photographing the ultraviolet spectrum or claiming to photograph the entire light spectrum from the ultraviolet through visible and into the infrared, referred to as *'Full Spectrum'* photography and video.

The Invisible Light Spectra

Light forms part of the overall electromagnetic spectrum and comprises a series of waves of differing frequencies or wavelengths; usually stated in nano-metres (nm). A nano-metre is 1×10^{-9} Metres. Usually, the colour of the wavelength is substituted for a specified wavelength i.e., Red, Green, or Blue when describing the frequency of light. The visible light spectra are those wavelengths of light that can be detected by normal human vision and lie between approximately the upper part of the ultraviolet range (380nm) and the bottom of the infrared (760nm). The shortest wavelengths are seen as deep violet, whilst the longer wavelengths appear as a deep red. Beyond this visible spectra are two regions of invisible light, the ultraviolet (UV) and the infrared (IR). Ultraviolet light extends down from the visible spectra toward x-rays, whilst the infrared region extends up into the thermal radiation spectrum.

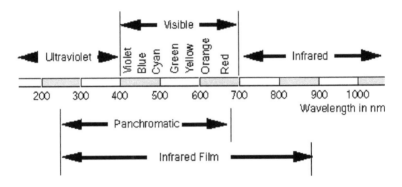

The visible light spectrum and beyond

Photographing the Invisible - Ultraviolet

Johann Ritter discovered the existence of the ultraviolet spectrum in 1801. It is considered to be from around 10nm to 400nm, the upper regions of which extend just into the visible portion of the light spectrum. Physicists often further divide the ultraviolet spectrum into four bands. In ascending order of wavelength they are the: UVD, UVC, UVB and UVA. All wavelengths of ultraviolet light have harmful exposure effects including skin burning, cellular and eye damage. Accordingly, sustained or cumulative exposure to ultraviolet light should be avoided. It is only the UVA band (320nm-400nm) within which photography is considered possible. It is also worth noting that certain materials may be excited by the high-energy ultraviolet radiation and emits light within the visible spectrum, this effect is known as fluorescence. Ultraviolet photography dates to 1903, the year when Professor Robert Wood demonstrated a filter that passed ultraviolet light whilst excluding visible light. When undertaking photography, it is necessary to fit the camera with a filter that permits only the UVA light to pass but blocks all other wavelengths, this is known as an ultraviolet transmission filter. This should not be confused with the 'UV' (or Skylight) filter that is often added by photographers to the front of a lens in order to block ultraviolet light from reaching the film or sensor and preventing a blue cast as blue shadows can often spoil colour photographs taken in bright daylight or when using electronic flash. Camera and lens manufacturers also normally add an ultraviolet absorbent coating to the lens optics which may be seen as a purple, blue, or green sheen on the front of a lens when it is viewed from the front in bright light. Regardless of the presence or otherwise of any ultraviolet absorbing lens coating, the glass used to make the individual lens elements increasingly absorb ultraviolet light below around 320nm, eventually becoming opaque to those wavelengths below about 200nm. Specialist ultraviolet camera lenses made of Quartz or Fluorite crystal do exist for specialist medical photography applications and these can pass light down to around 150nm, such lenses are enormously expensive to produce and buy. Although there are a small number of specialist cameras and lenses available, to undertake successful ultraviolet photography can be challenging, as a result of the inherent properties of the materials within the optics of consumer cameras. Moreover, in recent years the availability of ultraviolet transmitting filters has greatly diminished and many manufacturers have now ceased production entirely. Kodak continues to make the Wratten 18A filter in a limited number of sizes and this has become the standard ultraviolet transmission filter, allowing UVA light between 300nm and 400nm to pass whilst blocking the visible light spectrum. The Wratten 18A is also commonly called the Wood's filter named after Prof. Wood. However, the Wratten 18A and many other similar filters do not just permit UVA light to pass but they also permit Infrared light in the 700nm-900nm region to pass.

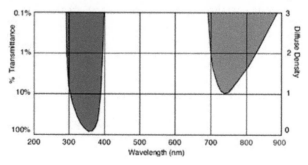

The Transmission Spectra of a Wratten 18A (Wood's) Filter

Photographing the Invisible, Infrared

Discovered by William Herschel in 1800, the infrared spectrum extends upwards from around 700nm. Infrared photography is principally concerned with the near infrared region (700nm-1400nm). The infrared spectrum above 1400nm can be visualised but requires a specially made converter tube, this technique is known as infrared thermography (commonly called Thermal Imaging). Infrared photography is not new; infrared sensitive films have been readily available since the 1920's. Early applications for infrared photography included the forensic examination of documents and paintings to detect fraud and, pioneer psychical investigators such as Harry Price, also used infrared photography as it permitted photographs to be taken in the prevailing conditions of near darkness during séances. Infrared photography makes use of both direct and reflected light, although direct imaging is more consistent with thermography. The simplest technique for infrared photography uses an infrared transmission filter fitted over the lens. Several filter types are available that permit more or less of the infrared spectrum to pass. The most commonly used filter is the Hoya R72 or equivalent which permits all infrared light above 720nm to pass, other types include the R85 (850nm) and R95 (950nm) filters which block successively more of the IR wavelengths. For specialist applications, filters that block all infrared light below 1000nm such as the R100 may be used.

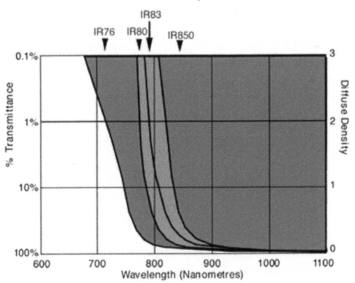

The Transmission Spectra of various IR pass filters

Sources of Invisible Light

The Sun is the most obvious source of illumination, daylight being an excellent source of both ultraviolet and infrared light, even under cloudy skies or indoors. Indoors, specialised lighting is normally required. For ultraviolet photography the most practical illumination is typically a specially constructed ultraviolet fluorescent tube or Black light, which is both inexpensive and efficient. Xenon flash tubes fitted to many cameras may also be a good source of UVA light although manufacturers normally apply an ultraviolet absorbing coating to the flash in order to prevent an oversaturation of blue in colour photography. Ultraviolet light emitting diodes have become available in recent years and provide controlled emissions, but their comparatively low output makes them suitable only for short-range applications. Continuous sources of high intensity ultraviolet light require care when working with to avoid skin burning or eye damage. Tungsten and halogen lamps generally emit a large amount of light in the infrared spectrum. When conducting infrared photography, it may be preferable in some circumstances to remove the visible light from artificial light sources, such as for security or wildlife observation applications and this is done by filtering the light source using the same type of infrared pass filter that is fitted to the camera lens, such as the R72 type etc. In recent years light emitting diodes have also become available that provide controlled infrared illumination, this type of illumination may be found in many CCTV and video camera systems. The heat generated by Tungsten and halogen infrared lights can be a serious consideration and, in addition to potential overheating of the lights themselves, extended exposure to high intensity infrared radiation may result in skin burns.

Digital Photography and Video

The early techniques for photography within the invisible light spectra involved using specially made film and modified equipment but since the advent of electronic photography it has become possible to greatly simplify the process. Modern digital cameras and video cameras use an electronic image sensor, which have an inherent sensitivity to both ultraviolet and infrared light. For consumer level sensors this sensitivity is generally within the region of 380nm up to around 1100nm. At the ultraviolet wavelengths this is similar to the way the human eye sees light and it is really only at the infrared wavelengths that the electronic sensor offers an ability to see much beyond normal human vision. The discovery that electronic imaging techniques could be used for invisible light photography is also certainly not new. In the late 1920's, television pioneer John Logie-Baird demonstrated a working infrared television system which he called the Noctovisor. This used a modified television tube and is perhaps better considered as an early thermal imaging camera, nonetheless, it permitted instantaneous infrared images to be obtained for the first time. One of the people Baird demonstrated his Noctovisor system to was the eminent physicist and psychical researcher Sir Oliver Lodge who seems to have either missed the opportunity or failed to realise the potential for such a system to support investigations of paranormal claims.

Baird demonstrates the Noctovisor to Sir Oliver Lodge

Pictures obtained with early digital cameras frequently suffered from poor colour rendition as a result of their inherent sensitivity to ultraviolet and infrared light and manufacturers needed to use filtering to prevent the invisible light spectra from reaching the sensor. In addition to the ultraviolet blocking layers usually added to the lens protective coating, the camera makers also placed an infrared blocking filter directly in front of the image sensor. This additional filter is sometimes known as a hot mirror, the term deriving from the thermal aspects of infrared radiation. Both of these techniques are necessary in order to improve the colour response of the sensor in order to produce pictures that better reflect the way the human eye responds to light thus making the pictures more acceptable to the user. One or two camera makers have recognised that that there may be commercial advantages to having an infrared filter that is capable of being moved into or out of the light path, in particular Sony, who used this method when developing their NightShot mode. The system worked by operating a single switch which caused the infrared blocking filter to physically move away from its normal position in front of the sensor whilst at the same time turning on additional on-camera infrared light emitting diodes. The initial Sony camcorders (those made prior to 1998) gained the reputation of apparently being able to see through clothing and this caused a media storm with headlines proclaiming the camera's x-ray abilities and calls for them to be banned from sale. This ability was much over-stated although, under certain circumstances, the camera might appear to show detail beneath clothing. Sony responded by altering the exposure system of cameras fitted with the NightShot system, preventing the mode from being used except in conditions of near or complete darkness. The modified technique fixed the shutter speed to either 1/30th or 1/60th of a second and also fixed the lens to the widest aperture available ensuring that under any normal lighting conditions the camera would over-expose the image thereby rendering it unusable.

A number of other camera manufacturers have also utilised the sensitivity of the image sensor at invisible light wavelengths to provide specialist cameras for use in medical and scientific photography applications. Typically, these cameras do away with completely, or make switchable the infrared and the ultraviolet filters, in addition to modifications that control both the focus and exposure systems. Some manufacturers also provide modified sensors that increase the sensitivity to either the ultraviolet or infrared spectra, but not both. While it is relatively simple to provide a switchable infrared capability that retains the camera's ability to take good quality pictures or videos under visible lighting, it is much more difficult to do the same with ultraviolet modified photography. To date there are no consumer digital cameras or video cameras that have been designed to permit ultraviolet photography. The technical considerations of such cameras would be costly to implement and infrared photography provides users with many of the desired capabilities i.e., low or no (visible) light photography.

Some Problems with Invisible Light Photography

A simple method of determining if a digital camera or camcorder can be used for infrared photography is simply to point an infrared remote control (e.g. a TV remote) directly toward the camera in a darkened room. Press any button on the remote control whilst watching the camera's screen. If the screen or the recorded image shows a bright emission of light from the remote control's light emitting diode then infrared light is reaching the sensor. All Sony NightShot equipped models will demonstrate this ability when in NightShot mode but also a surprising number of other camcorders and cameras without any apparent night vision will demonstrate this sensitivity to infrared light. By placing an infrared pass filter in front of the lens, an enhanced sensitivity to infrared may also be observed with digital still cameras. The sensitivity of different electronic sensors varies enormously and the actual exposure settings must be determined by experimentation. The lengthy exposure times also create additional problems for those wishing to try invisible light photography. The first is fairly obvious, that of blurred images, caused either by movement of the camera or of the subject. This is not so much of a problem with Sony's NightShot cameras, which use a fixed shutter speed of 1/30th of a second and are therefore capable of reducing motion blur to an acceptable degree. However, this is not the case with the Super NightShot mode that is also found on many Sony models and which uses a 1/8th of a second exposure which will result in considerable motion blur when used. The longer exposures required for successful infrared photography and video also creates a second problem, that of anomalies within the pictures as a result of electronic noise and the physical heat generated within the sensor and the electronics needed to amplify the signal coming from the sensor. Referred to as photon noise, this can generally be seen as blotchy or patchy areas in dark parts of the image and is more common in hot conditions or in low light situations. Another frequently observed anomaly of electronic infrared and ultraviolet photography is the appearance of bright spots or points within the image.

Image Aberrations

Camera lenses are primarily designed to focus visible light and must be adjusted in order to be able to bring either the infrared or ultraviolet light wavelengths into correct focus on the surface of the sensor. This is not necessarily a problem in modern still and video cameras as the autofocus systems will normally operate successfully provided there is sufficient contrast within the overall scene. Real-time LCD viewfinders also mean the photographer is able to visually check and confirm the focus and make any necessary manual adjustments if required. However, achieving a properly focussed image is made more difficult when the scene is lit by different wavelengths of light and the camera is being used for invisible light photography. This is common in situations where visible light sources such as the ambient room lighting or hand torches are being used. This inability of the lens to bring all the wavelengths of light into sharp focus at the same point at the sensor is referred to as Chromatic aberration.

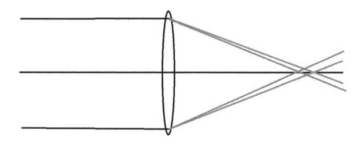

Different wavelengths of light are brought into focus at different points

Under these mixed light conditions the camera will try to focus on either the infrared or visible light within the scene, leaving the other wavelengths slightly out of focus. Sometimes, the focus may continually shift back and forth slightly as the autofocus system tries to bring the different light frequencies into sharp focus. All too often, the autofocus will simply give up and refuse to properly focus on anything within the scene, a situation that is commonly encountered by investigators using this technique and can often be seen when watching footage taken under such mixed lighting in which the camera intermittently loses focus. These focus-induced aberrations may be further exacerbated by the large lens aperture typically used by the camera, which results in a very shallow depth of field. Once the autofocus system or the user have decided on the desired point of focus within a scene, the shallow depth of field results in large areas of the image not being fully in focus; generally speaking, the central area will tend to be sharpest with the focus quickly falling off for objects away from the focal plane. Those who wish to take infrared images or videos under mixed lighting conditions can use a filter such as the R72 to remove the visible light from the scene and ensure they minimise chromatic aberrations and focus problems. For those with cameras that offer control over the exposure, they may also opt to select a smaller aperture to maximise the depth of field; this also offers some control over chromatic aberrations but at the cost of increased exposure times. The ability to control the exposure is not available in Sony's NightShot mode but the addition of an R72 filter can help the camera to focus more reliably as the autofocus system does not attempt to bring both the visible light and infrared wavelengths into focus at the same time. In conditions where there is little or no visible light within a scene, focus may also be improved using this method. Unfortunately, many low cost infrared pass filters are inefficient and also allow ultraviolet light to pass; in effect behaving more like a Wratten 18A (Wood's filter). Using such a filter may actually exacerbate the chromatic and focus aberrations in scenes where any ultraviolet light source is present. Another problem is caused by light, including invisible wavelengths, entering the lens away from its central-axis. This can create distortions and produce a smear or comet-like tail that is often mistaken for movement of the light source. This is called Coma aberration and is particularly noticeable when point or bright sources of light are present within a scene. The materials and coatings used to control such aberrations are not as effective at the non-visible wavelengths and coma aberration can become a serious problem in both IR and UV photography.

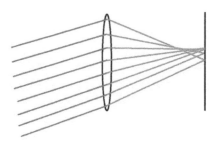

Coma aberrations produce distorted highlights

The lenses of many lightweight consumer digital cameras and camcorders use either optical resin or plastic instead of glass for the individual elements within the lens. Plastic and resin lenses create few problems for visible light photography but the material is very poor at passing light at the ultraviolet and infrared wavelengths. This means that, regardless of what the user tries to achieve, little or no invisible light is able reach the sensor, being almost totally absorbed within the lens and the various optical coatings applied. Most camera lenses are designed to acceptably control light and minimise aberrations at visible wavelengths. Coatings and lens materials are selected to produce the best possible image quality for a given price point. Thus a cheaply made lens will not control light as well as a more expensive model. Regardless of cost, many lenses may still be susceptible to aberrations at the non-visible wavelengths, a problem that is exacerbated in the simple lenses found in many low-end consumer cameras. A further but important consideration for those wishing to use NightShot mode equipped Sony cameras is that since around 2005, Sony have altered the overall sensitivity of the NightShot mode and reduced the number of on-camera infrared light emitting diodes from two down to one in order to provide better control of the inherent electronic noise problems. This has had the effect of losing around 30% of the effective shooting range of these cameras. Users of such cameras now need to add additional IR light sources to obtain properly illuminated objects at distances greater than about ten feet from the camera.

Full Spectrum Photography and Video

So-called full spectrum photography and video has in recent years become a popular technique for ghost and general paranormal investigation. In this context however, full spectrum actually refers to cameras and video cameras that have been modified in such a fashion that removes much of the visible light spectrum. Several companies and individuals are offering various modified cameras for sale and, in addition, there are websites that offer instructions and advice to those wishing to modify their own camera or provide a modification service for a fee. The majority of the commercial sites selling full spectrum cameras provide very little information about the actual modifications they undertake. Instead, they make vague claims about the prowess of their particular modification and the camera's ready ability to obtain pictures of ghosts, spirits, UFO's and various otherworldly subjects. Modified full spectrum models generally sell for between £100 and £400 and are sold via online stores and auction sites. Many of these modified cameras start as out as low-specification models, typically unbranded and retailing unmodified for less than £50. There are also one or two modified consumer cameras available, also normally based on entry-level cameras. The sales pitch for these modified FS cameras is certainly impressive:

> What lurks within the invisible spectrum? Spirits exist on many frequencies or dimensions other than our own. These dimensions also contain frequencies of light unseen by the human eye. This custom modified digital video camera has been modified to allow the maximum amount of invisible light into the camera in order to best capture images of the spirit world.

> Modified Full Spectrum Camcorder with 8MP Camera. This video camera offers 640x480 needed to capture clear evidence. This camcorder has been professionally modified with UV and IR sensitivity to view the full spectrum of light including light not seen with the human eye. This Full Spectrum Digital Video Camera will capture images reflected within both ends of the light spectrum - where theories suggest that spirits reside! Enhancing the camera's ability to capture light reflected in these frequencies has made this camera an effective and essential photographic Full Spectrum Camcorder with 8MP Camera. This video camera offers 640x480 needed to capture clear evidence. This camcorder has been professionally modified with UV and IR sensitivity to view the full spectrum of light including light not seen with the human eye. This Full Spectrum Digital Video Camera will capture images reflected within both ends of the light spectrum - where theories suggest that spirits reside! Enhancing the camera's ability to capture light reflected in these frequencies has made this camera an effective and essential photographic evidence gathering tool.

The advertised specifications rarely make any mention of actual modification that has been carried out or have details of the camera's enhanced light gathering ability. Generally, where specifications are provided they are simply a copy of the manufacturer's specifications for the original un-modified camera, for instance:

- SD or MMC Card supports up to 8GB
- Image Sensor: 5.0 MP CMOS sensor
- VGA 640x480
- Lens: F/2.8 f=8.5mm
- 0.5m. ~ Infinity
- Macro mode: 11cm ~ 18cm
- Zoom: 8x Digital Zoom
- Flash strobe: Built-in (Auto / force / off)
- Storage Memory: SD card Up to 8GB
- File format: Picture: JPEG, Video: AVI

From the provided specifications, it is usually possible to determine that the camera is a low specification model with low-resolution image. However, for those who are prepared to spend a little more cash, higher specification models such as one of the Sony NightShot mode equipped cameras are available. Here, again, the seller provides scant information about either the modification or the enhanced invisible light capability:

- Video recording: HD-1920x1080 (30fps)
- Photo Resolution: 12MP, 5MP or 3MP (Fine/Standard/Economy)
- Aperture: F3.2~F6.8
- Focal Length: 6mm~18"
- 20X zoom (5x Optical, 4X Digital)
- External Memory: SD/MMC card; tested Up to 32 GB (SDHC)
- Image format: JPEG; Video format: MOV
- Interface: USB 2.0 connector
- Power supply: NP120 Rechargeable Lithium-ion battery

No mention is made of the actual Sony model used and a generic Sony advertising picture was used in the advert.

For those wishing to see examples of photographs taken with these modified cameras it is a simple matter to search the Internet for *"Full Spectrum Camera"* or search the numerous web based stores selling ghost hunting gadgets and equipment. The various modifiers and sellers are unsurprisingly competitive and, in addition to their own vague claims, they often include some form of warning in their promotion to the buyer to avoid other retailers who might offer similarly modified cameras:

Don't get stuck investigating with blinders on! Other units claiming to be 'full spectrum' that block the visible light are what we refer to as 'multi-spectrum' - not full spectrum. Why block visible light in low light situations when evidence may happen? Capture everything with this true Full Spectrum camcorder.

This warning seems to be somewhat at odds with the reality of the specifications (the few that are provided) and advertising pictures of the cameras which demonstrate that most are using the same unmodified donor cameras as their starting point. Further at odds with these warnings, is that in a number of cases the same individual is carrying out the actual modification on behalf of a number of sellers. It might be imagined that where some indication of invisible light performance is provided, the user would be able to determine which camera would best suit their needs. Unsurprisingly, this also proves not to be almost impossible. In one example, three Internet stores clearly offer the same camera model and it is also clear that the same person undertook the modifications. One site claims the camera has an ultraviolet capability down to 100nm, the second site claims sensitivity to 200-250nm, whilst the third states sensitivity to be around 300nm. All of these claims are actually way beyond the capability of the electronic sensors and also the optics and each case no mention of the infrared performance is even provided. The various sellers provide sample images and video that promote the capability of their modified cameras, some may also provide pictures taken with unmodified cameras or competitor's models to demonstrate why their camera is superior. What is interesting is that in every case the video or photographs that are provided are all taken under direct sunlight, bright artificial lighting, or by using one of their own (offered for sale) "special full spectrum" lights. This choice of lighting to demonstrate the camera is unsurprising given the physics of invisible light and the nature of the actual modifications. Simply put, in order to take a photograph or shoot video it is necessary to have a suitable light source. This may be visible light such as daylight or artificial illumination or it may be invisible light from the same general sources. Although sellers are reluctant to reveal the nature of their camera modifications the sample images they provide offer some clues as to what has been done to alter the camera's light response. Many of the pictures have an overall pink hue, a fact that is referred to by at least one seller: "Note: This camcorder is not suitable for everyday use such as family gathering and sporting events as the hardware modifications to the unit make the picture constantly a 'pinkish' hue during use in daylight".

This overall pink hue is the natural response of the sensor and is due to its inherent sensitivity to infrared wavelengths of light, which results in the unnatural colour cast. As already described, digital camera makers use an infrared blocking filter placed directly in front of the image sensor in order to improve the colour response of the sensor in the visible wavelengths and provide images that are more realistic and acceptable to the typical (non-ghost investigating) user. The infrared blocking filter in most equipment is attached to the electronic sensor and forms an important part of the physical protection for the device. The pink cast in the sample images clearly demonstrates that the blocking filter has been removed from in front of the sensor. No additional modification is required to be carried out to increase ultraviolet sensitivity in these budget cameras as the cheap lens usually has a poor quality or no ultraviolet absorbing lens coating applied. The seller also relies upon the fact that sensor has an inherent sensitivity in the top end of the ultraviolet spectrum, around 380nm (which in fact lies within the range of human vision). In this configuration the sensor allows all light between about 380nm to about 1100nm to be visualised. A note of caution is needed here, the colour cast of sample images may in some cases be misleading and many sellers appear to have modified the advertising picture by using photo editing software with some pictures appearing on websites as either monochrome images or exhibiting a range of colourful hues. A number of sellers of full spectrum cameras have clearly made an additional physical modification to the camera, which may be determined by simply looking at their photographs of the actual cameras on sale or in use. This is in the form of an additional visible light-blocking filter in front of the cameras lens. Although it is rarely stated what exactly this filter is, its appearance as a black opaque disc gives away its function. Such a filter must be either an infrared pass filter such as an R72 or similar or, in rare cases, a Wratten 18A filter, both of which appear black and opaque under visible light.

Hoya R72 IR Filter   Wood's (Wratten 18A) Filter

The simple addition of either filter removes most of the visible light spectrum but unless the camera's exposure system is also modified, the photographs or videos will be greatly underexposed. This modification is generally extremely unsatisfactory. The camera's exposure system has been designed to provide sufficient amounts of ambient visible light to ensure that electronic noise artefacts are well controlled. Reducing the amount of light reaching the sensor means that the output from the sensor must be amplified to a much greater extent, resulting in increased levels of electronic noise, and a corresponding increase in the number of potential aberrations in the recorded images. Budget cameras tend to have very small sensors and poorer quality lenses having a fixed aperture. Such cameras tend to use changes to the amplification of the sensor output signal in order to produce an acceptable image. It is therefore hardly surprising that the sellers of these full spectrum cameras show only samples taken under bright visible light and frequently stress the need for the user to purchase their accessory of full spectrum lights. Such lights generally consist of a mixed array of visible (white), ultraviolet, and infrared LED's and in some cases other colours too, green being common. They fail to mention that simply turning on the normal room lighting or using a standard white video light will generally provide adequate illumination at all wavelengths for these cameras to function without the need to add a disco-like bank of colourful LED lighting.

Perhaps the most revealing detail about the efficacy of these claimed full spectrum modifications is that of cost. As mentioned, ghost hunting full spectrum cameras are generally offered for sale for between £100 and £400. Specialist ultraviolet or infrared lenses that are manufactured for medical or scientific purposes and which have either Quartz or Fluorite crystal lens elements and a modified optical design such as the Jenoptik UV-VIS 105mm, sell for around £5,000 new. The now discontinued Medical Nikon UV lens can sometimes be found as cheaply as £15,000 for a good used model. It is therefore highly unlikely that the performance claims being made for these cheap full spectrum cameras, particularly with regard to their ability to operate in the ultraviolet spectrum are accurate. Whilst these cheap full spectrum cameras may exhibit some improvement in their overall response to some invisible light frequencies, any improvement is biased heavily in favour of the infrared wavelengths with little to be gained at ultraviolet wavelengths. Using them in bright daylight or with suitable artificial lighting, the addition of filters on the lens and removal of the filtering in front of the sensor may offer some very slight improvement to both the infrared and ultraviolet sensitivity but this is at the cost of increased image noise and aberrations.

Fortunately, for those wishing to undertake effective invisible light photography, there are one or two well-designed options that are available. Camera maker Fujifilm has for a number of years exploited the inherent sensitivity of their sensor and has optimised this in a modified version of their S-series professional digital cameras. The most recent model being the IS PRO, aimed primarily at users within forensics, law enforcement, science, medicine, and art forgery. The camera costs around £3,000 (body only), with various lens, filter, and lighting options being available that add considerably to the cost of the system. The camera, based on their S5 Pro model, has a modified sensor filter and is stated to be sensitive to ultraviolet and infrared light between 380nm and 1000nm. Fujifilm provide detailed specifications for the camera as might be expected from a reputable manufacturer. It can be seen from the stated wavelength sensitivity of this camera that the ultraviolet spectrum below 400nm has only limited coverage whilst the infrared spectrum above 700nm has much greater sensitivity. Such sensitivity figures are somewhat different and considerably at odds with many of the claims for invisible wavelength sensitivity being made for the full spectrum cameras being offered by ghost hunting equipment stores. In order to successfully take pictures at these wavelengths, the Fujifilm IS PRO requires specially constructed lenses, additional filters and lighting with each lens, filter pack, and lighting set-up all being specific to the wavelengths that the user wishes to photograph. Fujifilm also acknowledge the limitations of the camera and the difficulties that successful invisible light photography entails:

Dark opaque filters that cover the lens often render the viewfinder useless, so the IS Pro carries specialized features useful for investigative photography, such as a special quick activate one touch Live Image Preview (black and white) mode that can be activated by pressing the "Display/Back" button for three seconds. This makes fast access to Live Preview mode much easier when used on forensic copy stand tables in dark room environments. Its Mirror Lock-Up and Shutter Delay features also aid in reducing image blur during long exposures. It also has a specially formulated protective CCD glass filter that was designed to help protect the Super CCD Pro from dust and general maintenance damage while maximising its UV and IR gathering potential. The technology designed into the Fujifilm IS PRO was initially designed for traditional visible wavelength imagery. However, the natural low noise signature of the Fujifilm Super CCD produces high quality high-resolution images within a limited band of Visual to Infrared. Because of the wide range of light spectrums captured, focusing and exposure are often done manually. However if enough visible light is available auto focusing will work.

(FUJIFILM PRESS RELEASE, 2007)

More recently Fujifilm announced a second camera with a reduced cost but also with a reduced capability, the IS-1. This costs under £2500 and includes the cost of the modified lens. The IS-1 and its lens are optimised for infrared photography using filters built-in to the lens itself. The camera's built-in flash has also been modified to provide some limited additional infrared illumination. A low-resolution movie mode is also available. Fujifilm cameras are the basis of some full spectrum photography that has been shown on television ghost hunting shows together with the erroneous claim of the photography being full spectrum, as the photography is undertaken only within the infrared portions of the light spectrum and does not include the visible light wavelengths that are blocked by the applied filters. It is interesting to observe the nature of the image anomalies that are being presented on programmes and social media as providing evidence of a paranormal interaction or the existence of some alternative dimension or reality. In most cases they resemble anomalies that are clearly caused by chromatic aberrations, focus problems and other well-understood visible light phenomena.

Chroma aberration presented as a paranormal anomaly

Some of the explanations on the discussion forum regarding the above image neatly illustrates the effects such representations have on viewers:

> It looks just like a UFO, it sure would help awaken the ufology field out there that the possibility that they are actual beings, flying around. Not just crafts. Micro and macro. There are actual other worldly beings on some that you might catch if you look, I saw at least two or three times different forms of the human format. Different forms of human walking around.

> I was thinking the exact same thing... It just looks too similar to a craft... Different forms of the human format? Care to elaborate? Sounds intriguing!

Of course, in the dozens of comments, nobody mentioned the anomaly is really just a good example of coma aberration!

There are further options available to those wishing to use invisible light photography and video, such as the previously discussed Sony NightShot equipped cameras. This mode uses a moveable IR pass filter in front of the sensor and adjustments within the exposure and focus system to increase the overall sensitivity of the camera to infrared light above 700nm. Almost twice as much infrared light is able to reach the sensor when this mode is enabled, furthermore, the sensitivity peak value of a camcorder in visible light mode is roughly about 700nm while the sensitivity peak value of the Sony NightShot mode is roughly about 800nm. There is a 100nm difference in these two modes. In short, if the internal infrared filter is removed, much more IR can reach the sensor. Prior to 1998, all NightShot models offered the ability to shoot infrared video or take stills with full control over the exposure system, meaning that infrared pictures could be obtained under all lighting conditions including daylight. The media storm surrounding claims that these cameras were capable of seeing through clothing resulted in Sony making modifications to the Night-Shot mode and seriously restricting the cameras ability to be used in bright daylight. Over the years a number of fixes have been developed and published on the Internet to get around this restricted capability, some involve partial dismantling of the camera, whilst others provide less risky options. The simplest of all methods and one that is also remarkably effective uses an R72 filter in front of the lens together with one or more Neutral Density (ND) filters in front of the lens to control the over-exposure in bright natural light. In dull overcast daylight an ND8 is generally considered to provide a reasonable level of exposure but in brighter conditions the use of an ND16 or even an ND32 filter may be needed to restrict the amount of light reaching the sensor in order that a useable image can be obtained. Such adaptations and alterations offer the user the ability to carry out photography or video in the infrared spectrum between 720nm-1100nm. Different infrared pass filters may be used to more precisely photograph progressively higher regions of the IR spectrum, for example, an R85 will block all light below 850nm whilst an R1000 will block all light below 1000nm (1mm). Users and owners of digital cameras can also take advantage of the services of several specialist modifiers who offer to permanently convert almost any digital camera to take infrared biased pictures by removing the infrared filter from in front of the sensor. This modification permits use up to around 1100nm. The modification can be carried out on just about any DSLR and some compact models too. The modification is permanent but will permit the normal focus and exposure controls to be used. Owners of some Sigma DSLR's are even more fortunate as the camera actually has a user removable infrared blocking filter placed behind the lens.

Daylight infrared photograph taken using Sony
NightShot mode camera and applied filters

Invisible Light Options and Considerations

It is clear that there are a number of options available for those wishing
to undertake photography using parts of the invisible light spectrum.
All of which require to a greater or lesser extent some modification
to the visible light operations of the camera. It is also clear that none
of the major camera manufacturers provide equipment that can take
pictures or video of both the ultraviolet and infrared spectra simultaneously and certainly none that also offer a simultaneous visible light
capability too.

True full spectrum, photography using all the available wavelengths
of light currently does not exist outside of one or two highly specialised
scientific applications costing several millions of pounds. It has long
been known that all electronic sensors and even cathode tubes have
the ability to detect light over a large range of wavelengths, from the
higher regions of the ultraviolet spectrum, through the visible wavelengths and into the infrared regions. One might reasonably expect

that the simple act of removing all of the ultraviolet coatings from the cameras lens and the additional removal of the infrared blocking filter from in front of the sensor would permit the sensor to respond to all light wavelengths between 380nm and 1100nm. Technically, to achieve this whilst adequately controlling the image aberrations would be highly complex and would provide no significant advantage over existing methods of obtaining images under invisible light conditions. All conventional forms of visible and invisible light photography require additional light to provide the illumination levels necessary to obtain good quality images, this is also true of systems that use light amplification technology such as night vision cameras and scopes. Light sources such as natural daylight, modified electronic flash or specifically filtered artificial light (including LED's) all proving satisfactory to a greater or lesser degree.

Other Methods of Invisible Light Imaging

Light intensifiers also called night vision or starlight scopes; amplify the available light within a scene tens of thousands or even hundreds of thousands of times. Developed originally for military use during WW2 and in continuous development ever since, affordable consumer versions have now been available for about twenty years. These models tend to make use of earlier versions of the technology. Consumer image intensifier scopes often lack any means of recording the observed scene but some models are now available that use sensitive electronic sensors rather than the conventional light-intensifier tube method and allow the user to take either still or moving images. These digital night vision devices are very similar to the Sony NightShot system in the way they operate. They have been designed with the consideration that just being able to see in the dark is more important than the actual picture quality and use very high levels of electronic amplification to the sensor output signal. This produces grainy and noisy pictures that lack any real definition and image detail. All night vision devices work by boosting the available light and cannot work in situations where there is no ambient light. In such circumstances it is necessary to add some form of additional illumination and this is normally done using infrared lights either in the form of a filtered accessory light or built-in. There is one type of imaging technology that requires no additional light as the illumination comes directly from the objects being photographed either as emitted infrared energy or in the form of reflected infrared energy. Thermal imaging cameras use the higher frequencies of the infrared spectrum in the form of heat radiation that is emitted by almost every object. Thermography is a truly passive system of imaging that needs no additional illumination to a scene in order to operate.

Thermal Imaging

In the late 1920's, television pioneer John Logie-Baird demonstrated a working infrared television system which he called the Noctovisor. This used a modified television tube. The manner of its operation and the wavelengths of infrared light it used means that the Noctovisor is perhaps better considered as being an early thermal imaging camera. The Noctovisor was never developed and it wasn't until 1965 that the first commercial thermal imaging camera appeared, designed for high voltage power line inspection. The modern thermal camera works by recording emissions within the infrared spectrum (8000-15,000nm), which it converts into a visible image. The main source of infrared energy is heat or thermal radiation. Every object that has a temperature above Absolute Zero Kelvin (-273.15 Celsius) emits infrared thermal energy. The camera detects these emissions, which are focussed by special optics onto the infrared detector. Like the visible light spectra hitting the imaging sensor in a digital camera the infrared emissions are converted into a visible image, which can be viewed on the viewfinder and recorded for later use. Thermal cameras are primarily designed for industrial, surveillance, military, and medical use and range from basic models costing a few hundred pounds to advanced versions costing tens of thousands.

Thermal cameras designed for police surveillance or military applications, are not currently permitted to be used by the public, even for ghost investigating, and all but the most basic models are prohibitively expensive. There are several manufacturers of thermal cameras but perhaps the best known is FLIR Systems. Their name derives from the acronym 'Forward Looking Infra Red', a term which is used for military airborne thermal imaging systems. FLIR Systems was formed in 1978 following the merger between several European and American thermal image camera manufacturers. FLIR, together with other manufactures, provide a series of consumer thermal imaging products that are more affordable and a number of ghost investigators now include a thermal imager in their investigation kit.

Currently, the image specifications for these cameras are quite basic with a resolution of between 3,600 and 19,600 pixels. Compare that to a basic digital camera with a resolution of 8 million pixels or more (8 Mega-pixels). Thermal sensitivity, the camera's ability to detect changes in the emitted temperature of an object, is typically 0.1 degree Celsius with a stated accuracy of around +/- 2 Celsius. All models allow the user to record still images to either an internal memory or a plug-in memory card, a number of models also allow video to be recorded. The images can be easily transferred to a computer and can be examined with manufacturer-supplied software that permits detailed thermal information to be obtained about the scene. The thermal camera has become a much sought after and highly prized gadget for modern ghost investigators following their use on television programmes such as *Most Haunted* and *Ghost Hunters*. However, due to their portrayal on such shows, ghost investigators have tended to seriously misunderstand the capabilities and usefulness of these devices. Rather than using the thermal imager to examine the location with respect to the thermal information that the device provides, the majority of investigators concentrate solely on the forms and shapes that may appear in the thermal pictures and videos. In order to interpret thermal images correctly the user needs to know how different materials and conditions can influence temperature readings from the thermal camera. A number of factors must be considered when obtaining and understanding the information from every thermal imager, these include the thermal conductivity, emissivity and thermal reflection of almost every object.

Thermal Conductivity

Different materials have differing thermal properties, some warm slowly or cool quickly. Brick and stone for instance will heat up slowly but once warmed, can store the heat for several hours. Most metals heat up comparatively quickly but cool down equally rapidly. This difference in thermal conductivity can sometimes lead to the appearance of large temperature differences under some circumstances.

Emissivity

In order to correctly read the temperature and render the scene accurately, the emissivity of a material also needs to be taken in account. Emissivity is the efficiency with which an object emits infrared radiation. It is important and necessary that the correct emissivity is set or the subsequent measurements will be erroneous. If the object has a low emissivity and there is a large temperature difference between the object and the ambient temperature the reflection of the ambient temperature will influence the performance of the thermal camera resulting in erroneous readings and unexpected anomalies within the image. Modern thermal cameras have adjustments for emissivity and ambient temperature compensation that must be correctly set before the camera can be properly used and the images correctly interpreted. Moreover, these settings must be constantly adjusted as the investigator moves around a location and encounters different materials, construction methods, and conditions. The camera manufacturers normally provide instructions for making these adjustments and it is important that the instructions are fully read, understood, and applied correctly. Failure to do this will result in erroneous information and greatly increase the possibility of the image being misinterpreted by the investigator.

A further factor that needs to be considered is thermal reflection. Much like a mirror reflects visible light, many materials reflect thermal energy. Such reflections can lead to a misinterpretation of the thermal image. Often, the thermal reflection of the user can lead to the unexpected appearance of a figure within a picture where no one was standing and is a common cause found in thermal pictures offered as evidence by investigators.

FLIR Systems and other manufacturers provide courses for operators of thermal cameras. The courses are sometimes offered at a discount to new purchasers and while some might consider them costly, the information they provide is invaluable and highly recommended.

Thermal Reflectivity

Like a mirror, which reflects visible light, almost every object reflects thermal energy. Such reflections can lead to a misinterpretation of the thermal image. This not only affects the accuracy of the temperature measurements but often, the thermal reflection of the user can lead to the unexpected appearance of objects or figures within a picture where no one was standing. The figures are of course most likely to be the investigators themselves and their thermal reflection is a common cause of anomalies found in thermal pictures offered as evidence by investigators.

FLIR Systems and other manufacturers provide courses for operators of thermal cameras. The courses are sometimes offered at a discount to new purchasers and while some might consider them costly, the information they provide is invaluable and highly recommended.

The low resolution of the thermal camera is also a potential problem. Models such as the FLIR i3 and i5 that are a current favourite of ghost investigators offer a resolution of just 60x60 (3,600 total) pixels. This means that detail within the captured image is correspondingly low. Fine or even moderate levels of detail within the images are absent and overall. In terms of image quality, thermal cameras compare badly to even the most basic digital cameras, for example, a computer webcam typically has more than 1,200,000 total pixels (1.2 Mega-pixels). Accordingly, it is simply not possible to discern subtle details within a thermal image.

Image from an FLIR Systems i7 with a resolution of 19,600 pixels

A thermal image is a synthetic or false image that is constructed within the software of the camera. Colours or scales of grey are used to represent the temperature range of the subject. Most thermal cameras have an automatic calibration mode, which permits it to produce a good overall image but can and does cause colours to suddenly change. The colour palette and grey scale range is limited and this inevitably leads to the same object appearing as a variable range of colours as the camera adjusts its calibration. As with any camera, the dynamic range (thermal exposure) of the image will affect the overall image and thus an object that appears warm (red) against a cool (blue) background will appear as cool (blue) against a hotter (red) background. The same effect is also seen in grey scale images with sudden changes occurring within the shades of grey being used to represent the temperature. Disconcertingly for the unwary investigator, an object might suddenly appear to change its apparent temperature and has been the cause of several anomalies presented by investigators. A manual thermal exposure mode can provide greater clarity and cause less colour changing, some basic models do not have a manual mode, for those that do, the mode needs to be used correctly for proper results to be obtained.

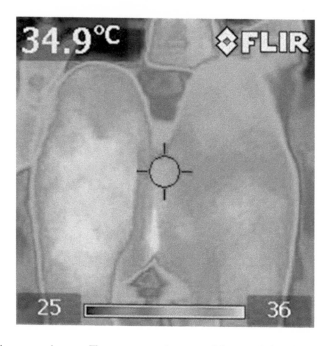

FLIR i5 screen image. Temperature in central 'gunsight' is shown in top left corner. The dynamic range of 25 - 36 Celsius is shown along the bottom. The overall low image resolution can also be seen (image shows a man doing sit-ups).

Focussing an IR image uses the same principle as focussing visible light. A lens is used to bring the wavelengths into the correct plane of focus on the sensor. Some models allow the user to adjust the focus for objects that are nearer or further from the camera but some of the basic models have a pre-set focus. This typically is pre-set for objects between around 4 to 8 feet from the camera, obviously objects outside of this range will become increasingly out of focus and therefore even less well defined.

In terms of their use in ghost investigation, the thermal camera really only has anecdotal evidence to support its use. Based upon the assumption that paranormal activity is linked to changes in temperature, either real or imagined, investigators have speculated that it might be possible to visualise a ghost or spirit using this technology.

This assumption lead approach is a significant issue as there is simply no evidence as yet that ghosts or spirits have any thermal properties.

Fraud

Thermal Imaging cameras and thermography can be a useful asset for the ghost investigator but generally this is not in the way that many of them are using their expensive gadgets when trying to capture images of ghosts. Used correctly, a thermal camera can permit the investigator to obtain a great deal of useful thermal data from a location. In addition, the thermal camera can also be useful in the detection of fraud, as it permits images to be obtained in total darkness without introducing any additional lighting. All night vision cameras require additional lighting which in the case of infrared night vision models is very dim but it may still be seen as a dim glow by the human eye and therefore can alert others to the fact that a camera is in use. The thermal camera is totally passive and with its screen turned off (some models permit this) or with the screen covered, it is not possible to know if the thermal camera is being used. On a number of occasions I have personally recorded instances of malpractice and fraud during investigations by using this technique. The thermal camera can be used to determine whether an object has been touched or moved from its original position. It is possible for the camera to clearly see the heat that is left behind, even following a short duration contact between a warm object and a cooler object, such as a warm hand on a cold wall or a jacket for instance. The sensitivity of just 0.1 degree Celsius can often mean the thermal evidence remains visible for several minutes. The following pair of images was taken as part of a sequence and neatly illustrates how a thermal camera can be used in the detection of fraudulent practice during an investigation.

The hand in this image belong to an investigator / medium who is tapping a member of the public as the group ask for the spirits to indicate their presence by touching someone.

The investigator / medium denied touching the person and claimed that the first picture was deliberately misleading and created by using a clever camera angle. Unfortunately, the warm hand of the investigator left a thermal imprint on the jacket of the person. Irrefutable proof that contact had been made.

One particularly false assumption is that a thermal imager can see ghosts, a claim that many investigators believe to be true without ever considering the actual claim that is being made. Some people have speculated that perhaps ghosts or spirits are made up from particles of some type of matter that is capable of emitting or absorbing infrared energy, and so the ghost would become visible and measurable using a thermal camera. That is entirely speculation and it would first need to be demonstrated that:

a) Ghosts and spirits actually exist.

b) They have some physical properties that allow them to emit or absorb infrared energy i.e., they have an emissivity value.

One further claim regarding thermal cameras that is frequently encountered on some television shows and in investigation reports is that the thermal imager detected a cold spot. This is simply not possible due to the design of the device itself. A thermal camera relies upon emitted infrared energy and it cannot see thermal changes in air. FLIR Systems actually design their cameras to include filters that prevent the temperature fluctuations of the ambient air currents from interfering with the correct production of the thermal image. A series of highly specialised thermal imagers are made that are designed to detect thermal information within gaseous emissions, such as the GasFind (GF) series cameras. These models are seriously expensive and are only capable of detecting a specific narrow range of emission wavelengths to aid the detection of gas emissions from ruptured pipes for instance.

FLIR Systems note this in their training for operators:

> Instrument designers do this by designing the instruments to be sensitive to wavelengths of IR where gases are highly transparent and do not emit IR well. This allows the radiation of surfaces that are of interest (like building surfaces) to suffer minimum attenuation as they travel through the atmosphere on the way to the IR camera. To view gases, a different camera design approach is desired. We want to view gases at wavelengths where they emit and absorb well. This is precisely what is done with the FLIR GasFind IR cameras.
>
> (INFRARED TRAINING CENTER, FLIR SYSTEMS)

Perhaps the greatest drawback to the use of thermal imagers is that the users are simply not familiar with the unusually coloured low-resolution images that these camera's produce. As such, it is commonplace that normal artefacts within the image are misunderstood and misinterpreted as being anomalous and even paranormal. Used with care, the thermal imager can be a genuine asset in many investigation situations but when they are used without training and a proper understanding the thermal imager can quickly confuse the investigator and mislead the investigation results. There are several good reasons for using thermal imagers in support of ghost investigations and it is not necessary to go any further here than to state once again that as yet there is no device that can demonstrate the existence or otherwise of ghosts or even that ghosts exist at all. To therefore claim that ghosts can then be detected using a thermal camera is simply erroneous.

Searching for the Invisible

There has been an upsurge of interest in invisible light or extended light spectrum photography in recent years by those with an interest in areas of paranormal investigation such as ghost investigation and ufology. Having largely failed to find what they were looking for using conventional photographic methods, investigators have turned increasingly to these newer technologies. This move has to a great extent been spurred on by the appearance of incorrectly labelled full spectrum cameras within the media and the various claims that are made for the successes of such equipment. Shows such as *Ghost Hunters International*, which were among the first to showcase full spectrum photography, have claimed that they have been able to detect genuine paranormal anomalies in pictures taken with their 'full spectrum camera'. Other investigators claim that by using cameras capable of seeing beyond the ability of human sight it is possible to capture proof that ghosts and otherworldly entities such as demons actually exist. Paranormal groups and individuals showcase the pictures taken with their full spectrum cameras and use them to support their belief that they demonstrate important evidence. Often, the pictures are backed up with testimony and explanation about the presented pictures, stating that they have been analysed and that they are simply beyond all possible explanation. As an example, here are a couple of comments from an Internet forum that discusses paranormal evidence and claims:

I use a digital full spectrum camera on our Investigations and I have to say that it is one of my best pieces of gear. I have caught some really good photos with this equipment. On the last investigation our team did, I captured a moving apparition about 15 seconds after one of our members described seeing a white misty light about two feet off the floor. I have also captured a still picture that is really good. Through my own experience, I believe the energy, or spirits, can be seen better in the UV range

Of course, the real prize was the "full spectrum" photograph. I immediately saw what they were referring to in the picture, and I have to admit that it's very suggestive of a human figure. I also like the fact that they presented a reference photograph of the same exact location where nothing was captured.

Such claims are highly contentious and more likely to be based on a misunderstanding of the physics of light and the operation of the camera, compounded by the numerous image problems that are inherent with invisible light photography that have already been discussed. Focusing errors, normal aberrations within the image, and poor resolution are just some of the problems that occur both from operating the camera equipment outside of the manufacturers designed parameters and carrying out modifications to the equipment itself. Given the strong likelihood that invisible light cameras produce image aberrations and that any photograph or piece of video footage taken using non-visible light wavelengths appears alien to the way we are used to seeing our surroundings, it is not surprising that all too frequently the investigator is faced with an image anomaly that they were not expecting. Objects may appear to change colour, dark objects may look light, and some materials apparently become see-through. The inability of the camera's optics to properly focus within the scene creates strange highlights and halos or the auto-focus system may give up altogether and appear to malfunction. Faced with the numerous image anomalies, many ghost investigators make a rudimentary attempt to analyse the images using conventional photo or video editing software. Belief and expectation also play a large part in the investigator's subsequent determination of what the anomaly actually shows. They know the images are being taken in a haunted location, and, they are there with the sole intent of capturing some proof of the existence of a paranormal realm, thus they are taken unawares by the anomalies that appear. In order to try and understand the anomaly, they often resort to changing the colour and contrast of the image until they obtain a picture that fits in with their existing expectations or beliefs and supports their pre-conceived notion that, if it is unusual, it is most likely to be paranormal, rather than just the result of a poorly modified camera operating way outside of it's designed capabilities.

Some investigators offer the argument that ghosts and spirits exist outside of our realm of awareness in a dimension that we are unable to see or hear by any normal means and, in order to capture evidence of such entities, it is necessary to extend the search beyond our normal sensory range. Such ideas are counter-productive to the general direction of good investigation methods, which must start by the examination and testing of the original testimonies of those claiming experience of the paranormal. It is entirely logical to assume that if a witness claims to have seen an apparition, it is extremely unlikely that they were using a vision-enhancing device at the time, and this is especially true of cases that pre-date such equipment. Thus the investigator is dealing with an apparition that exists either as a hallucination or, if it had a physical reality, it must be within the visible light spectrum, otherwise, the witness could never have reported it. Many recent investigations have been conducted with little or even no existing prior reports of anomalous activity ever having taken place at the location. The investigators simply turning up on the assumption that because a site is either old, derelict, historically significant, or conforms to their own criteria of what a haunted location should be like, then it must be worth investigating. They are then rarely surprised to discover when viewing their camera footage that they have obtained something that is unusual. They certainly cannot claim their discovery to be unexpected, after all, why else are they there? It is clear that the numerous claims being made for the detection of ghosts, spirits, and other assorted paranormal phenomena are being made by those using modified cameras and this must be questioned as it is most likely only the result of wishful thinking by the investigator compounded by the hype and marketing of television programme makers and those offering modified full spectrum cameras.

Any investigations that rely on this type of technology have effectively become bogged down in a mire of pseudo-scientific or nonsensical beliefs. So, is there any case at all for using invisible light photography and video as a useful tool for paranormal investigation? The simple answer is of course yes. Investigators in the early twentieth century recognised that such photographic techniques allowed them to record images in the dim light or apparent darkness of the séance room. They used infrared sensitive film to capture evidence, not of spirit visitations and manifestations, but of mediums and their accomplices undertaking acts of fraud and manipulation. There are also some instances in which photography and video may need to be obtained but circumstances may prevent any form of lighting that allows successful visible light photography to be undertaken. This is the true value of invisible light photography and where its key advantage to the investigator of ghost claims truly lies.

CHAPTER 19

ORBS, SOME DEFINITIVE EVIDENCE

D evelopments in digital camera technology permitted an experiment to be undertaken that demonstrated conclusively that airborne material located close to the camera and reflecting the camera flash is responsible for creating orbs.

The evolution of digital imaging, which began in the late 1990's, resulted in a revolution in ghost research. Investigators began to report a phenomenon previously almost unseen on images that had been taken using conventional film based cameras. By common consent, this apparently paranormal phenomenon was dubbed the 'orb'. Orbs are generally bright circular anomalies within an image, although other shapes such as angular and elongated forms are known. They may appear as single or multiple anomalies and may vary both in colour and intensity. To date, many thousands of orb pictures have been offered by investigators and members of the public as evidence and proof of something truly paranormal being captured by the camera. The orb debate has dogged ghost research for many years now with both believers and non-believers each putting their respective arguments and presenting their evidence.

Proffered explanations as to what orbs actually represent vary widely. For example, many investigators believe they are evidence of, and for, ghost and spirit manifestations. Others consider orbs to be the energetic emissions of angelic and otherworldly beings. The Internet is filled with pictures containing orbs presented as evidence of some type of ghostly manifestation. Newspapers and magazines regularly publish pictures of orbs, repeating the claims for their paranormality and occasionally adding a celebrity endorsement just for good measure. Such was the case of television star Noel Edmonds who, during a television interview in September 2008, claimed that his deceased parents "Are melon sized orbs" which he described as "Little bundles of positive energy" and "Conventional photography can't pick them up but digital cameras can"[1] There have been a number of books written describing in great detail the supernatural nature of orbs and how to interact with orbs thereby gaining spiritual enlightenment such as, *Ascension Through Orbs* (Cooper & Crosswell, 2010). Many investigators have now resolved to try and steer a middle ground through the orb dilemma; accepting that dust, flying insects, water vapour, and other airborne particles are the likely cause of most orbs they find on their digital pictures. They acknowledge the likelihood that the majority of orbs can be explained but then, all too often, they go on to say that there remain a number of orbs that cannot be explained and are therefore evidence of something paranormal. Generally a figure of around one or two per cent being unexplainable is favoured and, interestingly, this small percentage is usually to be found on pictures they themselves have taken and present on their Internet sites and social media pages.

Early Experiments

Between 2001 and 2003, I undertook a series of studies that attempted to determine the nature of orbs and also why they appear on digital cameras. The results demonstrated the strong probability that orbs were simply the result of airborne dust, moisture, and other particles reflecting the light from the camera flash back toward the imaging sensor, resulting in the characteristic of a bright anomaly. The results also indicated that in order to produce an orb anomaly within a picture a number of conditions needed to be met. For example, the camera flash

---

[1]   *Daily Mail* Online: http://www.dailymail.co.uk/tvshowbiz/article-1055732/My-dead-parents-melon-sized-orbs-New-Age-Noel-Edmonds-bizarre-airrant.html .

must have been used at the time of picture taking and the airborne material must be located within a few centimetres of the camera lens and also be within a narrow range of angles relative to the lens centre axis for the material to be able to reflect the light from the flash into the lens (figure 1).

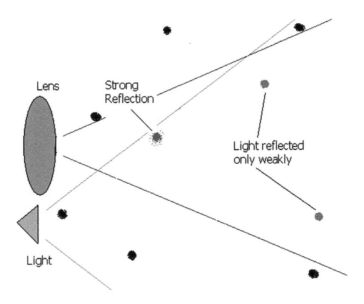

(Figure 1) Relative positioning of airborne particles needed to produce orbs

Other researchers have also carried out similar studies and experiments examining the orb phenomenon, reaching the same conclusion that orbs are simply the result of dust and other airborne matter reflecting the light from the camera mounted source back toward the image sensor.[2] These initial studies did result in many people questioning the true nature of orbs and led others to carry out their own experiments with the result that the probability that orbs are the result of airborne dust and other material has now been widely acknowledged. However, it was also clear that all of these early experiments had failed to conclusively show that airborne matter and moisture is responsible for orb production. This allowed the debate between the orb believers and sceptics to continue, to the obvious detriment of ghost research

---

[2]   http://www.theorbzone.com

and the continued confusion of all concerned. Camera manufacturers also recognised the problem that was resulting from the increased use of the much smaller digital cameras and many included cautions in the instruction manuals they provided (figure2).

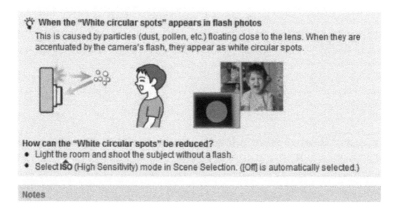

Flash

1. Press ⚡ (Flash) on the control button.
2. Select the desired mode with the control button.

✓	⚡AUTO (Auto)	Flash automatically operates in dark locations or when there is backlight.
	⚡ (On)	Flash always operates.
	⚡SL (Slow Synchro)	Flash always operates. The shutter speed is slow in a dark place to clearly shoot the background that is out of flash light.
	⊘ (Off)	Flash does not operate.

☼ **When the "White circular spots" appears in flash photos**
This is caused by particles (dust, pollen, etc.) floating close to the lens. When they are accentuated by the camera's flash, they appear as white circular spots.

How can the "White circular spots" be reduced?
- Light the room and shoot the subject without a flash.
- Select ISO (High Sensitivity) mode in Scene Selection. ([Off] is automatically selected.)

Notes

(Figure 2) Extract from Sony Cybershot® camera online manual

Stereo Camera Experiments

An experiment I had originally considered was the use of stereo photography to explore the orb phenomena. The technique should make it possible to test the hypothesis that orbs are airborne matter located physically close to the camera. I hypothesised that any object appearing on only one of the stereo pictures must be physically close to the camera. It would appear on both of the stereo pictures only if it were located more than a short distance (typically less than 5cm) from the camera, the actual distance being determined by the separation of the two lens axes. This may be simply demonstrated by placing a finger close to one of the eyes whilst alternately opening and closing each eye in turn. The finger will appear and disappear from view. Moving the finger an increasing distance from the front of the same eye will cause it to be seen with both eyes. Returning to orbs, in addition, the anomaly must also be located within the angle of view formed between the flash and the lens in order that the camera mounted illumination is reflected from the object causing the orb anomaly to appear on the final picture.

Stereo photography is a well-understood technique that has been used with film photography for over a century. However, the technical difficulties applying the technique to digital photography and ensuring that the resulting images were identical proved technically and practically insurmountable at that time. Difficulties included, finding a means of ensuring that both pictures were taken simultaneously, that both pictures had identical photographic settings, i.e., focus and exposure, and that both pictures had identical post image processing applied such as scene pre-sets, colour balance, file compression, etc. The use of a stereo lens fitted to a digital camera was considered but discounted, as the lens attachment partially blocked the light from the camera's built in flash. Also, the use of a single lens / sensor arrangement within the camera meant that it would not be possible to fully exclude any artefacts and errors caused by these two components.

In 2009, Fujifilm released the very first consumer stereo digital camera, the Fujifilm W1 3D digital camera, which comprised two separate lenses and high-resolution image sensors forming a matching pair of image taking systems integrated within the same camera body. The two image taking systems share a single common flash positioned equidistant between the lenses. Crucially, both image taking systems are activated using a single shutter button and use the same focus, exposure, and flash settings, thereby ensuring that the two resulting images produced for each press of the shutter are identical in every respect except for the parallax separation between the left and right pictures. The camera permitted the hypothesis to finally be tested that orbs are the result of nearby airborne matter reflecting the flash light toward the camera. I was also fortunate in being able to secure one of the first examples of this new type of camera shortly after its launch in order to begin a renewed investigation of the orb phenomenon.

The camera was used extensively at more than twenty locations widely spread throughout the United Kingdom and Eire between 2009 and 2011. The locations were selected to encompass a broad representation of allegedly haunted venues, for example, castles, industrial sites, houses, and modern retail premises. It also included a number of outdoor and indoor locations. Photographs were taken at several well-known ghost hunting locations, such as Mary King's Close, Edinburgh, Margam Castle, Wales, and Wicklow Gaol in Eire. In most instances the photography was undertaken whilst ghost investigators or members of the public conducted some form of paranormal investigation but at the same time they were unaware of the particular nature of the camera or the focus of the experiment that was being undertaken. This subsequently led to an interesting incident when a psychic medium at one location noticed an orb on the screen of the camera and promptly declared the orb to be precisely where he had perceived the spirit of a young girl. Upon request he was happy to write a note confirming that the picture showing the orb floating in mid-air was proof of the spirit of the young girl who haunted the location.

In order to replicate this simple point and shoot technique of most digital photography that is undertaken during ghost investigations the camera was only used in the fully automatic exposure and focus mode. The use of the fully automated mode also ensured that the resulting stereo pair of images were identical in terms of any software processing of the images that were applied in-camera, such as those affecting colour balance, scene pre-sets, file compression, etc. The paired images were downloaded from the camera to a laptop computer. No enhancement or manipulation of the resulting images was undertaken. Each simultaneous stereo pair of images were viewed side by side and compared visually for the presence of orb anomalies on either side of the pair.

During the course of the original experiment, 1,870 stereo pairs of images were taken and examined in this manner. Orb anomalies were found on 630 pairs. In 491 pairs, an orb or multiple orbs were seen to be present only in the left or right image. In 139 stereo pairs, orbs were seen to be present in both of the stereo images (left & right) but not in a position that corresponded to the individual orb being the same object. Interestingly, a further four stereo pairs of images show other anomalies that are frequently offered up as evidence of the paranormal. Two were images of the camera strap, whilst two more show breath condensation as the photographer exhaled. As with the orb photographs, these four anomalies appear on only one side of the stereo pair, again showing that they were quite normal in origin.

Orbs Are Dust

This comprehensive survey[3] strongly supports the hypothesis that orbs appearing on digital photographs are simply the result of dust and other

---

[3]   http://www.parascience.org.uk/articles/orbs.htm

airborne material drifting close to the camera thereby reflecting flash illumination back toward the image sensor thus providing long over-due evidence that their origin lies firmly within the mundane and ex-plainable and not the paranormal or supernatural. Before concluding, it is also worth bearing in mind the original statistical claims of some researchers that one or two per cent of all orb pictures represent unex-plainable and potentially paranormal orbs. The survey captured over six hundred orbs, so it might be expected that if their assertion was correct, it might be reasonable to have found between six and twelve orb anomalies that did not conform to the expected outcome during the experiment. In fact, all of the orb anomalies that were obtained during the survey were readily explained using the stereo photogra-phy technique. Statistically speaking that is zero per cent paranormal and one hundred per cent explainable. It is hoped that this extensive series of pictures will finally remove much of the confusion and non-sense that has surrounded the orb and similar classes of photograph-ic anomaly, and permit psychical research to move forward from this long-standing debate.

Following the completion of the initial survey and publishing the results in 2011, the original camera, together with a second Panasonic stereo digital camera has continued to be used in a longer-term study of the orb phenomenon. As of January 2015, the number of stereo-paired pictures has risen to over 9,000 (over 18,000 separate pictures), of which orbs can be found in around 5,800 pairs. To date not a single orb has appeared that is coincident in both pictures of a stereo pair (allowing for parallax) and no orb has appeared that does not immediately con-form to the hypothesis.

CHAPTER 20

SMART GHOST HUNTING

Modern ghost investigators have always used technology to assist them in their exploration of haunted sites. Ghost hunting kits include cameras, sound recorders, and thermometers. Many investigators also include items borrowed from crime scene investigation and the séance room. Other investigators have added more inventive and unusual items, from interactive toys to bars of soap marketed specifically for ghost hunters to 'spiritually cleanse' them beforehand! In recent years there has been an explosion of devices that claim to assist the ghost investigator in their quest for proof and there are now a number of companies in the UK and the USA that build and market such devices. But is it now possible to replace many of these devices and reduce the number of flight cases full of ghost hunting equipment? Such a possibility is certainly an attractive proposition. The fleet of vehicles that are required to transport the ghost tech is reduced, as is the need to spend hours setting up and packing away equipment. The number of batteries consumed is also reduced. Of course there will always be those investigators who consider that owning a veritable arsenal of equipment is important. More than just adding to their investigative ability they seem to believe that having large amounts of equipment also adds to their credibility as investigators.

Just such a device might already exist and most people now have a smart phone or tablet (portable computer) device. Can a mobile phone or tablet replace many of the traditional items in the ghost investigator's kit? Is it an effective tool for the investigator and can it produce reliable information?

Ghostly Apps

There are many smart phones and tablet devices that are available with several software operating systems but the most commonly encountered are Apple's iOS operating system designed to work with their iPhone, iPad, and iPod devices and the Android operating software used by numerous manufactures in a wide range of tablets and phones. In order to simplify matters and avoid repetition, this chapter will mainly consider the fifth and sixth generation iPhone (iPhone 5 and iPhone 6), although much of the discussion can be applied equally to those devices that use the Android operating system. Smart phones have been in use at the margins of the ghost-hunting scene for several years now. Typically they are scorned and much maligned by those who consider themselves to be serious investigators and possibly for good reason too. Many will have seen a large number of ghost photographs in the newspapers and on the social media over recent years. Hardly a week goes by without one or more amazing pictures of a ghost caught being caught using their smart phone camera by some unwitting person. Such pictures rapidly go viral and become much discussed and argued over in the social media, they are supported and debunked, blogged about, and shared endlessly. Eventually, each picture is in turn is replaced by another. In many instances it can be shown that these pictures have certainly been the result of one of the numerous apps that have appeared for smart phones and tablets. Apps are simply small programmes that can be downloaded and installed on the device to carry out a particular task including inserting the image of a ghostly figure into the user's pictures and videos. A quick search in the Apple iTunes store revealed over 160 such apps offering the iPhone user the ability to add a huge choice of spooky ghosts to their pictures or videos in near real time. The Google Play store for devices using the Android operating system offers nearly as many.

iPhone app ghost

But smartphones are so much more than mere devices that allow users to capture compelling images of ghosts. App developers have used their talents to develop a wide range of specialist ghost hunting tools for smartphones. It is possible to download apps that can seemingly transform the device into an EMF meter or EVP Recorder and there are many more interesting and sometimes original ways to detect ghosts together with a range of assorted other paranormal phenomena. One such app is the Ghost Hunter M2® which according to the description in the Apple store was "...developed by a team of professional engineers and is an advanced, yet very easy to use, paranormal investigation toolkit that has been specially designed for both the advanced and novice paranormal investigator". The developers provide brief descriptions of the various instruments that are included:

EVP Instrument:
The Electronic Voice Phenomena instrument presents words, in both audio (voice) and visual format, based on an advanced phonetic selection algorithm.

Sensor Sweep Instrument:
The Sensor Sweep instrument utilises a complex pattern detection algorithm, coupled with your device's advanced sensor array, to provide a spatial representation of potential paranormal activity.

EMF Instrument:
The EMF instrument uses the iPhone's magnetometer to measure fluctuations in the surrounding magnetic

Audio Detection Instrument:
The Audio Detection Instrument utilises your device's acoustic to electric traducer system, driven by extremely powerful algorithms, to analyze complex audio

FFT-V Instrument:
The Fast Fourier Transform Visualiser utilises your device's acoustic to electric transducer system, driven by powerful algorithms, to analyse complex audio.

Geoscope Instrument:
Using an advanced triple-axis redundancy filter, the Geoscope instrument has the ability to magnify even the slightest terrainial, and sub-terrainial fluctuations.

Spatial Displacement Instrument:
The Spatial Displacement instrument uses a powerful, and proprietary algorithm to analyse the data presented by the system's electro-mechanical sensor array.

Smart Sensors

Putting aside any particular claims that are made about the possibility of using a smart phone and the various apps to detect ghosts and spirits, exactly what sensors are available as standard in the iPhone

5 and 6? Both models have 8 Megapixel (MP) main cameras that are capable of recording both still pictures and full 1080 HD video. Both also have 1.2 MP cameras that face toward the user, again capable of taking stills or video. Each has a built in microphone, in fact there are two built-in microphones to permit effective noise cancelling during phone calls. They also have the ability to add an additional mono or stereo microphone via the 3.5mm audio jack socket.

Both models are fitted with a three-axis accelerometer capable of detecting acceleration or g-forces, vertically, laterally or horizontally in addition to an electronic gyroscope that allows motion and orientation in any plane to be detected and measured. Each has a magnetometer, which is capable of detecting and measuring a static or moving magnetic field in any axis when used in conjunction with the gyroscope. A sensor is also fitted which can measure changes in the ambient lighting levels. The iPhone 6 adds a barometer for measuring changes in the air pressure and it is worth mentioning that the iPhone 6 also has upgraded versions of all the main sensors and improved processing.

It almost goes without saying that smartphones can also access external systems such as the mobile phone network, Wi-Fi, and the global positioning satellite (GPS) systems. GPS allows the phone to calculate its geographical location to a very high degree of accuracy. Data retrieval and uploading to home computer systems and the World Wide Web (WWW) is now possible in most locations where a signal of some form is available. Bluetooth, which uses a short-range radio frequency connection, also allows the smartphone to directly access other nearby devices that are suitably equipped for this mode of communication.

The heart of any smart device is the processor, the internal computer that performs the complex calculations. Devices such as the iPhone 5 and 6 have processors that can easily outperform many home and portable computer systems from just two or three years ago. In the case of the latest smart devices, additional processors that are dedicated to particular tasks and functions support the primary processor.

All recent iPhone models have a multi-purpose input / output port, known as the Lightning port. This allows a wide range of external devices and sensors to be attached to the iPhone as well as permitting the more mundane task of charging the battery. On non-Apple products, a mini USB port serves much the same role. The Lightning port can be used to attach external sensors that are currently available as either internal components or provide additional measurement accuracy over the internal sensors. One such example is an external temperature measuring system with a wide range of sensors. Other sensors that can be connected via the Lightning port or USB include a fully functioning thermal imaging camera and biophysical sensors.

In order to utilise any of the sensors, specialised software programmes are required. These programmes can be downloaded from various websites and the already mentioned online stores. Often they can be freely obtained but more advanced or specialist apps are generally charged for.

The camera really requires little additional discussion here. It combines a high quality stills camera with a full HD video camera. Apps are available to extend its functionality to include low light, time-lapse, slow motion, and also sound or motion triggering of either video or stills. Many professional broadcasters make use of this technology and electronic news gathering (ENG) is now routinely being carried out using smartphones. The ease of use and ready portability means that it is often quicker, easier, and sometimes safer to obtain pictures and video with such a device than with a conventional camera.

Using either the built-in microphone, the 3.5mm stereo audio jack or the lightning port it is possible to record audio with high quality in many formats. These include the usual compressed formats such as MP3 or uncompressed lossless formats such as .wav. This permits the smartphone to record audio that is suitable for use by broadcasters and in some instances smartphones are beginning to replace conventional portable recording devices. Additional hardware is available that includes very high quality microphones and other audio input devices that improves the quality of the recorded audio still further.

Smart Apps

Apps can also be used to extend the basic recording functions and are capable of replicating or even exceeding the capabilities of many professional recording devices. Combined with additional hardware, apps also permit extremely complex acoustic measurement to be carried out. The combination of purpose designed hardware and dedicated app means that measurements can be made that conform to the various recognised International standards. Measurements include, sound pressure measurement, sound spectrum analysis, and frequency measurements. There are serious limitations relating the smartphone's built-in microphone but, by using the correct external microphones, it is now possible to make accurate sound pressure level measurements that cover the acoustic range from very high to very low frequencies. Calibration of both the hardware and the software data to recognised standards is also possible and such smart device based systems are now being used routinely to capture data for use within scientific and industrial applications.

The solid-state three-axis accelerometer that is fitted to the iPhone can be used as a standalone tool for making measurements of inertia. The sensitivity and reliability of this sensor now permits several research facilities to use smartphones as portable seismometers for scientific field observations. The same sensor can also be used to detect and measure vibration. The sensor was developed from sensors used in many unmanned aerial vehicles (UAV's) and in missile control systems. The accelerometer is also capable of working in conjunction with the gyroscopic sensor enabling the device to detect and measure motion and the forces applied in any direction. Measurements of lateral accelerations can be made over a broad range of frequencies; currently available systems are able to make calibrated measurements down to 0.01Hz. Several manufacturers offer plug-in seismic and vibration detection sensor systems that connect via the lightning port and provide increased functionality and additional features. A number of these external sensors operate to recognised measurement standards and are capable of calibration and the data that is obtained can be used for high quality and accurate measurements.

The three-axis gyroscope permits real-time observations and measurements to be made of rotational motion. The data can be logged to the device's internal memory, or transmitted to another computer via Wi-Fi, Bluetooth, or the cellular phone network.

The three axis magnetometer operates primarily as a compass within the iPhone although the data can also be integrated to work with the accelerometer, gyroscope, and GPS. Its sensitivity is such that it can be used to measure field strength variations of less than 1 picoTesla. The magnetometer can also be used to measure deviations in moving magnetic fields such as low frequency electromagnetic sources. It will also respond to changes caused by the presence of nearby magneto-conductive materials. This allows it to be used for applications such as the detection of metals and wiring.

The iPhone 6 and latest iPad models also include a barometer that has a stated accuracy of +/- 0.1 hPa or 0.1 mBar. Sampling rates are adjustable within the software and pressure data can be updated once per second. In addition to air pressure it is possible to use this sensor to measure relative changes in altitude. As with all the sensors, the data can be logged or streamed and by combining the sensor data it is possible to undertake some measurements that are really very advanced. The data can be used in real time or it can be stored for later use. It can be accessed directly or remotely. Used appropriately and with care, the resulting information can be a genuine asset to the investigator or researcher who needs to be able to make objective measurements of a location. For those who are so inclined, it is also possible to extract the raw data from each of the sensors for use with external software or even hardware.

Modern smartphone use has its potential problems too, not least of these being that they are battery-powered devices and battery life is finite. Typically, a smartphone that is being used as a data-gathering tool will have a usable battery life of several hours. This will be dramatically reduced if additional functions of the device are enabled. Bluetooth, Wi-Fi, and cellular network connections use power, as does the screen, and a have multiple apps running in the background. This also highlights a second potential problem with smartphone use. By design they are essentially devices for communicating, and often the device will prioritise an incoming call, text, or email over any data gathering that is being carried out which can result in the partial or even total loss of the measurement data. Unless the user is using the Bluetooth or Wi-Fi to connect to an external sensor or specifically streaming the data, it is always wise to turn off or disable connections that are not required. IPhones and most Android devices allow the user to select which connection features they require from the options menu.

Some ghost investigators have already begun to embrace the extra possibilities that smart devices provide. Unfortunately, with rare exceptions, this is not yet done in a way that may prove helpful to the overall area of study.

Many of the investigators use one or more of the currently available apps that are promoted for use in paranormal investigation, of which there are hundreds. In reality, none of them are providing or obtaining information that can be shown to be reliable or even helpful to the investigative process. Whilst many of them use one or more of the sensors built into the device, the information is provided in a format that does not generally represent the data accurately. For instance, some apps claim to permit the magnetometer to measure the apparent ability of ghosts and spirits to manipulate magnetic fields, these measurements are then translated into words and phrases by the app and permit the ghost or spirit to communicate. Other apps use the magnetometer measurements to detect the ghost or spirit as they disrupt or manipulate the magnetic fields around the device, presenting the intruder's relative position or location in a graphic form. Many other apps are nothing more than software trickery and attractive visuals.

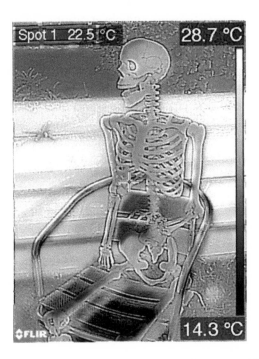

A combined thermal imager and x-ray camera built into an iPhone? Wishful thinking perhaps for the x-ray camera but a thermal imager for iPhone is a reality (picture taken using the FLIR One camera for iPhone and iPad)

Smart Users

When it comes to actually measuring anything related to reported spontaneous experiences, what iPhone features may be useful? Certainly the camera, the microphone and external audio hardware, the Lightning port, the magnetometer, accelerometer, gyroscope, and the barometer are all helpful.

I would add one very important additional item to the sensor list, the user. Any smartphone or other smart device is in reality just a dumb machine with some features that permit its use as a tool for undertaking some task or objective. Measuring anything requires an understanding of that which is being observed and measured. All measuring devices have limitations inherent in their design and usage. The sensor package inside a smart device is extensive and can be used to carry out a number of objective measurements and observations that may be required by the ghost investigator but only if the investigator understands the reasons why they might need to observe and measure something and how the measurements should be obtained. Most importantly of all is a good understanding of what any measurement data actually means.

As the makers of smartphones and smart devices offer greater processing power and a wider range of ever improving sensors with each new generation of devices, it becomes increasingly possible that future ghost investigators will no longer require carrying so much technology. Certainly, it is now possible for many of the basic investigation observations and even a number of advanced measurements to be obtainable using a smartphone with just a small number of additional add-on hardware accessories. Of course the capabilities of these smart devices will in all likelihood do little to seriously dent the sales of or the desire for ghost gadgets. Ghost investigators love their gadgets and just carrying a smartphone on a ghost investigation perhaps doesn't impress in quite the same way as a truckload of flight cases full of tech.

CHAPTER 21

AND FINALLY...

It has often been said that ghost investigation is boring, let's face it at 3am most people would prefer to be in bed than stalking ghosts in gloomy corridors or staring mindlessly at a monitor in the hope of seeing a headless orb float past. Well if you have reached the end of *Ghostology* and you still have several hours to wait until the lockdown is released and you can pack away the ghost gadgets, here is a little word search to keep you occupied...

Good luck and thank you for reading *Ghostology*

```
P  A  R  A  N  O  R  M  A  L  G  H  O  S  T  O  E  L  O  G  Y  S  G  A
P  G  Q  L  Q  A  C  W  K  I  E  J  P  S  P  R  N  F  S  G  L  C  P  H
P  A  R  A  C  O  U  S  T  I  C  S  K  E  E  R  T  O  P  H  Y  C  D  A
P  N  M  W  R  L  T  Z  D  V  I  W  R  O  V  L  I  G  O  O  W  D  A  M
E  V  H  E  I  E  T  A  Q  O  T  Q  D  J  L  H  T  X  O  S  M  T  R  I
I  O  H  A  L  T  A  H  B  H  L  Y  N  Q  D  I  Y  A  K  T  A  D  K  T
I  O  B  E  U  E  C  L  I  O  M  U  G  Y  R  V  K  P  Y  T  G  W  X  Y
I  L  J  R  M  N  C  H  I  N  R  A  F  L  J  P  I  P  W  N  I  B  J  V
N  S  B  B  Y  I  T  T  C  T  V  L  N  Q  U  P  Q  A  J  A  C  N  K  I
F  Q  O  M  L  T  C  I  R  R  Y  E  E  G  M  G  T  R  P  J  G  N  D  L
R  L  B  K  E  H  R  L  N  O  A  D  S  Y  E  E  M  I  Q  J  H  K  M  L
A  E  D  E  C  N  C  X  C  G  N  F  Z  T  Q  L  D  T  I  J  O  A  E  E
S  V  C  Y  I  Q  F  U  S  F  E  I  T  V  I  T  T  I  X  V  S  C  T  D
O  Z  E  O  P  A  N  I  L  S  A  Y  C  K  I  G  D  O  U  G  T  O  A  V
U  R  E  Z  R  N  Y  I  E  P  S  Y  C  H  I  C  A  N  G  M  O  U  P  E
N  Q  G  B  Y  D  U  Q  M  L  W  M  X  O  Q  V  D  T  L  N  L  S  H  A
D  F  H  X  M  B  E  Y  Z  Z  D  J  L  S  A  M  I  O  O  L  O  T  Y  J
R  I  R  X  X  K  T  R  H  Q  J  S  S  K  W  G  P  N  C  R  G  I  S  P
Q  A  Z  S  D  T  B  W  P  H  R  U  N  Y  M  V  O  E  I  A  Y  C  I  T
E  M  Q  E  S  U  P  E  R  N  A  T  U  R  A  L  L  Y  Z  P  S  V  C  V
D  E  M  O  N  O  S  A  M  P  L  E  T  C  W  B  O  M  Y  P  R  M  S  M
U  S  T  H  K  X  Q  M  B  S  X  J  E  B  M  Q  J  L  A  H  K  B  W  F
B  P  H  O  T  O  G  R  A  P  H  P  P  B  Q  O  R  P  S  O  H  E  V  Q
G  E  A  F  T  E  R  L  I  F  E  X  E  V  P  J  K  J  L  L  F  P  M  S
```

In the spirit of all good investigations there are no clues to assist you.
Well perhaps just one.........you should be able to find thirty-one words.

SUGGESTED FURTHER READING

The History and Reality of Apparitions (Andrew Moreton (Daniel Defoe), 1727. Modern reprints and e-books are available).

The Night Side of Nature (Catherine Crowe, 1848). Modern reprints and e-books are available.

Leaves from a Psychist's Case Book (Harry Price, 1933).

Confessions of a Ghost-Hunter (Harry Price, 1936).

Search for Truth (Harry Price, 1942).

The Haunting of Borley Rectory (E.J. Dingwall, K. Goldney, T. Hall, 1956).

The Founders of Psychical Research (Alan Gauld, 1968).

Ghost Hunting, a Practical Guide (Andrew Green, 1973).

Poltergeists (Alan Gauld & A.D. Cornell, 1979).

Ghostwatching (J. Spencer & T. Wells, 1994).

Investigating the Paranormal (Tony Cornell, 2002).

Paracoustics: Sound and the Paranormal, Steven T. Parsons and Callum E. Cooper, (2015). White Crow Books.

Paperbacks also available from
White Crow Books

Elsa Barker—*Letters from
a Living Dead Man*
ISBN 978-1-907355-83-7

Elsa Barker—*War Letters from
the Living Dead Man*
ISBN 978-1-907355-85-1

Elsa Barker—*Last Letters from
the Living Dead Man*
ISBN 978-1-907355-87-5

Richard Maurice Bucke—
Cosmic Consciousness
ISBN 978-1-907355-10-3

Arthur Conan Doyle—
The Edge of the Unknown
ISBN 978-1-907355-14-1

Arthur Conan Doyle—
The New Revelation
ISBN 978-1-907355-12-7

Arthur Conan Doyle—
The Vital Message
ISBN 978-1-907355-13-4

Arthur Conan Doyle with
Simon Parke—*Conversations
with Arthur Conan Doyle*
ISBN 978-1-907355-80-6

Meister Eckhart with Simon Parke—
Conversations with Meister Eckhart
ISBN 978-1-907355-18-9

D. D. Home—*Incidents in my Life Part 1*
ISBN 978-1-907355-15-8

Mme. Dunglas Home; edited,
with an Introduction, by Sir
Arthur Conan Doyle—*D. D.
Home: His Life and Mission*
ISBN 978-1-907355-16-5

Edward C. Randall—
Frontiers of the Afterlife
ISBN 978-1-907355-30-1

Rebecca Ruter Springer—
Intra Muros: My Dream of Heaven
ISBN 978-1-907355-11-0

Leo Tolstoy, edited by Simon
Parke—*Forbidden Words*
ISBN 978-1-907355-00-4

Leo Tolstoy—*A Confession*
ISBN 978-1-907355-24-0

Leo Tolstoy—*The Gospel in Brief*
ISBN 978-1-907355-22-6

Leo Tolstoy—*The Kingdom
of God is Within You*
ISBN 978-1-907355-27-1

Leo Tolstoy—*My Religion:
What I Believe*
ISBN 978-1-907355-23-3

Leo Tolstoy—*On Life*
ISBN 978-1-907355-91-2

Leo Tolstoy—*Twenty-three Tales*
ISBN 978-1-907355-29-5

Leo Tolstoy—*What is Religion
and other writings*
ISBN 978-1-907355-28-8

Leo Tolstoy—*Work While
Ye Have the Light*
ISBN 978-1-907355-26-4

Leo Tolstoy—*The Death of Ivan Ilyich*
ISBN 978-1-907661-10-5

Leo Tolstoy—*Resurrection*
ISBN 978-1-907661-09-9

Leo Tolstoy with Simon Parke—
Conversations with Tolstoy
ISBN 978-1-907355-25-7

Howard Williams with an Introduction
by Leo Tolstoy—*The Ethics of Diet:
An Anthology of Vegetarian Thought*
ISBN 978-1-907355-21-9

Vincent Van Gogh with Simon Parke—
Conversations with Van Gogh
ISBN 978-1-907355-95-0

Wolfgang Amadeus Mozart with Simon
Parke—*Conversations with Mozart*
ISBN 978-1-907661-38-9

Jesus of Nazareth with Simon Parke—
Conversations with Jesus of Nazareth
ISBN 978-1-907661-41-9

Thomas à Kempis with Simon
Parke—*The Imitation of Christ*
ISBN 978-1-907661-58-7

Julian of Norwich with Simon
Parke—*Revelations of Divine Love*
ISBN 978-1-907661-88-4

Allan Kardec—*The Spirits Book*
ISBN 978-1-907355-98-1

Allan Kardec—*The Book on Mediums*
ISBN 978-1-907661-75-4

Emanuel Swedenborg—*Heaven and Hell*
ISBN 978-1-907661-55-6

P.D. Ouspensky—*Tertium Organum:
The Third Canon of Thought*
ISBN 978-1-907661-47-1

Dwight Goddard—*A Buddhist Bible*
ISBN 978-1-907661-44-0

Michael Tymn—*The Afterlife Revealed*
ISBN 978-1-970661-90-7

Michael Tymn—*Transcending the
Titanic: Beyond Death's Door*
ISBN 978-1-908733-02-3

Guy L. Playfair—*If This Be Magic*
ISBN 978-1-907661-84-6

Guy L. Playfair—*The Flying Cow*
ISBN 978-1-907661-94-5

Guy L. Playfair —*This House is Haunted*
ISBN 978-1-907661-78-5

Carl Wickland, M.D.—
Thirty Years Among the Dead
ISBN 978-1-907661-72-3

John E. Mack—*Passport to the Cosmos*
ISBN 978-1-907661-81-5

Peter & Elizabeth Fenwick—
The Truth in the Light
ISBN 978-1-908733-08-5

Erlendur Haraldsson—
Modern Miracles
ISBN 978-1-908733-25-2

Erlendur Haraldsson—
At the Hour of Death
ISBN 978-1-908733-27-6

Erlendur Haraldsson—
The Departed Among the Living
ISBN 978-1-908733-29-0

Brian Inglis—*Science and Parascience*
ISBN 978-1-908733-18-4

Brian Inglis—*Natural and Supernatural:
A History of the Paranormal*
ISBN 978-1-908733-20-7

Ernest Holmes—*The Science of Mind*
ISBN 978-1-908733-10-8

Victor & Wendy Zammit —*A Lawyer
Presents the Evidence For the Afterlife*
ISBN 978-1-908733-22-1

Casper S. Yost—*Patience
Worth: A Psychic Mystery*
ISBN 978-1-908733-06-1

William Usborne Moore—
Glimpses of the Next State
ISBN 978-1-907661-01-3

William Usborne Moore—
The Voices
ISBN 978-1-908733-04-7

John W. White—
The Highest State of Consciousness
ISBN 978-1-908733-31-3

Stafford Betty—
The Imprisoned Splendor
ISBN 978-1-907661-98-3

Paul Pearsall, Ph.D. —
Super Joy
ISBN 978-1-908733-16-0

All titles available as eBooks, and selected titles available in Hardback and Audiobook formats from www.whitecrowbooks.com

Lightning Source UK Ltd.
Milton Keynes UK
UKHW012033090619
344114UK00001B/67/P